Lecture Notes in Computer Sci

Commenced Publication in 1973
Founding and Former Series Editors:
Gerhard Goos, Juris Hartmanis, and Jan van Leeuwen

George Danezis   Sven Dietrich
Kazue Sako (Eds.)

Financial Cryptography and Data Security

FC 2011 Workshops, RLCPS and WECSR 2011
Rodney Bay, St. Lucia, February 28 - March 4, 2011
Revised Selected Papers

 Springer

Volume Editors

George Danezis
Microsoft Research Cambridge
Roger Needham Building
7 J J Thomson Avenue
Cambridge, CB3 0FB, UK
E-mail: gdane@microsoft.com

Sven Dietrich
Stevens Institute of Technology
Department of Computer Science
Castle Point on Hudson
Hoboken, NJ 07030, USA
E-mail: spock@cs.stevens.edu

Kazue Sako
Central Research Laboratories
NEC Corporation
1753 Shimonumabe Nakahara
Kawasaki 211-8666 Japan
E-mail: k-sako@ab.jp.nec.com

ISSN 0302-9743   e-ISSN 1611-3349
ISBN 978-3-642-29888-2   e-ISBN 978-3-642-29889-9
DOI 10.1007/978-3-642-29889-9
Springer Heidelberg Dordrecht London New York

Library of Congress Control Number: 2012937455

CR Subject Classification (1998): C.2, K.4.4, K.6.5, D.4.6, E.3, J.1

LNCS Sublibrary: SL 4 – Security and Cryptology

Typesetting: Camera-ready by author, data conversion by Scientific Publishing Services, Chennai, India

Printed on acid-free paper

Springer is part of Springer Science+Business Media (www.springer.com)

Real-Life Cryptographic Protocols and Standardization

Preface

This workshop, "Real-Life Cryptographic Protocols and Standardization," is intended to gather the experiences of the designers and implementers of cryptographic protocols that are deployed in real-life systems. Designing and implementing real-life systems puts forth many challenges – not only technical issues regarding the use of hardware and software, but also usability, manageability, interoperability and timing to deploy the system. Designing to fulfil all these restrictions while not degrading security frequently requires tremendous efforts. The resulting cryptographic protocols may not always be interesting at the theoretical cryptography level, but the documentation of the challenges they face and the ways such challenges were met are important to be shared with the community. Standardization also promotes the use of cryptographic protocols where the best practices from these experiences are condensed in a reusable way.

We were happy to organize the second workshop in conjunction with the Financial Cryptography and Data Security Conference 2011 in St. Lucia. The selected papers focus on real-life issues and discuss all the design criteria and relevant implementation challenges. We hope the proceedings from the series of this workshop serve as a place where researchers and engineers find the documentation of the necessary know-how for designing and implementing secure systems that have a tangible impact in real life; ultimately, we hope that this contributes to a future generation of usable real-life systems where security would be one of their intrinsic qualities.

April 2011   Kazue Sako

Workshop on
Ethics in Computer Security Research

Preface

The second Workshop on Ethics in Computer Security Research (WECSR 2011, http://www.cs.stevens.edu/~ spock/wecsr2011/), organized by the International Financial Cryptography Association (IFCA, http://www.ifca.ai/), was held in Rodney Bay, St. Lucia, on March 4, 2011. It was part of the second multi-workshop event co-located with Financial Cryptography 2011.

The goal was to continue searching for a new path in computer security that is acceptable for Institutional Review Boards at academic institutions, as well as compatible with ethical guidelines for professional societies or government institutions. The first results are beginning to appear, such as initial drafts of the Menlo Report, the equivalent of the Belmont Report for this domain.

We mixed the three papers and one panel selected from six submissions with two invited papers and one invited panel. Each submission was reviewed by at least four Program Committee members. The Program Committee carefully reviewed the submissions during an online discussion phase in fall 2010. I would like to thank the Program Committee for their work. We would like to thank all submitters for the papers and efforts, and hope that the comments received from the reviewers will allow them to progress with their work.

The workshop brought together about 35 participants, including computer security researchers, practitioners, policy makers, and legal experts, and fostered often fervent ethical and philosophical debates among participants, in order to shape the future of ethical standards in the field. The relaxed local atmosphere allowed for many continued discussions beyond the day itself, including the island excursion the following day kindly organized by the Local Arrangements Chair Fabian Monrose.

I would like to thank George Danezis, Steven Murdoch, Rafael Hirschfeld, Andrew Patrick, Jon Callas, Burton Rosenberg, and last but not least Fabian Monrose for their hard work and help in organizing this workshop. Many thanks also to those who traveled far to this island in the Eastern Caribbean.

I look forward to many more discussions at future instances of the workshop.

March 2011   Sven Dietrich

Organization

The 15th International conference on Financial Cryptography and Data Security (FC 2011) was organized by the International Financial Cryptography Association (IFCA).

Organizers

General Chair

Steven Murdoch — University of Cambridge, UK

Local Arrangements Chair

Fabian Monrose — University of North Carolina Chapel Hill, USA

Real-Life Cryptographic Protocols and Standardization

Program Chair

Kazue Sako — NEC

Program Committee

Josh Benaloh	Microsoft Research
Aline Gouget	Gemalto and CryptoExperts
Hongxia Jin	IBM Almaden
Aggelos Kiayias	University of Connecticut
Helger Lipmaa	Cybernetica AS and Tallinn University
Sandra Marcello	Thales
Jean-Francois Misarsky	Orange Labs
David Naccache	ENS
Kaisa Nyberg	Aalto University and Nokia
Satoshi Obana	NEC
Pascal Paillier	Gemalto and CryptoExperts
Benny Pinkas	Bar Ilan University
Ahmad-Reza Sadeghi	TU Darmstadt and Fraunhofer SIT
Kazue Sako	NEC

Workshop on Ethics in Computer Security Research

Program Chair

Sven Dietrich   Stevens Institute of Technology

Program Committee

Michael Bailey	University of Michigan
Elizabeth Buchanan	University of Wisconsin-Stout
Aaron Burstein	University of California Berkeley
Nicolas Christin	Carnegie Mellon University
Michael Collins	RedJack, LLC
Marc Dacier	Symantec Research
Roger Dingledine	The Tor Project
David Dittrich	University of Washington
Kenneth Fleischmann	University of Maryland
Rachel Greenstadt	Drexel University
Erin Kenneally	UC San Diego/CAIDA/Elchemy
Engin Kirda	Northeastern University
Howard Lipson	CERT, Software Engineering Institute, CMU
John Mchugh	RedJack LLC and University of North Carolina
Peter Neumann	SRI International
Vern Paxson	ICSI and LBNL
Len Sassaman	K.U. Leuven ESAT-COSIC
Angelos Stavrou	George Mason University
Michael Steinmann	Stevens Institute of Technology
Paul Syverson	Naval Research Laboratory

Sponsors

Gold	Office of Naval Research Global
Silver	Research in Motion
Bronze	East Caribbean Financial Holding
	Google
In Kind	Lime
	WorldPay
	Financial Services Technology Consortium BITS

Table of Contents

Financial Cryptography and Data Security Workshops

Real-Life Cryptographic Protocols and Standardization

Workshop on Ethics in Computer Security Research

Cryptographic Protocols: From the Abstract to the Practical to the Actual

Moti Yung

Google Inc. and Department of Computer Science, Columbia University
moti@cs.columbia.edu

Abstract. We identify three levels of cryptographic research and development: Starting from the general "abstract" design level, the first layer includes much of theoretical cryptography, and general engineering principles (most present in cryptographic conferences). The second level is of designs which are contributed to systems and international standards, and include mechanisms ready to be implemented in hardware and software; we call this level "practical." Finally, the third level which we call "actual," includes fielded cryptography as external contribution to, and part of "general (hardware/ software) engineering projects," requiring cryptographic participation and supervision throughout the life cycle of the constructed system. I briefly review these three levels and their connections; (the treatment is based on personal experience and is, therefore, subjective). The position expressed here motivates the need for a scientific forum on "real life cryptographic designs and protocols," to deal with the interactions between the three levels from actual real life perspective.

Cryptographic Protocol Design on Three Levels

Abstract Cryptography. The field of cryptography is multi disciplinary and has many connections to other areas. Cryptographic designs have mathematical nature, and in modern computer science, cryptography is a field, and cryptographic protocols typically build on (assumed) hard problems in mathematics (or other physical limitations). They essentially solve problems involving secrecy, authenticity, symmetry breaking, timeliness, fairness, and other requirements involving partial information constrains. The area involves design of cryptosystems, signature systems, and interactive protocols. It includes defining and refining definitions of basic primitives, realizing them, improving their complexity and their properties (e.g., their security against increasingly strong adversary), and investigating the assumptions upon which the primitives can be realized. Research in the area, conducted in the last few decades, has revealed numerous interesting connections of the science of cryptography and other areas of mathematics and theoretical computer science (for example, there are strong connections with algebra, number theory, computational complexity, and distributed systems). There are numerous forums dedicated to the basic nature and scientific connections of cryptography.

G. Danezis, S. Dietrich, and K. Sako (Eds.): FC 2011 Workshops, LNCS 7126, pp. 1–2, 2012.

Practical Cryptography. In the last few decades computing systems have been evolving in an interesting direction: networked computers involving remote communication and transactions. Thus, the need for cryptographic tools has increased. In practical cryptography the task is to evaluate the tools and systems that are suitable for practical use. The demand for a tool can come from an application domain, standard bodies, or from a community recognizing a need.

The typical activity in practical cryptography involves identifying primitives/ variants ready for practical use, implementing them, measuring their performance, and standardizing them. Creating cryptographic software systems is another activity (typically including: random and pseudorandom generation, symmetric ciphers and basic asymmetric cryptography), as well as embedding cryptography in hardware, and designing utility protocols to be used as black box in environments (e.g., the SSL/TLS protocol). Practical cryptographic research involves methodologies for the above activities in general and emerging systems/ environments. At times this area is called cryptographic engineering, but there are cross fertilization and no clear boundary between this research and the more applied results in abstract cryptography.

Actual Cryptography. Much of the activities described above are pretty much "actual," but what I mean here is the *external contributions* of cryptography to general engineering, i.e., the activity of fielding cryptographic protocols in actual working systems. In some projects, like the national lottery project I participated in, the need for cryptography is clear, but, on the other hand, in other projects I participated in, cryptography was not in the original specifications, and the need was recognized in the middle of the project, as partial information constraints became clear. I have learned a few crucial things as part of participation in general engineering projects, and I will mention some of them. First, the security needs and requirements, while understood by engineers intuitively, are not often presented correctly (they are not as sophisticated as in abstract cryptography, but quite subtle and interesting). Secondly, often, important issues are missing (e.g., fault tolerance issues), and the cryptographers have to design them. Thirdly, the need for cryptographic solution may not come out of pure security need, but implicitly out of business and engineering constraints. Thus, the cryptographer has to be involved early on to understand the global needs of the entire project, to make sure that sub-optimal and misleading "solutions" are avoided. Also, resistance to incorporating new technology like cryptography in a general project is always expected; the long term involvement in a project may find opportunities to allow the introduction of cryptography, either since security constraints start to dominate, or when cryptography helps and is not in contradiction with usability, performance and function.

Final Note. Given the above level classification, a scientific forum for real life cryptographic protocols, treated as a field of study, seems to be needed to close the gaps among the three levels identified above, so that cryptographic contributions can be more effective.

Toward Real-Life Implementation of Signature Schemes from the Strong RSA Assumption

Ping Yu and Rui Xue

State Key Laboratory of Information Security
Institute of Software, Chinese Academy of Sciences
Beijing, China 100190
{yuping,rxue}@is.iscas.ac.cn

Abstract. This paper introduces our work on performance improvement of signature schemes based on the strong RSA assumption for the purpose of real-life implementation and deployment. Many signature schemes based on the strong RSA assumption have been proposed in literature. The main advantage of these schemes is that they have security proofs in the standard model, while the traditional RSA scheme can only be demonstrated secure in the Random Oracle Model. However, the downside is the loss of efficiency among these schemes. Almost all these schemes double the computational cost of signature generation in the RSA scheme. So far the research in this area is more focusing on theoretical aspect. In this paper, we introduce techniques which greatly improve the performance of available schemes, and obtain a state-of-the-art signature scheme in the strong RSA family. In a typical setting where the RSA modulus is 1024 bits, it needs only one exponentiation calculation at the cost of about 160 modular multiplications, and a 162-bit prime number generation. This cost is even lower than the RSA signature scheme. Our work brings the current theoretical results into real-life implementation and deployment.

Keywords: Digital Signature, Efficiency, Real-life Implementation, Strong RSA Assumption.

1 Introduction

The digital signature concept is a fundamental primitive in modern cryptography. A digital signature scheme is a triple of algorithms: $(\text{Gen}, \text{Sig}, \text{Ver})$. $\text{Gen}(1^k)$ is called the key generation algorithm, which generates a pair of verification and signing keys (vk, sk) based on the security parameter k. $\text{Sig}(sk, m)$ is called the signing algorithm, which produces a signature σ on message m. $\text{Ver}(vk, m, \sigma)$ is called the verification algorithm, which checks if σ is a valid signature of message m. A basic requirement for a signature scheme is that a valid signature can only be produced by the signer who knows the signing key.

It is a challenging task to demonstrate the security of cryptographic schemes, including signature schemes. A popular method for carrying out security analysis is the Random Oracle Model, in which a public random oracle is set up to be accessed by all parties. Since random oracles are a mathematical convenience for the sake of analysis, when such an algorithm is implemented in practice the random oracle is typically

G. Danezis, S. Dietrich, and K. Sako (Eds.): FC 2011 Workshops, LNCS 7126, pp. 3–12, 2012.

replaced by a cryptographic hash function. The random oracle methodology facilitates design and analysis of many cryptographic schemes. For example, the RSA scheme with the Optimal Asymmetric Encryption Padding (OAEP), which is one way the RSA scheme is used for encryption in practice, has been proved secure in the Random Oracle Model [2,15]. Unfortunately, Canetti *et al.* showed that there exist schemes which can be proved secure in the Random Oracle Model, but any instantiation of the random oracle will result in a broken construction [5]. Their work shows the Random Oracle Model fundamentally has some issues.

Another model is called the real world model, or the standard model, in which the behaviors of all involved parties in the environment of a proof are the same as or indistinguishable from those in the real protocol in the view of attackers. No additional assumptions are needed to carry out the proof. It is always desirable for a scheme to be secure in the standard model since the Random Oracle Model is in essence a heuristic method for security proofs.

1.1 Signature Schemes from the Strong RSA Assumption

The first signature scheme is the well known RSA scheme [14]. The RSA scheme combined with a padding technique (e.g., the technique due to Bellare and Rogaway [3]) can be proved secure in the Random Oracle Model.

In 2000, Cramer and Shoup proposed the first practical signature scheme from the RSA family which has a security proof in the standard model [6]. It is based on a stronger assumption called the strong RSA assumption. Later, many schemes have been proposed in the strong RSA family with different types of enhancement for the purpose of efficiency and simplicity. Among those are the Camenisch-Lysyanskaya scheme [4], Zhu's scheme [17,18], Fischlin's scheme [7], the Yu-Tate scheme [16], Joye's scheme [11], and others.

The major advantage of these schemes is that they all have security proofs in the standard model. The discouraging side is that they have much higher computational cost compared to the RSA scheme. For example, the computational cost for the Camenisch-Lysyanskaya scheme is about three times higher than the RSA scheme. It has been a continuous effort in this area to adjust design to improve efficiency with the hope of obtaining a scheme at least as efficient as the standard RSA scheme.

The performance issue in these schemes hampers people's interest to implement and deploy them in the real world. So far, we are not aware of any of these schemes being deployed in practice. Even though the RSA scheme can only be demonstrated secure in the Random Oracle Model, it has been working so well in the real world for more than twenty years and people are satisfied with the current situation. To encourage real-life deployment of signature schemes in the strong RSA family which have better security property, it is critical for a candidate being at least as efficient as the RSA scheme. Otherwise, people might not show much interest in these theoretical results.

1.2 Contributions

In this paper, we propose a new signature scheme, which is the state-of-the-art signature scheme in the strong RSA family. We discuss techniques on parameter tuning on current schemes in the family. Even though these tricks are not theoretically significant, the performance improvement is not marginal. The new scheme is the first construction in the strong RSA family that is even more efficient than the standard RSA scheme.

In a typical setting in which the RSA modulus is 1024 bits, to produce a signature, the new scheme only needs one modular exponentiation whose cost is about 160 modular multiplications, plus the cost of a 162-bit prime number generation. This cost is the lowest one among all signature schemes in the strong RSA family, even lower than the standard RSA signature scheme which needs about 1024 modular multiplications. In addition, the new scheme can produce signatures in an online/offline manner. The majority of computation can be done before a message appears, and the online computation only needs a multiplication of two 160-bit integers. This is the best online performance which can be achieved so far. Joye's scheme has already achieved such a level of online performance, but its offline computation is about six times more expensive than the new scheme.

Our work brings the current theoretical results into real-life implementation and deployment. The rest of the paper is organized as follows. Section 2 reviews some cryptographic notations and definitions. We analyze the Camenisch-Lysyanskaya scheme in Section 3, and propose a method to improve its performance. Section 4 analyzes the Yu-Tate scheme, and discusses another way for performance improvement. We introduce the new scheme in Section 5. Section 6 gives a brief comparison on some typical signature schemes from the strong RSA assumption. Finally, we give the conclusions in Section 7.

2 Preliminaries

This section reviews some notations, definitions and security assumptions which are related to the discussion in this paper.

One of the first public key cryptographic systems published was the RSA scheme [14], which uses computations over modular group $\mathbb{Z}_n^*$, where $n = pq$, p, q are both prime, and n should be constructed in a way such that the factorization of n is infeasible. This type of n is called an RSA modulus. Many different ways exist to construct n such that the resulting modular groups exhibit different properties which can be used in cryptographic constructions. Many constructions adopt a special RSA modulus which is defined as follows.

Definition 1 (Special RSA Modulus). *An RSA modulus $n = pq$ is called special if $p = 2p' + 1$ and $q = 2q' + 1$ where p' and q' are also prime numbers.*

Most signature schemes in the RSA family which have security proofs in the standard model rely on a well-accepted complexity assumption called the strong RSA assumption. This assumption was first introduced by Baric and Pfitzmann [1] and Fujisaki and Okamoto [8].

Assumption 1 (Strong RSA Assumption). *(SRSA Assumption) Let n be an RSA modulus. The flexible RSA problem is the problem of taking a random element $u \in \mathbb{Z}_n^*$ and finding a pair (v, e) such that $e > 1$ and $v^e = u \mod n$.*

The strong RSA assumption *says that no probabilistic polynomial time algorithm can solve the flexible RSA problem for random inputs with non-negligible probability.*

Even though the first signature scheme, i.e., the RSA scheme, was proposed back in 1977, a formal definition of a secure signature scheme appeared much later. The well accepted definition is called existential unforgeability under adaptive chosen message attacks, which was proposed by Goldwasser, Micali and Rivest in 1988 [10]. The definition we give here is due to Gennaro *et al.* [9].

Definition 2 (Secure Signatures [9]). *A signature scheme* $S = \langle \text{Gen}, \text{Sig}, \text{Ver} \rangle$ *is existentially unforgeable under an adaptive chosen message attack if it is infeasible for a forger who only knows the public key to produce a valid (message, signature) pair, even after obtaining polynomially many signatures on messages of its choice from the signer.*

Formally, for every probabilistic polynomial time forger algorithm $\mathcal{F}$, *there exists a negligible function* $\text{negl}(\cdot)$ *such that*

$$\Pr\begin{bmatrix} \langle vk, sk \rangle \leftarrow \text{Gen}(1^k); \\ for\ i = 1 \ldots n \\ \quad m_i \leftarrow \mathcal{F}(vk, m_1, \sigma_1, \ldots, m_{i-1}, \sigma_{i-1});\ \sigma_i \leftarrow \text{Sig}(sk, m_i); \\ \langle m, \sigma \rangle \leftarrow \mathcal{F}(vk, m_1, \sigma_1, \ldots, m_n, \sigma_n), \\ s.t.\ m \neq m_i\ for\ i = 1 \ldots n,\ and\ \text{Ver}(vk, m, \sigma) = accept \end{bmatrix} = \text{negl}(k).$$

Intuitively speaking, an adaptive chosen message attack for a signature scheme is that a signature forger is allowed to adaptively choose any messages a polynomial number of times, asking the signer to produce signatures for these messages. If the forger can create a signature which is not produced by the signer before, the attack succeeds and the scheme is broken. Otherwise, we say that the signature scheme is secure.

3 Analysis of the Camenisch-Lysyanskaya Signature Scheme

In 2002, Camenisch and Lysyanskaya proposed a signature scheme secure in the standard model under the strong RSA assumption [4], which is referred to as the CL scheme in the rest of the paper. We discuss a way to improve the CL scheme in this section.

3.1 The CL Scheme

Like all digital signature schemes, the CL scheme has three procedures: key generation, signing and verification algorithms.

Key Generation. On input 1^k, choose a special RSA modulus $n = pq$, $p = 2p' + 1$, $q = 2q' + 1$ of length $l_n = 2k$. Choose uniformly at random, $a, b, c \in QR_n$. Output public key (n, a, b, c), and private key (p', q').

Signing Algorithm. On input message $m \in [0, 2^{l_m})$, choose a random prime number e of length $l_e \geq l_m + 2$, and a random number s of length $l_s = l_n + l_m + l$, where l is a security parameter. Compute the value v as

$$v = (a^m b^s c)^{e^{-1}} \mod n.$$

Verification Algorithm. To verify that the triple (e, s, v) is a signature on message m in the message space, check that $v^e \equiv a^m b^s c \mod n$, and $2^{l_e} > e > 2^{l_e - 1}$.

As specified in their paper, one parameter setting for the CL scheme is $k = 512$, so n is 1024 bits long. l_m can be chosen as 160, and messages longer than 160 bits can first be sent through a collision-resistant hash function (e.g., SHA-1) to produce a 160-bit message digest, which is then signed. The security parameter $l = 160$ so $l_s = 1024 + 160 + 160 = 1344$. For this setting of parameters, the cost of the signing algorithm is about $(160 + 1022 + 1344)$ modular multiplications and the generation of a 162-bit prime number. The verification requires $(1344 + 162 + 160)$ modular multiplications. Notice in the CL scheme s is required to be a very large integer, which contributes to a large portion of computational cost for signature generation.

3.2 Improvement of the CL Scheme

If we look at the CL scheme carefully, one interesting observation would be uncovered. A valid CL signature satisfies

$$v^e \equiv a^m b^s c \mod n.$$

Notice, since $s > e$, s can always be represented as $s = k'e + s'$ for some k', and $s' < e$. Then we have

$$v^e \equiv a^m b^s c \equiv a^m b^{k'e + s'} c \equiv a^m b^{k'e} b^{s'} c \mod n.$$

Subsequently we obtain $v^e b^{-k'e} \equiv v'^e \equiv a^m b^{s'} c \mod n$, with $s' < e$, and $v' = v b^{-k'} \mod n$. This transformation shows that from a valid CL signature, we can always obtain a new valid signature with much shorter s. Therefore, we are able to obtain a variant of the CL scheme with $s < e$, which is obviously equivalent to the CL scheme in terms of security properties, since both schemes can be converted into each other by a trivial transformation. This implies that the length of s actually has no impact on the security properties of the scheme. Following the similar analysis, we can observe that s can be a random integer with the length between l_e and l_s.

We summarize our analysis as the following lemma.

Lemma 1. *The length requirement of s in the CL scheme has no impact on the security properties of the scheme. That is, s can be any random integer with the length between l_e and l_s as defined in the scheme. Therefore, we can adjust the length of s as needed to improve computational efficiency.*

4 Analysis of the Yu-Tate Signature Scheme

In 2008, Yu and Tate proposed an online/offline signature scheme which is referred to as the YT scheme [16]. Their scheme is similar to the CL scheme at the structural level. Both of them have the same verification algorithm and similar parameter choices. For example, the YT scheme also requires s being 1344 bits long for a typical setting where the RSA modulus is 1024 bits long. The major difference is that the YT scheme takes a different approach on signature generation. In the YT scheme, v is first calculated as $v = b^\gamma \mod n$, then s is computed out based on the relationship among exponents of a, b, c. More specifically, in the YT scheme, $a = b^\alpha \mod n$, and $c = b^\beta \mod n$. Therefore

$$\gamma \times e \equiv \alpha \times m + s + \beta \mod p'q'.$$

s can be calculated out based on this equation, and the verification algorithm is

$$v^e = a^m b^s c \mod n,$$

which is the same as the CL scheme.

The YT scheme only needs one exponentiation of 1022-bit exponent for signature generation in a typical setting. In comparison, the CL scheme needs three exponentiation calculations: one with 160-bit exponent, one with 1344-bit exponent, and one with 1022-bit exponent. Therefore the YT scheme is much more efficient than the CL scheme.

Our consideration is how to further improve the YT scheme. In the YT scheme, computing operations are conducted in the group of QR_n, since all parameters in the scheme are randomly chosen in QR_n. For example, when computing v, γ is picked up as a 1022-bit integer. We can consider to choose a smaller exponent to reduce computational cost. For example, we could pick a 160-bit integer instead of a 1022-bit integer. However, we need to address one issue for this consideration. The security proofs for the CL scheme and the YT scheme require v being randomly distributed in QR_n for the purpose of simulation. We should argue that this change will not affect an attacker's view in the proof.

The soundness of this consideration relies on the fact that it is infeasible to distinguish elements with short exponent and those with full size exponent. That is, informally speaking, if we have two elements $(a = g^x, b = g^y)$, where g is a generator of a group, $x \in_R (0, order(g))$, $y \in_R (0, 2^l)$, and $l < l_{order(g)}$, it is assumed impossible to make a decision whether a and b are generated based on different sizes of exponents. There is a well-known assumption called the discrete logarithm assumption with short exponent (DLSE) [13], which states that no efficient algorithms can calculate the exponent of an element if the exponent is larger than a threshold value for a large group. For example, it is assumed impossible to calculate the exponent r of a random element v such that $v = g^r$ where the length of r is longer than certain threshold length (e.g., 160 bits). Many secure problems related to the short exponent problem have been proposed, such as short exponent Diffie-Hellman problem, short exponent DDH problem, etc. Interested readers may refer to [13,12] for detailed discussion.

Koshiba and Kurosawa proved that, based on the DLSE assumption, it is infeasible to distinguish elements with short exponent and those with full size exponent [12]. Their result is applied to groups whose order is known to attackers. For constructions in the strong RSA family, the order of the underlying group is not known. However, a simple observation shows this indistinguishable property still holds for a group with unknown order. Suppose we have two elements, one has a short exponent, while the other has a full size exponent. Since the order of the group is not known to the attacker, we can simply tell the attacker the order of the group, which at least provides more information for him to use. Using the same proof by Koshiba and Kurosawa, we can show even when the order is known to the attacker, he still cannot distinguish these elements. Now, without the knowledge of the order of the group, this certainly makes the attacker's strategy more stringent. Therefore, we have the following lemma.

Lemma 2 (Indistinguishability between Short Exponent and Full Exponent). *Let g be a generator of G where the discrete logarithm problem with short exponent is assumed hard. Let l_f be the bit length of $order(g)$. Let $l_s < l_f$ and is greater than a threshold value so the DLSE assumption holds (e.g., $l_s > 160$). Let $(a = g^x, b = g^y)$, where $x \in_R (0, order(g)), y \in_R (0, 2^{l_s})$. Under the DLSE assumption, no probabilistic polynomial time algorithm can distinguish a, b with non-negligible probability.*

5 The New Signature Scheme

In this section, we introduce the new signature scheme based on the analysis in the previous sections.

5.1 The Scheme

- **Public System Parameters.** Let k be the security parameter. l is the length of a specific exponent used in the signing algorithm, which ensures the DLSE assumption holds (in practice, $l = 160$ is sufficient). l_m is the bit length of messages. l_e is the bit length of parameter e which is a prime number. It is required $l_e > l_m$.

- **Key Generation.** On input 1^k, pick two k-bit safe RSA primes p and q (so $p = 2p' + 1$, and $q = 2q' + 1$, where p' and q' are also prime), and let $n = pq$. Let $l_n = 2k$ be the length of the public modulus, QR_n be the quadratic residue group of $\mathbb{Z}_n^*$, and select a random generator b of QR_n. Select $\alpha, \beta \in_R [0, 2^l)$ and compute $a = b^\alpha \bmod n, c = b^\beta \bmod n$. Output public key (n, a, b, c), and private key $(p'q', \alpha, \beta)$.

- **Signing Algorithm.** The signing procedure includes two steps.
  STEP ONE: The signer picks a random $\gamma \in_R [0, 2^l)$, and a random prime e with length l_e, then computes

$$v = b^\gamma \bmod n, \quad \lambda = \gamma \times e - \beta.$$

  STEP TWO: When a message $m \in [0, 2^{l_m})$ appears, the signer computes

$$s = \lambda - \alpha \times m.$$

  The signature is (v, e, s) for message m.

- **Verification Algorithm.** To verify that (v, e, s) is a signature on message m, check that

$$v^e \equiv a^m b^s c \bmod n.$$

5.2   Performance Analysis

This new scheme is very efficient. A typical setting is that $l_n = 1024$, $l = 160$, $l_e = 162$, and $l_m = 160$. The major computation happens at STEP ONE, which needs about 160 modular multiplications and the cost of a 162-bit prime number generation. STEP TWO needs one multiplication of two 160-bit integers and an addition. Notice in the new scheme, s is about 322 bits long, and is much shorter than that in the CL ans YT schemes which is 1344 bits long.

The experiments in [6] show in the CS scheme the cost of generating a 161-bit prime is roughly one third of total cost of signature generation, and the CS scheme is 1.4 times slower than standard RSA scheme. In addition to prime number generation, the new scheme needs roughly 160 modular multiplications, where the CS scheme needs 1342 modular multiplications[1]. A simple calculation shows the new scheme runs faster than the RSA scheme $(1.4 \times (\frac{160}{1342} \times \frac{2}{3} + \frac{1}{3}) = 0.58)$. This is the first scheme from the strong RSA family that is more efficient than the RSA scheme.

The new signature scheme produces signature in two steps. The first step does not need to know a message, so can be done offline. The second step can be done when the message is known, which only needs a multiplication of two 160-bit integers. So far the best online performance among online/offline signature schemes is due to Joye's scheme [11]. The new scheme achieves the same level of online performance as Joye's scheme. However, the offline computation of Joye's scheme is about six times more expensive than the new scheme.

In summary, the new scheme is the state-of-the-art signature scheme from the strong RSA assumption, with best online and offline performance.

5.3   Security Property

Based on our analysis on the CL scheme and the YT scheme, we have the following theorem for the security of the new scheme.

Theorem 1. *The new scheme is existentially unforgeable under an adaptive chosen message attack, assuming the strong RSA assumption and the DLSE assumption, in the standard model.*

Proof. The CL scheme has been proved secure in the standard model based on the strong RSA assumption (Theorem 1 in [4]). As showed in Lemma 1, we can reduce the length of s to the setting in the new scheme without any impact on the security of the scheme. In the new scheme, b is a random generator of QR_n, and v, a, c are produced by choosing short exponents. By Lemma 2, v, a, c in the new scheme are indistinguishable from those in the CL scheme.

As a result, the new scheme is also secure in the standard model based on the strong RSA assumption and the DLSE assumption.   □

---

[1] The basic CS scheme needs 1502 modular multiplications. However, the implementation technique in Section 3 of [6] can reduce this cost to 1342 modular multiplications.

6 A Brief Comparison among Signature Schemes from the Strong RSA Family

In this section, we give a brief comparison among signature schemes from the strong RSA family. We also use the RSA scheme as the base for comparison. The parameter choices are based on a typical setting in the RSA based schemes in which n is chosen as a 1024-bit integer. For simplicity, we can use the number of modular multiplications in a scheme to estimate computational cost. For example, for a modular exponentiation $g^x \bmod n$, if x is a 160-bit integer, we can estimate its cost as 160 modular multiplications. All strong RSA based schemes need to produce a large prime number, and we consider that all schemes have the same cost for prime number generation. In the following table, we use "+ e" to represent the cost of prime number generation. For schemes which need hash computation, we take the bit length of hash value as 160. The comparison is showed in the following table. Clearly, the new scheme is the most efficient scheme so far.

Table 1. Comparison of Signature Schemes from the Strong RSA Family

Signature Scheme	Cost of Signature Generation	Support Online/Offline
RSA	1024	No
the CS scheme	1342 + e	No
the CL scheme	2526 + e	No
Zhu's scheme	1342 + e	No
Joye's scheme	1342 + e	Yes
the YT scheme	1022 + e	Yes
the new scheme	160 + e	Yes

7 Conclusions

In this paper, we discussed techniques on performance improvement of signature schemes based on the strong RSA assumption, and proposed a new signature scheme, which is state-of-the-art among constructions in the strong RSA family. It is the first signature scheme based on the strong RSA assumption that outperforms the standard RSA scheme. Before that, all available schemes in this family have low computational performance compared to the RSA scheme. Moreover, the new scheme can be proved secure in the standard model, while the standard RSA construction can only be demonstrated secure in the Random Oracle Model. Furthermore, the new scheme supports online/offline signing, and online performance stands in line with the best online/offline scheme so far (Joye's scheme).

Our work brings the current theoretical results into real life practice. Our next work will be implementation, field testing and verification, and future standardization.

Acknowledgments. This work is supported partially by NSFC No. 60903210 and No. 60873260, China national 863 project No. 2009AA01Z414, and China national 973 project No. 2007CB311202.

References

1. Baric, N., Pfitzmann, B.: Collision-Free Accumulators and Fail-Stop Signature Schemes without Trees. In: Fumy, W. (ed.) EUROCRYPT 1997. LNCS, vol. 1233, pp. 480–494. Springer, Heidelberg (1997)
2. Bellare, M., Rogaway, P.: Optimal Asymmetric Encryption. In: de Santis, A. (ed.) EURO-CRYPT 1994. LNCS, vol. 950, pp. 92–111. Springer, Heidelberg (1995)
3. Bellare, M., Rogaway, P.: The Exact Security of Digital Signatures — How to Sign with RSA and Rabin. In: Maurer, U.M. (ed.) EUROCRYPT 1996. LNCS, vol. 1070, pp. 399–416. Springer, Heidelberg (1996)
4. Camenisch, J., Lysyanskaya, A.: A Signature Scheme with Efficient Protocols. In: Cimato, S., Galdi, C., Persiano, G. (eds.) SCN 2002. LNCS, vol. 2576, pp. 268–289. Springer, Heidelberg (2003)
5. Canetti, R., Goldreich, O., Halevi, S.: The random oracle model, revisited. In: 30th Annual ACM Symposium on Theory of Computing, pp. 209–218 (1998)
6. Cramer, R., Shoup, V.: Signatures schemes based on the strong RSA assumption. ACM Transaction on Information and System Security, 161–185 (2000)
7. Fischlin, M.: The Cramer-Shoup Strong-RSA Signature Scheme Revisited. In: Desmedt, Y.G. (ed.) PKC 2003. LNCS, vol. 2567, pp. 116–129. Springer, Heidelberg (2002)
8. Fujisaki, E., Okamoto, T.: Statistical Zero Knowledge Protocols to Prove Modular Polynomial Relations. In: Kaliski Jr., B.S. (ed.) CRYPTO 1997. LNCS, vol. 1294, pp. 16–30. Springer, Heidelberg (1997)
9. Gennaro, R., Halevi, S., Rabin, T.: Secure Hash-and-Sign Signatures without the Random Oracle. In: Stern, J. (ed.) EUROCRYPT 1999. LNCS, vol. 1592, pp. 123–139. Springer, Heidelberg (1999)
10. Goldwasser, S., Micali, S., Rivest, R.: A digital signature scheme secure against adaptive chosen-message attacks. SIAM J. Computing 17, 281–308 (1988)
11. Joye, M.: An Efficient On-Line/Off-Line Signature Scheme without Random Oracles. In: Franklin, M.K., Hui, L.C.K., Wong, D.S. (eds.) CANS 2008. LNCS, vol. 5339, pp. 98–107. Springer, Heidelberg (2008)
12. Koshiba, T., Kurosawa, K.: Short Exponent Diffie-Hellman Problems. In: Bao, F., Deng, R., Zhou, J. (eds.) PKC 2004. LNCS, vol. 2947, pp. 173–186. Springer, Heidelberg (2004)
13. van Oorshot, P.C., Wiener, M.J.: On Diffie-Hellman Key Agreement with Short Exponents. In: Maurer, U.M. (ed.) EUROCRYPT 1996. LNCS, vol. 1070, pp. 332–343. Springer, Heidelberg (1996)
14. Rivest, R.L., Shamir, A., Adleman, L.: A method for obtaining digital signatures and public-key cryptosystems. Commnuications of the ACM 21, 120–126 (1978)
15. Shoup, V.: OAEP Reconsidered. In: Kilian, J. (ed.) CRYPTO 2001. LNCS, vol. 2139, pp. 239–259. Springer, Heidelberg (2001)
16. Yu, P., Tate, S.R.: Online/Offline Signature Schemes for Devices with Limited Computing Capabilites. In: Malkin, T. (ed.) CT-RSA 2008. LNCS, vol. 4964, pp. 301–317. Springer, Heidelberg (2008)
17. Zhu, H.: New digital signature scheme attaining immunity to adaptive chosen-message attack. Chinese Journal of Electronic 10(4), 484–486 (2001)
18. Zhu, H.: A formal proof of Zhu's signature scheme (2003),
   http://eprint.iacr.org/

Detailed Cost Estimation of CNTW Attack against EMV Signature Scheme

Tetsuya Izu[1], Yoshitaka Morikawa[2], Yasuyuki Nogami[2],
Yumi Sakemi[2], and Masahiko Takenaka[1]

[1] Fujitsu Laboratories Ltd.
4-1-1, Kamikodanaka, Nakahara-ku, Kawasaki, 211-8588, Japan
{izu,takenaka}@labs.fujitsu.com
[2] Okayama University
3-1-1, Tsushima-naka, Kita-ku, Okayama, 700–8530 Japan

Abstract. EMV signature is one of specifications for authenticating credit and debit card data, which is based on ISO/IEC 9796-2 signature scheme. At CRYPTO 2009, Coron, Naccache, Tibouchi, and Weinmann proposed a new forgery attack against the signature ISO/IEC 9796-2. They also briefly discussed the possibility when the attack is applied to the EMV signatures. They showed that the forging cost is $45,000 and concluded that the attack could not forge them for operational reason. However their results are derived from not fully analysis under only one condition. The condition they adopt is typical case. For security evaluation, fully analysis and an estimation in worst case are needed. This paper shows cost-estimation of CNTW attack against EMV signature in detail. We constitute an evaluate model and show cost-estimations under all conditions that Coron et al. do not estimate. As results, it has become clear that EMV signature can be forged with less than $2,000 according to a condition. This fact shows that CNTW attack might be a realistic threat.

1 Introduction

EMV is an international specification of IC card and IC card capable POS terminals and ATMs, for authenticating credit and debit card transaction. The name of EMV comes from the initial letters of Europay, MasterCard, and VISA, and the first version of EMV specification is decided by these three companies. Now, version 4.2 EMV is effect and is widely adopted by financial facilities around the world[4].

EMV defines the interaction of various level specifications between IC card and IC card processing devices for financial transactions, which are not only physical, electrical, logical specification, but also that of application. EMV signature that is included in these specifications is a digital signature scheme conform to ISO/IEC 9796-2 Scheme 1.

At the 29th International Cryptology Conference CRYPTO 2009, Coron et al. proposed a new forgery attack against ISO/IEC 9796-2 Scheme 1 (CNTW

G. Danezis, S. Dietrich, and K. Sako (Eds.): FC 2011 Workshops, LNCS 7126, pp. 13–26, 2012.
© IFCA/Springer-Verlag Berlin Heidelberg 2012

attack)[2]. This attack creates a forged signature from multitude of correct signatures. In case of ISO/IEC 9796-2 Scheme 1 signature with 2048-bit RSA, a forged signature can be calculated for two days using 19 servers on the Amazon EC2 grid for a total cost of about $800.

Since EMV signature scheme is conform to ISO/IEC 9796-2 Scheme 1, CNTW attack can be applied to it. Therefore, Coron et al. also showed the technique of applying their attack against EMV signature scheme. And they showed assumption applying the attack against EMV signature scheme to estimate the cost by using their experimental results of forging signature. In their estimation, a message format of EMV signature scheme was shown. The message is constituted plural fields that is set various information and data to be authenticated. They assumed to be classified these fields into alterable and locked fields for an adversary, which the cost increases according to amount of locked fields increases. They estimated the cost under the assumption. As results, they estimated the cost for forging signature by CNTW attack is $45,000. And, because large amount of correct signature must be used in attacking process, they concluded that forgery of EMV signature is hard in the operational condition.

The consensus of their assumption, however, is not completely obtained, and it is a possibility that the attack can use another classifications according to issuer of IC cards or IC card processing devices for EMV signature. Therefore, cost estimations by using assumptions of various classifications are necessary for security evaluation of EMV signature.

This paper shows cost estimations in detail under all classifiable conditions of EMV signature scheme, which were not evaluated by Coron et al. Especially, this paper also estimates the cost under the condition that have an advantage for adversary, and it is clearly beneficial for security evaluation of EMV signature scheme. In addition, in order to estimate in detail, this paper contributes a computation method of parameters for CNTW attack. As the result, we show that forgery attack can be applied to EMV signature scheme with practical cost in case of specific conditions.

This paper is organized as follows: in section 2, we show ISO/IEC 9796-2 Signature and CNTW attack. Section 3 shows EMV signature scheme is shown and CNTW attack is applied to EMV. In section 4, a calculating model is introduced for estimate the cost of the attack. And finally, we show results of cost estimation and discuss the security evaluation of EMV signature scheme.

2   ISO/IEC 9796-2 Signature and Attack

This section shows a specification of ISO/IEC 9796-2 Scheme 1 [5] and a forgery attack against the signature scheme by Coron, Naccache, Tibouchi, and Weinmann (CNTW attack)[2].

2.1   ISO/IEC 9796-2 Scheme 1

ISO/IEC 9796 specifies digital signature schemes giving partial (or total) message recovery. Now, there are ISO/IEC 9796-2 and ISO/IEC 9796-3 in ISO/IEC

9796 standard, which the security based on the difficulty of factorizing large numbers and based on the difficulty of discrete logarithm problem respectively. ISO/IEC 9796-2:2002 specifies three digital signature schemes (Scheme 1, 2, 3), two of which are deterministic (non-randomized) and one of which is randomized[5]. All three schemes can provide either total or partial message recovery. This paper targets only ISO/IEC 9796-2 Scheme 1 and describes it as "ISO/IEC 9796-2 signature". Followings show the specification of ISO/IEC 9796-2 signature.

Scheme1.KeyGen. According to security parameter k, this algorithm chooses a pair of private and public key $(\mathsf{sk}, \mathsf{pk})$, and $\mathsf{sk} = (p, q, d)$, $\mathsf{pk} = (N, e)$. Here, p, q are $k/2$-bit prime numbers, $N = p \cdot q$ is a k-bit composite number, and d, e are integer that $d \cdot e \equiv 1 \,(\mathrm{mod}\,(p - 1) \cdot (q - 1))$.

Scheme1.Sign. This algorithm signs a message m and generate a signature σ as follows:

$$\sigma = \mu(m)^d \bmod N$$

Here, padding function $\mu(\cdot)$ is defined to

$$\mu(m) = \mathtt{0x6A}||m[1]||H(m)||\mathtt{0xBC}.$$

$H(\cdot)$ shows hash function with k_H (≥ 160) bits output, $m[1]$ is a most significant $(k - k_H - 16)$-bit value of message m. $\mathtt{0x6A}$ shows the header that this padding format is specified by ISO/IEC 9796-2 (partial message recovery), and $\mathtt{0xBC}$ shows the trailer that SHA-1 is used as hash function in this format. Function $\mu(\cdot)$ always generates $(k - 1)$-bit data.

Scheme1.Verify. Receiving a signature and a message m, this algorithm verifies the signature. $\mu(m) = \sigma^e \bmod N$ is calculated, and format-checked. In format check process, it is checked whether header, trailer, and $\overline{m[1]}$ of $\mu(m)$ are correctly included in m. Then, $\overline{H(m)}$ is extracted from $\mu(m)$. If $\overline{H(m)}$ is equal to $H(m)$, this algorithm outputs "valid". In another case, this algorithm outputs "invalid".

Note that $m[1] = m$ when the length of m is less than or equal to $(k - k_H - 16)$-bit. Therefore, ISO/IEC 9796-2 is a total message recovery signature in this case, and a verify algorithm dose not need a message m for verifying.

2.2 CNTW Attack

In the 29th International Cryptology Conference CRYPTO 2009, Coron, Naccache, Tibouchi, and Weinmann proposed a new forgery attack against ISO/IEC 9796-2 Scheme 1 (CNTW attack) and showed experimental results that forged signature can be created by the attack[2]. In this subsection, CNTW attack is introduced.

The main technique of CNTW attack is that forged message m^* is represented by a multiplicative combination of L messages $m_1, m_2, \dots, m_L$ as follows:

$$\mu(m^*) = \delta^e \mu(m_1)^{e_1} \mu(m_2)^{e_2} \cdots \mu(m_L)^{e_L} \bmod N,$$

and to derive a factor δ and each exponents $e_1, e_2, \ldots, e_L$ ($1 \leq e_1, e_2, \ldots, e_L < e$)[1]. In this instance, between forged signature σ^* and correct signatures $\sigma_1, \sigma_2, \cdots, \sigma_L$ according to these messages, following equation is satisfied:

$$\sigma^* = \delta \cdot \sigma_1^{e_1} \sigma_2^{e_2} \cdots \sigma_L^{e_L} \bmod N.$$

Therefore, forged signature σ^* is actually derived when an adversary obtains signatures $\sigma_1, \sigma_2, \ldots, \sigma_L$.

In order to derive the multiplicative combination mentioned above, Desmedt and Odlyzko proposed the method with prime factorization of $\mu(m_i)$ in 1985[3]. Because this method is based on prime factorization, it can use only less than 200-bit $\mu(m_i)$ in practice. Thus, this method cannot apply to ISO/IEC 9796-2 signature.

In 1999, Coron, Naccache, and Stern improved the method (CNS attack)[1]. They introduced alternative padding function instead of $\mu(\cdot)$,

$$\nu_{a,b}(\cdot) = a \cdot \mu(\cdot) - b \cdot N,$$

and proposed the method based on prime factorization of $\nu_{a,b}(\cdot)$. In their method, when parameters a, b and message m are properly chosen, the padding function $\nu_{a,b}(m)$ outputs at most $(k_H + 16)$-bit value. Therefore, minimum cost for forging signature is 2^{54} in case of $k_H = 128$ (with MD5), and 2^{61} in case of $k_H = 160$ (with SHA-1). As results, they showed that ISO/IEC 9796-2 signature can be forged. However, ISO/IEC 9796-2 signature was not actually forged, and they only showed the possibility. At that time, ISO/IEC 9796-2 signature specified the hash function that has to output at least 128-bit value ($k_H \geq 128$). By their proposal, the specification is changed to $k_H \geq 160$.

In 2009, Coron, Naccache, Tibouchi, and Weinmann proposed the optimization method of CNS attack to show that the padding function $\nu_{a,b}(m)$ can output at most $(k_H + |a|)$-bit value. Here, $|a|$ is a bit-length of parameter a and a few bits value. In addition, they succeeded an experiment of forging signature in actual[2]. Their conditions used in the experiment are follows:

- N is a 2048-bit composite number,
- exponent $e = 2$,
- SHA-1 is used as hash function,
- $|a| = 10$,
- only messages that padding function $\nu_{a,b}(m)$ outputs $(k_H + |a| - 8)$-bit values are used.

Under this condition, they actually showed that a forged signature was calculated for 2 days with Amazon EC2 (Elastic Compute Cloud) service, which cost about $800.

---

[1]   A derivation of a factor δ is omitted in detail in this paper. The derivation is shown in [2].

2.3   EMV Specification and EMV Signature

EMV is an international specification of IC card and IC card capable POS terminals and ATMs, for authenticating credit and debit card transaction. EMV signature scheme, one of EMV specifications, is a digital signature scheme conform to ISO/IEC 9796-2 Scheme 1. Therefore, CNTW attack can be applied to EMV signature scheme. EMV signature scheme specifies 7 different formats, depending on the message type. In [2], Coron et al. showed approximative cost-estimation to apply their attack to them, and especially described one of these formats, the Static Data Authentication Issuer Public-key Data (SDA–IPKD). In this paper, we discuss cost-estimation in detail to apply CNTW attack to SDA–IPKD.

2.4   Applying CNTW Attack to SDA–IPKD

SDA–IPKD is one of formats for static data authentication of EMV signature. SDA–IPKD specifies a format of message m as follows:

$$m = \texttt{0x02}||D_1||D_2||D_3||D_4||D_5||D_6||D_7||N_I||\texttt{0x03}.$$

Here, D_1 is Issuer ID(32-bit), D_2 is Certification Expiration Date (16-bit), D_3 is Certificate Serial Number (24-bit), D_4 is Hash Algorithm ID (8-bit), D_5 is Issuer Public Key Algorithm ID (8-bit), D_6 is Issuer Public Key Length (8-bit), D_7 is Issuer Public Key Exponent Length (8-bit), and N_I is Issuer's modulus to be certified.

Using this format, padding function $\mu(\cdot)$ of ISO/IEC 9796-2 signature is represented as follows:

$$\mu(m) = \texttt{0x6A02}||D_1||D_2||\cdots||D_6||D_7||N_I[1]||H(m)||\texttt{0xBC}.$$

Here, $N_I = N_I[1]||N_I[2]$, and bit size of $N_I[1]$ is $|N_I[1]| = (k - k_H - 128)$-bit.

Coron et al. assumed that D_1, D_2 and N_I are alterable value, and $D_3 - D_7$ are locked values for an adversary. Then they cost-estimated the forgery by CNTW attack. As results, they reported that the cost to forge an EMV signature is \$45,000 with Amazon EC2. Where, padding function $\nu_{a,b}(\cdot)$ outputs at most 204-bit value if minimum parameters a (this is represented as $\hat{a}$ in following sections) can be properly chosen. Note that, in order to calculate $\hat{a}$, they estimated that 13 years and extra \$11,000 with Amazon EC2 was needed besides the cost of CNTW attack.

3   Cost-Estimation for Forging SDA–IPKD in Detail

Coron et al. assumed only a condition of alterable and locked fields for an adversary and approximative cost-estimated of forgery by CNTW attack. The consensus of their assumption, however, is not completely obtained, and it is a possibility that the attack can use another conditions according to issuer of IC cards or IC card processing devices for EMV signature. Therefore, we think that cost-estimations in detail with various conditions are necessary for security evaluation of EMV signature.

As mentioned in subsection 2.4, it takes 13 years to calculate $\hat{a}$ under their condition. Thus cost to calculate $\hat{a}$ is not negligible. However, they cost-estimated only for CNTW attack without cost of calculating $\hat{a}$.

In this paper, we construct an evaluation model with all conditions that $D_1 - D_7$ fields are alterable or locked, and show the cost-estimation of CNTW attack in detail including cost to calculate parameter a.

3.1   Evaluation Model

In order to apply CNTW attack more efficiently, parameters a, b should be provided for output of $\nu_{a,b}(\cdot) = a \cdot \mu(\cdot) - b \cdot N$ to be as small as possible. Conditions of $D_1 - D_7$ directly concern the decision of these parameters. Therefore, to clearly show the effect of the condition, padding function $\mu_n(\cdot)$ is represented as follows:

$$\mu_n(m) = \texttt{0x6A02}||Y_1||X_1|| \cdots ||Y_n||X_n||N_I[1]||H(m)||\texttt{0xBC}$$

Here, X_i $(1 \leq i \leq n)$ are alterable values for an adversary, and Y_i $(1 \leq i \leq n)$ are locked values. n is a number of set of X_i and Y_i. X_n and Y_1 can be 0-bit values. For example, the condition of Coron et al., D_1 and D_2 are alterable values for an adversary and $D_3 - D_7$ are locked value, is represented as $n = 2$, $X_1 = D_1||D_2$, $Y_2 = D_3||D_4||D_5||D_6||D_7$, and Y_1, X_2 are 0-bit values in our model.

Since conditions are defined by 7 values $D_1 - D_7$, there are $2^7 = 128$ conditions. According to these conditions, 4 types $(n = 1, 2, 3, 4)$ of padding function $\mu_n(\cdot)$ are constructed. We calculate parameters and cost-estimate for CNTW attack according to these 4 types of $\mu_n(\cdot)$.

3.2   Calculating Parameters for EMV Signature

Cost to calculate parameter a is also considered in our cost-estimation. In this subsection, we describe the cost-estimation to calculate a that constitute a padding function $\nu_{a,b}(\cdot) = b \cdot N - a \cdot \mu_n(\cdot)$ for CNTW attack.

In CNTW attack, output length of a padding function $\nu_{a,b}(m)$ is minimized by choosing proper parameters a, b. For ISO/IEC 9796-2 signature, parameter b and output length are deterministically provided by parameter a. Thus, minimum parameter a that proper output length of $\nu_{a,b}(m)$ (that is $\hat{a}$) can be found by exhaustive search.

On the other hand, in order to obtain proper output length of $\nu_{a,b}(m)$ for EMV signature, proper parameters not only a, b but also X_i those are alterable values for an adversary should be found. Because of increasing a number of variables, it is difficult that proper output length of $\nu_{a,b}(m)$ can be found by exhaustive search.

Finding small values of plural variables so as to minimize the value of polynomial in these variables is a Closest Vector Problem (CVP). Coron et al. introduced the LLL algorithm [6] to solve this problem. The LLL algorithm is a polynomial time of lattice reduction algorithm. CVP can be easily solved using the LLL algorithm. Under their condition, Coron et al. found small b, X_1 and proper $\nu_{a,b}(m)$ regarding specified a. They used the LLL algorithm to solve CVP in a bi-dimensional lattice ($n = 2$). CVP in a multidimensional lattice ($n \geq 3$) can be easily solved by the LLL algorithm. We also use the LLL algorithm for calculating and cost-estimation of CNTW attack.

3.3 Cost-Estimation of Calculating Parameters with LLL Algorithm

When small b, X_i and proper $\nu_{a,b}(m)$ is found regarding specified k_a-bit a with the LLL algorithm, the length of proper $\nu_{a,b}(m)$ ($|\nu_{a,b}(m)|$) is less than ($k - \sum_{i=1}^{n} k_{X_i}$)-bit. Because b, X_i can take k_a-bit, k_{X_i}-bit values respectively. CNTW attack, however, needs a set of parameters a, b, X_i that $|\nu_{a,b}(m)| \leq (k + k_a - 16 - \sum_{i=1}^{n} k_{X_i} - \sum_{i=1}^{n} k_{Y_i})$. That is, most significant $(16 + \sum_{i=1}^{n} k_{X_i} + \sum_{i=1}^{n} k_{Y_i})$-bit of $a \cdot \mu(\cdot)$ want to be canceled by proper a, b and X_i. Here, $|\mu(\cdot)|$ is k-bit, $|a|$ and $|b|$ are both k_a-bit, and $|X_i|$, $|Y_i|$ are k_{X_i}-bit, k_{Y_i}-bit respectively.

Expectation of proper $|\nu_{a,b}(m)|$ is $(16 + \sum_{i=1}^{n} k_{Y_i} - k_a)$-bit larger than that necessary for CNTW attack. Therefore, LLL search is repeated about $2^{16 + \sum_{i=1}^{n} k_{Y_i} - k_a}$ times regarding various a. Then a set of parameters a, b, X_i that $|\nu_{a,b}(m)| \leq (k + k_a - 16 - \sum_{i=1}^{n} k_{X_i} - \sum_{i=1}^{n} k_{Y_i})$ is probably found by the heuristic search. And, $|a| = k_a$ satisfies following relation:

$$k_a \geq 16 + \sum_{i=1}^{n} k_{Y_i} - k_a,$$

the minimum k_a is provided

$$k_a = \frac{16 + \sum_{i=1}^{n} k_{Y_i}}{2}.$$

If a value to satisfy above condition is found, the most significant Z-bit of $\nu_{a,b}(m)$ can be adjusted to 0,

$$Z = 16 + \sum_{i=1}^{n} k_{X_i} + \sum_{i=1}^{n} k_{Y_i}.$$

Then, bit length of output of $\nu_{a,b}(m)$ is $(k + k_a - Z)$-bit. In addition, an adversary chooses proper $N_I[1]$, and the most significant $(Z + |N_I[1]|)$-bit of $\nu_{a,b}(m)$ can be adjusted to 0. Thus, using these techniques, $|\nu_{a,b}(\cdot)|$ is as follows:

$$|\nu_{a,b}(m)| = k + k_a - (Z + |N_I[1]|) = k_H + k_a + 8 \tag{1}$$

As mentioned above, in order to provide a proper $\nu_{a,b}(m)$, it is necessary to repeatedly calculate the LLL algorithm with various a. Such a that provides a proper $\nu_{a,b}(m)$ is represented by $\bar{a}$, here. In this paper, we estimate the cost of providing $\bar{a}$ by a number of searching with various a ($= \sharp\bar{a}$) and a cost par calculating the LLL algorithm as follows:

$$(\text{Cost of providing } \bar{a}) = \sharp\bar{a} \cdot (\text{cost par calculating LLL algorithm}) .$$

A cost of calculating the LLL algorithm, that is provided $O((n+1)^4)$, hardly depend on a number of variables. Table 1 shows the cost of calculating the LLL algorithm by n that is a number of variables X_i. Note that, a number of variables of the LLL algorithm is n because $X_i (1 \leq i \leq n-1)$ and b are the variables of CNTW attack. Note that, since X_n can be handled by concatenating to $N_I[1]$ as $X_n \| N_I[1]$, we assume that X_n is excluded in the variables. And, these costs are derived by experimental measurement with one core of Core 2 Quad 2.66 GHz. In addition, in case of $n = 1$, the cost is estimated as ~ 0 because parameters can be easily provided without the LLL.

Table 1. Cost of calculating the LLL algorithm by n

n	Cost [ms]
1	~ 0
2	1.6
3	6.2
4	15.5

On the other hand, $\sharp a$ is provided by search space of a (a number of k_a-bit integer) and existing probability of $\bar{a}$. We assume that the existing probability of $\bar{a}$ is constant, and search space increases in proportion to $(2^{k_a})^2$. Because b increases 1-bit as a increases 1-bit, the search space quadruples. Therefore, expectation of a number of $\bar{a}$ ($E(\bar{a})$) is provided as follows:

$$E(\bar{a}) = 4^{k_a - \frac{16 + \sum_{i=1}^n k_{Y_i}}{2}}$$

Here, we assume that $E(\bar{a}) = 1$ when $k_a = (16 + \sum_{i=1}^n k_{Y_i})/2$. This existing probability was provided by our experiments.

As mentioned above, $\sharp\bar{a}$ with just k_a-bit is provided as follows:

$$\sharp\bar{a} = \frac{2^{k_a - 1}}{4^{k_a - \frac{16 + \sum_{i=1}^n k_{Y_i}}{2}} - 4^{k_a - 1 - \frac{16 + \sum_{i=1}^n k_{Y_i}}{2}}} = \frac{2^{16 + \sum_{i=1}^n k_{Y_i} - k_a + 1}}{3} \quad (2)$$

These equation shows that it costs too large to find small $\bar{a}$ — and vice versa. Note that, all a are $\bar{a}$ in case $k_a \geq 16 + \sum_{i=1}^n k_{Y_i}$.

4   Results of Estimation and Discussion

In this section, we estimate the cost of CNTW attack against EMV signature. And, our estimation is compared with the results of Coron et al.

4.1   About Experimental Results of Coron et al.

Coron et al. computer experimented to find an $\bar{a}$ with $k_a = 52$ in [2]. They reported that $\sharp\bar{a}$ was $8,303,995 \simeq 2^{23}$ for 109 minutes with single-core 2 GHz

CPU to find an $\bar{a}$. And, they assumed that minimum $\bar{a}$ ($\hat{a}$) has $(16 + \sum_{i=1}^{n} k_{Y_i})/2$-bit, and estimated the cost to find $\hat{a}$ from their results. Under their conditions, $(16 + \sum_{i=1}^{n} k_{Y_i})/2 = 36$, the cost was provided as follows:

$$109 \cdot 2^{16+56-36}/2^{16+56-52} = 7.1 \cdot 10^6 \ [minutes] \simeq 13 \ [years] \qquad (3)$$

This is converted into \$11,000 on Amazon EC2 [2].

In our estimation, $\sharp\bar{a}$ with $k_a = 52$ is $\simeq 2^{20}$ from equation (2). Then, when we tried plural experiments with $k_a = 52$, we had results of $\sharp\bar{a}$ were 2^{19}—2^{20} values. And, equation (3) implies that Coron et al. estimated with 2^{20}. This contradicts their report that $\sharp\bar{a} \simeq 2^{23}$ for 109 minutes.

In addition, Coron et al. assumed that $\hat{a}$ is the best in $\bar{a}$. Using $\hat{a}$, the cost of CNTW attack is minimized certainly. They, however, consider the costs of CNTW attack and LLL algorithm independently. The cost of forgery against EMV signature includes both costs, and total cost should be estimated. Therefore, we define the best $\bar{a}$ as not $\hat{a}$ but $\tilde{a}$ that total cost is minimized with it, and estimate these costs.

As just described, their cost-estimation against EMV signature was inaccurate. In this paper, we estimate the cost in detail by using our evaluation model.

4.2 Cost-Estimation of CNTW Attack against EMV Signature

From above discussion, total costs of CNTW attack are estimated against all conditions of SDA–IPKD (with SHA-1). Our result is shown in Table 2. These results are arranged in ascending order of total cost.

Each column in Table 2 means as follows:

- "D_1–D_7" shows conditions of alterable (1) or locked (0) of D_1–D_7 fields.
- "n" is a number of set of X_i and Y_i.
- "$|\hat{a}|$" is bit size of minimum $\bar{a}$ that is provided $(16 + \sum_{i=1}^{n} k_{Y_i})/2$.
- "$|\tilde{a}|$" is bit size of optimal $\bar{a}$ that total cost is minimized with it.
- "$\sharp\tilde{a}$" is a logarithmic number of searching $\tilde{a}$.
- "$|\nu_{a,b}(\cdot)|$" is a bit size of output of padding function $\nu_{a,b}(\cdot)$.
- "LLL cost" is a cost of calculating LLL algorithm on Amazon EC2.
- "CNTW cost" is a cost of CNTW attack on Amazon EC2 that is converted from results of [2].
- "Total cost" is LLL cost + CNTW cost.

Here, $\sharp\tilde{a}$, $|\nu_{a,b}(\cdot)|$, LLL cost, CNTW cost, and total cost are provided corresponding to $\tilde{a}$. And, $|\nu_{a,b}(\cdot)|$ is 8-bit smaller than values provided equation (1) because we also introduce a same technique as [2]. This technique only choose values of which the most significant 8-bit is 0.

---

[2] Though this is $4.3 \cdot 10^8$ [minutes] in [2], $7.1 \cdot 10^6$ [minutes] is correct. And, $7.1 \cdot 10^6$ [minutes] = 119057 [hours]. According that a cost is \$0.1 par hour par single core CPU on Amazon EC2, it seems that their estimated cost on Amazon EC2 is \$12,000 correctly.

From Table 2, total cost increases according as a size of locked fields increases. Because size of a increases according as this size, both LLL cost and CNTW cost increase.

Table 2. Cost of CNTW attack against EMV signature under all conditions

D_1–D_7	n	$|\hat{a}|$ [bit]	$|\tilde{a}|$ [bit]	$\sharp\tilde{a}$ [log 2]	$|\nu_{a,b}(\cdot)|$ [bit]	LLL cost [$]	CNTW cost [$]	Total cost [$]
1111111	1	8	8	7.5	168	0	1,219	1,219
1110111	2	12	12	11.5	172	0	1,987	1,987
1111011	2	12	12	11.5	172	0	1,987	1,987
1111101	2	12	12	11.5	172	0	1,987	1,987
1111110	2	12	12	11.5	172	0	1,987	1,987
1011111	2	16	16	15.5	177	0	3,221	3,221
1110011	2	16	16	15.5	177	0	3,221	3,221
1111001	2	16	16	15.5	177	0	3,221	3,221
1111100	2	16	16	15.5	177	0	3,221	3,221
1110101	3	16	16	15.5	177	0	3,221	3,221
1110110	3	16	16	15.5	177	0	3,221	3,221
1111010	3	16	16	15.5	177	0	3,221	3,221
1101111	2	20	20	19.5	180	0	5,159	5,159
1110001	2	20	20	19.5	180	0	5,159	5,159
1111000	2	20	20	19.5	180	0	5,159	5,159
1010111	3	20	20	19.5	180	0	5,159	5,159
1011011	3	20	20	19.5	180	0	5,159	5,159
1011101	3	20	20	19.5	180	0	5,159	5,159
1011110	3	20	20	19.5	180	0	5,159	5,159
1110010	3	20	20	19.5	180	0	5,159	5,159
1110100	3	20	20	19.5	180	0	5,159	5,159
0111111	1	24	24	23.5	184	0	8,293	8,293
1100111	2	24	24	23.5	184	0	8,293	8,294
1110000	2	24	24	23.5	184	0	8,293	8,294
1010011	3	24	24	23.5	184	2	8,293	8,295
1011001	3	24	24	23.5	184	2	8,293	8,295
1011100	3	24	24	23.5	184	2	8,293	8,295
1101011	3	24	24	23.5	184	2	8,293	8,295
1101101	3	24	24	23.5	184	2	8,293	8,295
1101110	3	24	24	23.5	184	2	8,293	8,295
1010101	4	24	24	23.5	184	5	8,293	8,298
1010110	4	24	24	23.5	184	5	8,293	8,298
1011010	4	24	24	23.5	184	5	8,293	8,298
0110111	2	28	28	27.5	188	8	13,224	13,232
0111011	2	28	28	27.5	188	8	13,224	13,232
0111101	2	28	28	27.5	188	8	13,224	13,232
0111110	2	28	28	27.5	188	8	13,224	13,232
1001111	2	28	28	27.5	188	8	13,224	13,232
1100011	2	28	28	27.5	188	8	13,224	13,232

Table 2. (*continued*)

D_1–D_7	n	$|\hat{a}|$ [bit]	$|\tilde{a}|$ [bit]	$\sharp\tilde{a}$ [log 2]	$|\nu_{a,b}(\cdot)|$ [bit]	LLL cost [$]	CNTW cost [$]	Total cost [$]
1010001	3	28	28	27.5	188	31	13,224	13,255
1011000	3	28	28	27.5	188	31	13,224	13,255
1100101	3	28	28	27.5	188	31	13,224	13,255
1100110	3	28	28	27.5	188	31	13,224	13,255
1101001	3	28	28	27.5	188	31	13,224	13,255
1101100	3	28	28	27.5	188	31	13,224	13,255
1010010	4	28	28	27.5	188	77	13,224	13,301
1010100	4	28	28	27.5	188	77	13,224	13,301
1101010	4	28	28	27.5	188	77	13,224	13,301
0011111	1	32	32	31.5	192	0	20,906	20,907
0110011	2	32	32	31.5	192	127	20,906	21,034
0111001	2	32	32	31.5	192	127	20,906	21,034
0111100	2	32	32	31.5	192	127	20,906	21,034
1000111	2	32	32	31.5	192	127	20,906	21,034
1100001	2	32	32	31.5	192	127	20,906	21,034
0110101	3	32	32	31.5	192	493	20,906	21,400
0110110	3	32	32	31.5	192	493	20,906	21,400
0111010	3	32	32	31.5	192	493	20,906	21,400
1001011	3	32	32	31.5	192	493	20,906	21,400
1001101	3	32	32	31.5	192	493	20,906	21,400
1001110	3	32	32	31.5	192	493	20,906	21,400
1010000	3	32	32	31.5	192	493	20,906	21,400
1100010	3	32	32	31.5	192	493	20,906	21,400
1100100	3	32	32	31.5	192	493	20,906	21,400
1101000	3	32	32	31.5	192	493	20,906	21,400
0010111	2	36	36	35.5	196	2,036	33,164	35,200
0011011	2	36	36	35.5	196	2,036	33,164	35,200
0011101	2	36	36	35.5	196	2,036	33,164	35,200
0011110	2	36	36	35.5	196	2,036	33,164	35,200
0101111	2	36	36	35.5	196	2,036	33,164	35,200
0110001	2	36	36	35.5	196	2,036	33,164	35,200
0111000	2	36	36	35.5	196	2,036	33,164	35,200
1000011	2	36	36	35.5	196	2,036	33,164	35,200
1100000	**2**	**36**	**36**	**35.5**	**196**	**2,036**	**33,164**	**35,200**
0110010	3	36	36	35.5	196	7,890	33,164	41,054
0110100	3	36	36	35.5	196	7,890	33,164	41,054
1000101	3	36	36	35.5	196	7,890	33,164	41,054
1000110	3	36	36	35.5	196	7,890	33,164	41,054
1001001	3	36	36	35.5	196	7,890	33,164	41,054
1001100	3	36	36	35.5	196	7,890	33,164	41,054
1001010	4	36	38	33.5	197	4,931	41,773	46,704
0010011	2	40	42	37.5	201	8,145	65,128	73,273
0011001	2	40	42	37.5	201	8,145	65,128	73,273
0011100	2	40	42	37.5	201	8,145	65,128	73,273
0100111	2	40	42	37.5	201	8,145	65,128	73,273
0110000	2	40	42	37.5	201	8,145	65,128	73,273

Table 2. (*continued*)

D_1–D_7	n	$|\hat{a}|$ [bit]	$|\tilde{a}|$ [bit]	$\sharp\tilde{a}$ [log 2]	$|\nu_{a,b}(\cdot)|$ [bit]	LLL cost [$]	CNTW cost [$]	Total cost [$]
1000001	2	40	42	37.5	201	8,145	65,128	73,273
0001111	1	44	44	43.5	204	1,629	81,418	83,046
0010101	3	40	43	36.5	203	15,780	72,812	88,592
0010110	3	40	43	36.5	203	15,780	72,812	88,592
0011010	3	40	43	36.5	203	15,780	72,812	88,592
0101011	3	40	43	36.5	203	15,780	72,812	88,592
0101101	3	40	43	36.5	203	15,780	72,812	88,592
0101110	3	40	43	36.5	203	15,780	72,812	88,592
1000010	3	40	43	36.5	203	15,780	72,812	88,592
1000100	3	40	43	36.5	203	15,780	72,812	88,592
1001000	3	40	43	36.5	203	15,780	72,812	88,592
0000111	1	48	48	47.5	208	26,062	127,534	153,596
0010001	2	44	49	38.5	208	16,289	142,745	159,034
0011000	2	44	49	38.5	208	16,289	142,745	159,034
0100011	2	44	49	38.5	208	16,289	142,745	159,034
1000000	2	44	49	38.5	208	16,289	142,745	159,034
0010010	3	44	50	37.5	210	31,560	159,655	191,215
0010100	3	44	50	37.5	210	31,560	159,655	191,215
0100101	3	44	50	37.5	210	31,560	159,655	191,215
0100110	3	44	50	37.5	210	31,560	159,655	191,215
0101001	3	44	50	37.5	210	31,560	159,655	191,215
0101100	3	44	50	37.5	210	31,560	159,655	191,215
0101010	4	44	51	36.5	211	39,450	177,837	217,287
0000011	1	52	55	48.5	215	52,125	274,261	326,386
0001011	2	48	56	39.5	215	32,578	305,769	338,347
0001101	2	48	56	39.5	215	32,578	305,769	338,347
0001110	2	48	56	39.5	215	32,578	305,769	338,347
0010000	2	48	56	39.5	215	32,578	305,769	338,347
0100001	2	48	56	39.5	215	32,578	305,769	338,347
0100010	3	48	57	38.5	217	63,120	340,958	404,078
0100100	3	48	57	38.5	217	63,120	340,958	404,078
0101000	3	48	57	38.5	217	63,120	340,958	404,078
0000001	1	56	62	49.5	222	104,250	589,355	693,605
0000101	2	52	62	41.5	222	130,312	589,355	719,668
0000110	2	52	62	41.5	222	130,312	589,355	719,668
0001001	2	52	62	41.5	222	130,312	589,355	719,668
0001100	2	52	62	41.5	222	130,312	589,355	719,668
0100000	2	52	62	41.5	222	130,312	589,355	719,668
0001010	3	52	64	39.5	224	126,240	727,862	854,103
0000000	1	60	69	50.5	229	208,500	1,235,081	1,443,581
0000010	2	56	69	42.5	229	260,625	1,235,081	1,495,706
0000100	2	56	69	42.5	229	260,625	1,235,081	1,495,706
0001000	2	56	69	42.5	229	260,625	1,235,081	1,495,706

Then $\tilde{a}$ is compared with $\hat{a}$ in Table 2. Coron et al. assumed that the best $\bar{a}$ is minimum $\bar{a}$ ($\hat{a}$) because the cost of CNTW attack decreases according as a size of $\bar{a}$ decreases. However, $\tilde{a}$ (optimal $\bar{a}$) does not necessarily coincide as $\hat{a}$. LLL cost is negligible in case a size of locked fields is small. But, according as the size increases LLL cost increases and cannot be negligible. LLL cost can decrease by increasing the size of k_a. Therefore, decreasing LLL cost more improves total cost than minimizing CNTW cost in case of large size of locked fields.

4.3   Impact of CNTW Attack against EMV Signature

In this subsection, we discuss impact of CNTW attack against EMV signature. As mentioned in subsection 4.1, cost-estimation of Coron et al. against EMV signature was inaccurate. Table 2 shows that LLL cost is $2,036$, CNTW cost is $33,164$, and total cost is $35,200$ under their condition, which is indicated the row D_1–$D_7 = 1100000$. This estimation is compared with their results, which LLL cost is $11,000$ and CNTW cost is $45,000$. Our estimation is 40% lower than theirs.

From Table 2, EMV signature can be forged with less than $2,000$ according to a condition. this fact shows that CNTW attack is a realistic threat. Coron et al. assumed only a condition D_1–$D_7 = 1100000$, and concluded that CNTW attack is not a realistic threat. Their estimation, however, was inaccurate, and the consensus of their assumption is not completely obtained. It is a possibility that other conditions are used according to issuer of IC cards or IC card processing devices for EMV signature.

CNTW attack has been potential threat yet. However, a cause of such a problem depends on using traditional signature scheme such as ISO/IEC 9796-2 Scheme 1. Therefore, IC card of EMV specification should adopt provable secure signature methods such as ISO/IEC 9796-2 Scheme 2.

5   Concluding Remarks

This paper has shown cost-estimation of CNTW attack against EMV signature in detail. An evaluate model has been constitute and total cost included LLL cost has been estimated. In addition, we have shown cost-estimations under all conditions that Coron et al. do not estimate. As results, it has become clear that EMV signature can be forged with less than $2,000$ according to a condition. This fact shows that CNTW attack might be a realistic threat. A cause of such a problem depends on using traditional signature scheme such as ISO/IEC 9796-2 Scheme 1. Therefore, IC card of EMV specification should adopt provable secure signature methods such as ISO/IEC 9796-2 Scheme 2.

References

1. Coron, J., Naccache, D., Stern, J.: On the Security of RSA Padding. In: Wiener, M. (ed.) CRYPTO 1999. LNCS, vol. 1666, pp. 1–18. Springer, Heidelberg (1999)
2. Coron, J., Naccache, D., Tibouchi, M., Weinmann, R.-P.: Practical Cryptanalysis of ISO/IEC 9796-2 and EMV Signatures. In: Halevi, S. (ed.) CRYPTO 2009. LNCS, vol. 5677, pp. 428–444. Springer, Heidelberg (2009)
3. Desmedt, Y., Odlyzko, A.: A Chosen Text Attack on the RSA Cryptosystem and Some Discrete Logarithm Schemes. In: Williams, H.C. (ed.) CRYPTO 1985. LNCS, vol. 218, pp. 516–522. Springer, Heidelberg (1986)
4. Emv, Integrated circuit card specifications for payment systems, Book 2. Security and Key Management. Version 4.2 (June 2008), www.emvco.com
5. International Organization for Standardization (ISO): Information Technology – Security Techniques – Digital Signature Schemes Giving Message Recovery – Part 2: Integer Factorization based Mechanisms (2002)
6. Lenstra, A.K., Lenstra Jr., H.W., Lovász, L.: Factoring polynomials with rational coefficients. Mathematische Annalen. 261, 513–534 (1982)

Fast Elliptic Curve Cryptography in OpenSSL

Emilia Käsper[1,2]

[1] Google
[2] Katholieke Universiteit Leuven, ESAT/COSIC
emilia.kasper@esat.kuleuven.be

Abstract. We present a 64-bit optimized implementation of the NIST
and SECG-standardized elliptic curve P-224. Our implementation is fully
integrated into OpenSSL 1.0.1: full TLS handshakes using a 1024-bit
RSA certificate and ephemeral Elliptic Curve Diffie-Hellman key exchange over P-224 now run at twice the speed of standard OpenSSL,
while atomic elliptic curve operations are up to 4 times faster. In addition, our implementation is immune to timing attacks—most notably,
we show how to do small table look-ups in a cache-timing resistant way,
allowing us to use precomputation. To put our results in context, we
also discuss the various security-performance trade-offs available to TLS
applications.

Keywords: elliptic curve cryptography, OpenSSL, side-channel attacks,
fast implementations.

1 Introduction

1.1 Introduction to TLS

Transport Layer Security (TLS), the successor to Secure Socket Layer (SSL),
is a protocol for securing network communications. In its most common use, it
is the "S" (standing for "Secure") in HTTPS. Two of the most popular open-
source cryptographic libraries implementing SSL and TLS are OpenSSL [19]
and Mozilla Network Security Services (NSS) [17]: OpenSSL is found in, e.g.,
the Apache-SSL secure web server, while NSS is used by Mozilla Firefox and
Chrome web browsers, amongst others.

TLS provides authentication between connecting parties, as well as encryption of all transmitted content. Thus, before any application data is transmitted, peers perform authentication and key exchange in a TLS *handshake*. Two
common key exchange mechanisms in TLS are RSA key exchange and (authenticated) Diffie-Hellman (DH) key exchange. While RSA key exchange is computationally cheaper, DH key exchange provides the additional property of *perfect
forward secrecy*. Our work was motivated from a practical viewpoint: after analyzing the overhead associated with forward secure cipher suites, we set out to
improve the performance of Diffie-Hellman handshakes in OpenSSL. As a result,
we describe a new optimized elliptic curve implementation that is integrated into
OpenSSL and fully compatible with the elliptic curve flavour of DH handshakes
in TLS.

G. Danezis, S. Dietrich, and K. Sako (Eds.): FC 2011 Workshops, LNCS 7126, pp. 27–39, 2012.
© IFCA/Springer-Verlag Berlin Heidelberg 2012

1.2 Forward Secrecy in TLS

In a typical TLS handshake, say, when the client is a browser connecting to an HTTPS server, authentication is unilateral, meaning that only the server is authenticated to the client. In an RSA handshake, authenticated key exchange is achieved via the following mechanism: the server sends its RSA public key together with a corresponding certificate; the client, upon successfully verifying the certificate, replies with the pre-master secret, encrypted with the server's public key. Now, the server can decrypt the client's key exchange message and both parties derive a shared session key from the pre-master secret.

RSA handshakes exhibit a single point of failure: the security of all sessions relies on a single static key. If the server's private RSA key is compromised, the security of *all* sessions established under that key is violated. In other words, the attacker can record TLS traffic and decrypt these sessions later, should the key become compromised.

The complementary property, *forward secrecy*, which ensures that no long-term key compromise can affect the security of past sessions, is achieved in TLS via authenticated Diffie-Hellman (DH) handshakes. Contrary to RSA handshakes, the server's long-term RSA key now serves solely the purpose of authentication: it is only used to *sign* the server's DH value. If ephemeral DH is used, i.e., both parties generate a fresh DH value for every handshake, we achieve perfect forward secrecy, as the security of each session depends on a different instance of the DH problem.

While forward secrecy is undoubtedly a nice property to have, it comes at a cost. In an RSA handshake, the server needs to perform one private RSA operation (decryption); in a DH handshake, the server still needs a private RSA operation (signing) and, in addition, two exponentiations in the DH group. For more efficient Diffie-Hellman operations, TLS thus specifies an extension for elliptic curves, which achieve equivalent security with smaller group and field sizes (and hence, faster computation time).

Elliptic curve cryptography in TLS, as specified in RFC 4492 [7], includes elliptic curve Diffie-Hellman (ECDH) key exchange in two flavours: fixed-key key exchange with ECDH certificates; and ephemeral ECDH key exchange using an RSA or ECDSA certificate for authentication. While we focus our discussion on the ephemeral cipher suites providing perfect forward secrecy, our implementation results are also applicable to ECDH certificates and ECDSA signatures.

2 Motivation

2.1 Security Parameter Choices in TLS

An application choosing its TLS parameters should consider that the security of the session is bounded not only by the security of the symmetric encryption algorithm, but also by the security of the key exchange algorithm used to establish the session key—a session using AES-128 still achieves only roughly 80-bit security if 1024-bit RSA key exchange is used. According to various key length recommendations [12,18], in order to match 128-bit security, the server should use an RSA encryption key or a DH group of at least 3072 bits, or an elliptic curve over a 256-bit field, while a computationally more feasible 2048-bit RSA key/DH group or a 224-bit elliptic curve still achieves 112 bits of security.

In settings where 2048-bit RSA is considered prohibitively slow, ECDH key exchange with a 1024-bit RSA signing key offers a neat security-performance trade-off—it is faster than plain 2048-bit RSA key exchange (see Sect. 4 for exact timings), while offering perfect forward secrecy.[1] Yet ECDH key exchange is still significantly slower than 1024-bit RSA key exchange. Currently, one 224-bit elliptic curve point multiplication costs more in OpenSSL than a 1024-bit private RSA operation (and recall that the server needs *two* EC multiplications per handshake, while it needs only one RSA operation), so we focused our attention on optimizing the performance of the OpenSSL elliptic curve library. More specifically, as a lot of speed can be gained from implementing custom field arithmetic for a fixed field, we chose the NIST P-224 elliptic curve (`secp224r1` in [20]) as a target for our 64-bit optimized implementation.

2.2 Why NIST P-224?

Recently, several authors have published fast code for custom elliptic curves offering roughly 128 bits of security (see e.g. the SUPERCOP collected benchmarking results [11]). However, as our goal was to improve the performance of TLS handshakes in the OpenSSL library, we needed to ensure that the curve we choose is also supported by other common client libraries, and that the TLS protocol supports the negotiation of the curve.

Following the recommendations of the Standards for Efficient Cryptography Group [20], RFC 4492 specifies a list of 25 named curves for use in TLS, with field size ranging from 160 to 571 bits. Both OpenSSL and the Mozilla NSS library support all those curves. In addition, TLS allows peers to indicate support for unnamed prime and/or characteristic-2 curves (the OpenSSL elliptic curve library supports unnamed curves, while NSS does not). Yet the TLS specification has two important restrictions. First, it is assumed that the curve is of the form $y^2 = x^3 + ax + b$ (i.e., a Weierstrass curve), since the only parameters conveyed between the peers are the values a and b—many of the fastest elliptic curves today do not meet this format. Second, the client cannot indicate support for a specific unnamed curve in its protocol messages (that is, a client wishing to use unnamed curves must support all of them). Given these constraints, we chose to optimize one of the named curves, NIST P-224.[2]

Note that in order to provide 128-bit security, one of the two 256-bit named curves would have been a logical choice. Yet it happens that the 224-bit curve

---

[1] While the 1024-bit RSA key still offers only 80 bits protection, its use as a *signing-only* key is less of a paradox, as the compromise of this key does not affect the security of past legitimate sessions.

[2] As noted in RFC 4492, curve monoculture can lead to focused attacks on a single curve; yet NIST P-224 offers a comfortable 112-bit security level.

lends itself to a much faster implementation. Namely, an element of a 224-bit field fits easily in four 64-bit registers, while a 256-bit element needs five registers (it could fit in 4, but we also want to accommodate carry bits for efficient and timing-attack resistant modular reduction). An extra register, in turn, implies slower field arithmetic. For example, multiplication of two 5-register elements requires 25 64-bit multiplications, while multiplication of two 4-register elements requires only 16.

Aside from suitable field length, the NIST P-224 prime has a very simple format ($p = 2^{224} - 2^{96} + 1$) that further facilitates efficient field arithmetic.[3] Indeed, Bernstein has already made use of this by implementing NIST P-224 for 32-bit platforms, using clever floating point arithmetic [2]. However, we chose to reimplement the curve from scratch, using more efficient 64-bit integer arithmetic, as well as adding side-channel protection.

2.3   Side-Channel Concerns

In addition to providing a fast implementation, we wanted to offer one that was constant-time and thus verifiably resistant to timing attacks. The lack of side-channel protection in the current OpenSSL elliptic curve library has already been successfully exploited by Brumley and Hakala [6] who mounted a cache-timing key recovery attack on the ECDSA portion of the library. While the same attack may not be feasible for ephemeral ECDH key exchange (assuming single-use keys), we feel it is prudent to ensure side-channel resistance for other possible applications, including ECDSA and ECDH-certificate-based key exchange.

3   NIST P-224 Implementation

Our 64-bit implementation of the NIST P-224 elliptic curve is written in C—the 128-bit data type available in GCC allows us to make use of the 64-bit registers, as well as the 64-bit unsigned integer multiplication instruction MUL, which stores the 128-bit result in two 64-bit registers.

Our implementation does not rely on platform-specific instruction set extensions such as SSE. Of the SSE instructions, the one potentially useful to us is the packed multiplication PMULUDQ, which can do two unsigned 32-bit-to-64-bit integer multiplications in one cycle. While PMULUDQ is beneficial for Intel processors, MUL is best on AMDs [4]—we target both platforms, so opted to use the latter, as using 64-bit limbs also makes modular reduction simpler.

3.1   Field Arithmetic

We represent elements of the 224-bit field as polynomials $a_0 + 2^{56}a_1 + 2^{112}a_2 + 2^{168}a_3$, where each coefficient a_i is an unsigned 64-bit integer. (Notice that a

---

[3] In comparison, the P-256 prime ($p = 2^{256} - 2^{224} + 2^{192} + 2^{96} - 1$), which was also chosen with efficient *32-bit* arithmetic in mind, results in a much more cumbersome 64-bit modular reduction due to the "high" reduction term 2^{224}.

field element can have multiple such representations—we only reduce to the unique minimal representation at the end of the computation.) Outputs from multiplications are represented as unreduced polynomials $b_0 + 2^{56}b_1 + 2^{112}b_2 + 2^{168}b_3 + 2^{224}b_4 + 2^{280}b_5 + 2^{336}b_6$, where each b_i is an unsigned 128-bit integer. Using this representation, field multiplication costs 16 64-bit-to-128-bit multiplications and 9 128-bit additions, while squaring costs 10 multiplications, 3 scalar multiplications by 2, and 3 additions.

Aside from multiplications, we also need linear operations. Scalar multiplication and addition are straightforward. To perform subtraction $a - b$, we first add a suitable multiple of the field prime (i.e., a "multiple" of zero) to the left operand a, ensuring that the respective coefficients of a and b satisfy $a_i > b_i$—we can then perform unsigned subtraction.

Between two subsequent multiplications, we reduce the coefficients partially, ensuring that the four output coefficients satisfy $a_i < 2^{57}$. For each field operation, we also assert input bounds to guarantee that the output does not over- or underflow. For example, we need to ensure that all input coefficients to an addition satisfy $a_i < 2^{63}$, in order to guarantee that the output coefficients satisfy $b_i < 2^{63} + 2^{63} = 2^{64}$ and thus, fit in a 64-bit unsigned integer without overflow.

3.2   Elliptic Curve Point Operations

For elliptic curve group operations, we use the well-known formulae in Jacobian projective coordinates: point doubling in projective coordinates costs 5 field squarings, 3 field multiplication, and 12 linear operations (additions, subtractions, scalar multiplications), while point addition costs 4 squarings, 12 multiplications and 7 linear operations. Using alternative point addition formulae, it would in fact have been possible to trade one of the 12 multiplications with a squaring and several linear operations; however, in our experiments, this trade-off did not yield a performance improvement.

In order to minimize computation cost, we have manually analyzed the computation chain of point addition and doubling. By bounding inputs to each step, we perform modular reductions if and only if the next operation could overflow. For example, starting with partially reduced inputs x and y, we can compute $3(x+y)(x-y)$ without intermediate reductions. When computing $3(x+y)$, the coefficients of the output satisfy $a_i < 3 \cdot (2^{57}+2^{57}) < 2^{60}$. The largest scalar added to a coefficient of the left operand of a subtraction is $2^{58}+2$, so the coefficients of $x-y$ satisfy $a_i < 2^{57} + 2^{58} + 2 < 2^{59}$. Finally, as we use 4 limbs, each coefficient of the product is the sum of at most 4 atomic products: $b_i < 4 \cdot 2^{60} \cdot 2^{59} = 2^{121}$. The result fits comfortably in 128 bits without an overflow. We computed these bounds for each execution step: overall, the whole computation only needs 15 reductions for point addition and 7 for point doubling.

Finally, as elliptic curve points in TLS are transmitted using affine coordinates, we need a conversion routine from Jacobian to affine coordinates. As a Jacobian point (X, Y, Z) corresponds to the affine point $(X/Z^2, Y/Z^3)$, this conversion requires a field inversion—computing $Z^{-1} = Z^{p-2} \bmod p$ can be done in 223 field squarings, 11 field multiplications and 234 modular reductions [2].

3.3   Point Multiplication with Precomputation

Binary (schoolbook) elliptic curve point multiplication of nP requires 224 point doublings and on average 112 point additions for a 224-bit scalar n. In order to reduce the cost, we use standard precomputation techniques. By computing 16 multiples of the point P—$0 \cdot P, 1 \cdot P, \ldots, 15 \cdot P$—in 7 doublings and 7 additions, we bring the point multiplication cost down to 224 doublings and 56 additions (a total of 231 doublings and 63 additions, including precomputation). The precomputation table size of 16 points was deemed optimal for our implementation: aside from more expensive precomputation, larger tables would be affected by slower constant-time lookups (see Sect. 3.4).

For a fixed point G, we can perform interleaved multiplication by precomputing 16 linear combinations of the form $b_0 G + b_1 G^{56} + b_2 G^{112} + b_3 G^{168}$, where $b_i \in \{0, 1\}$.[4] As well as including precomputed multiples for the NIST standard generator G, our implementation allows the application to perform this precomputation for a custom group generator. After precomputation, each subsequent multiplication with the generator costs 56 doublings and 56 additions.

Finally, our implementation also supports batch multiplication. Namely, we amortize the cost of doublings by computing a linear combination of k points $n_1 P_1 + \cdots + n_k P_k$ in an interleaved manner [16]: the full computation still costs $56k$ additions, but only 224 (rather than $224k$) doublings. This technique is immediately useful in ECDSA signature verification.

3.4   Side-Channel Protection

Kocher [14] was the first to show that the execution time of a cryptographic algorithm may leak significant information about its secrets. In software implementations, two important leakage points have been identified: (i) conditional branching dependent on the secret input; and (ii) table lookups using secret-dependent lookup indices. Branching leaks information if the branches require different execution time, but even worse, the branch prediction used in modern CPUs causes a timing variance even for equivalent branches [1]. Table lookups are vulnerable as lookup results are stored in processor cache: simply put, multiple lookups into the same table entry are faster than multiple lookups into different locations, as the results are fetched from cache rather than main memory. Thus, the best way to ensure side-channel resistance is to avoid branching and table lookups altogether.

Our implementation is constant-time for single point multiplication. To ensure that it does not leak any timing information about the secret scalar, we have used the following techniques:

– Field arithmetic is implemented using 64-bit arithmetic and Boolean operations only—there are no conditional carries and no other branches;

---

[4] As this precomputation is almost as expensive as a full point multiplication, it is only useful when the point G is used more than once.

Listing 1. A routine for choosing between two inputs a and b in constant time, depending on the selection bit `bit`

```
int select (int a, int b, int bit) {
    /* -0 = 0, -1 = 0xff....ff */
    int mask = - bit;
    int ret = mask & (a^b);
    ret = ret ^ a;
    return ret;
}
```

Listing 2. A cache-timing resistant table lookup

```
int do_lookup(int a[16], int bit[4]) {
    int t0[8], t1[4], t2[2];
    /* select values where the least significant bit of the index is bit[0] */
    t0[0] = select(a[0], a[1], bit[0]); t0[1] = select(a[2], a[3], bit[0]);
    t0[2] = select(a[4], a[5], bit[0]); t0[3] = select(a[6], a[7], bit[0]);
    t0[4] = select(a[8], a[9], bit[0]); t0[5] = select(a[10], a[11], bit[0]);
    t0[6] = select(a[12], a[13], bit[0]); t0[7] = select(a[14], a[15], bit[0]);
    /* select values where the second bit of the index is bit[1] */
    t1[0] = select(t[0], t[1], bit[1]); t1[1] = select(t[2], t[3], bit[1]);
    t1[2] = select(t[4], t[5], bit[1]); t1[3] = select(t[6], t[7], bit[1]);
    /* select values where the third bit of the index is bit[2] */
    t2[0] = select(t2[0], t[1], bit[2]); t2[1] = select(t2[2], t2[3], bit[2]);
    /* select the value where the most significant bit of the index is bit[3] */
    ret = select(t3[0], t3[1], bit[3]);
    return ret;
}
```

- Rather than skipping unnecessary operations, point multiplication performs a dummy operation with the point-at-infinity whenever necessary (for example, leading zeroes of the scalar are absorbed without leaking timing information);
- Secret-dependent lookups into the precomputation table are performed in constant time, ensuring that no cache-timing information leaks about the secret scalar.

While branch-free field arithmetic and constant-time multiplication algorithms are also seen in some other implementations (e.g., in the constant-time implementations of Curve25519 [3,15]), combining secret-dependent lookups into the precomputation table with side-channel resistance is more tricky. Joye and Tunstall suggest to secure modular exponentiations by adding a random multiple of the group order to the secret exponent [13]. Using a different mask at every execution limits the leak, as multiple measurements on the same secret cannot be easily linked. The same technique could be employed for safeguarding the secret scalar in point multiplication, however, the masked scalar has a longer bit representation, thus requiring more operations—the overhead is worse for elliptic curves, which have shorter exponents compared to, say, RSA. Instead, we used standard techniques from hardware lookup tables to devise a software solution for performing lookups in a way that leaks no information even from a single execution.

Listing 1 shows sample code for implementing an **if**-statement in constant time: the routine `select()` returns input a if the input bit `bit` equals 0, and returns b if `bit` equals 1. By repeating `select()` 15 times on point inputs, we can thus select the correct precomputed point in a secure manner (see Listing 2)—independent of the lookup index (bit[3], bit[2], bit[1], bit[0]), we loop through the whole precomputation table in a fixed order. While the execution time is still dependent on cache behaviour, the timing variance is *independent* of the secret lookup index, thus leaking no valuable timing information. This strategy obviously does not scale for large tables, yet for us it is cheap compared to the cost of elliptic curve operations—we save more by precomputation than we lose by adding side-channel protection to the lookups.

4   Performance Results

4.1   The Benchmark Set-Up

As our goal was to provide a fully integrated implementation for applications using OpenSSL, we also chose to measure performance directly within OpenSSL. Rather than counting cycles for stand-alone point multiplication, the OpenSSL toolkit allows us to report timings for complete OpenSSL operations, from a single ECDH comutation to a complete TLS handshake. As these results take into account any overhead introduced by the library, they depict the actual performance gain when switching from the standard implementation to our optimized version. At the same time, they can be viewed as an upper bound to atomic elliptic curve operations.

Our benchmark machine was `ambre1`, with the following parameters:

Table 1. Our benchmark machine

ambre1			
CPU	Intel Core 2 Duo E8400	Lithography	45nm
CPU frequency	3.0 GHz	RAM	4GB
OS	Linux 2.6.18-194.11.4.el5 x86_64	Compiler	gcc 4.4.4

All benchmarks were performed, utilizing a single core.

4.2   Results

For atomic operations, we benchmarked ECDH key generation as well as shared secret computation. The former case corresponds to multiplication with a fixed basepoint; the latter amounts to one multiplication with a random basepoint, plus input point validation and output point conversion to its affine representation. Our benchmarks for the shared secret computation include all these operations. In order to complete an ephemeral ECDH handshake with single-use keys, both parties need to compute one operation of each type.

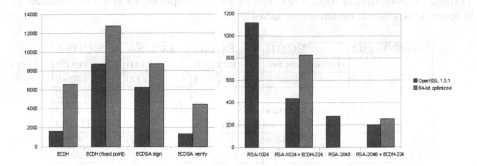

Fig. 1. Improved throughput (in operations/second) for elliptic curve operations (left) and TLS handshakes (right), measured on `ambrel`

In addition, we measured throughput for ECDSA signature generation and verification: ECDSA signing requires one fixed-point multiplication, while ECDSA verification makes use of batch multiplication to compute a linear combination of one fixed and one random point.

For benchmarking TLS handshakes, we chose the most common configuration: one-sided (server only) authentication using RSA certificates. The Qualys Internet SSL Survey from July 2010 [21] reveals that virtually all trusted SSL certificates contain either a 1024-bit or 2048-bit RSA key, so we restricted our attention to those key sizes. Since computing performance is crucial on the server side (and a typical browser client does not use the OpenSSL library anyway), we measured the time it takes a server to complete the handshake. Note that these timings include only computation time and do *not* reflect the communication latency. However, ephemeral ECDH key exchange or, more precisely, the requirement to maintain perfect forward secrecy can have an effect on handshake latency for typical TLS configurations—we discuss some latency reduction mechanisms in TLS, and their compatibility with forward secrecy in Section 5.

Figure 1 illustrates the increased throughput (in operations/second) when switching from standard OpenSSL to our optimized implementation; the corresponding precise measurements are given in Table 2. Since the OpenSSL library already contains optimized code for fixed-point multiplication, the gain is highest for random point multiplication, where throughput increases from 1600 to over 6500 operations/second. Also, Diffie-Hellman handshakes with a 1024-bit RSA signing key are nearly twice as fast when using the optimized code (435 vs 826 handshakes/second), allowing to switch from plain RSA to forward-secure cipher suites with only a 26% drop in server throughput.

4.3 Comparison with Other Results

We benchmarked Bernstein's implementation of NIST P-224 on `ambrel`, using the timing software provided with the code—raw point multiplication is about 1.5 times slower than our fully integrated OpenSSL implementation. Brown et. al.

Table 2. Throughput of NIST P-224 elliptic curve computations and TLS handshakes in operations/second, measured on `ambrel`

OpenSSL 1.0.1	ECDH shared secret	ECDH keygen	ECDSA sign	ECDSA verify
standard	1602.9	8757.1	6221.0	1309.9
64-bit opt	6552.9	12789.2	8757.6	4442.9
OpenSSL 1.0.1	RSA-1024 ECDH-224	RSA-1024 ECDH-224	RSA-2048 ECDH-224	RSA-2048 ECDH-224
standard	1118.6	435.5	277.6	199.4
64-bit opt	—	826.4	—	253.4

Table 3. Selected benchmarking results for various curves, reported in cycles/operation

curve	impl.	platform	benchmarking suite	keygen	shared secret	security	const. time
NIST P-224	this paper	ambrel	OpenSSL	234573	457813	112 bits	yes
NIST P-224	Bernstein	ambrel	Bernstein	662220	662220	112 bits	no
curve25519	donna	ambrel	donna	≈540000	≈ 540000	≈128 bits	yes
curve25519	mpfq	boing	SUPERCOP	394254	381375	≈128 bits	no(?)
gls1271	eBATS	boing	SUPERCOP	140355	314730	≈128 bits	no(?)

also report timings of several NIST curves [5]. This software appears to be much slower than Bernstein's but the measurements are obtained on a Pentium II, so we omit exact cycle counts to avoid comparing apples to oranges.

For the curious reader, we have also gathered some benchmarking data for other elliptic curves in Table 3. We benchmarked `curve25519-donna`, a 64-bit constant-time implementation of Curve25519 [15] on `ambrel`, noting that our NIST P-224 implementation outperforms it despite any OpenSSL overhead (admittedly, NIST P-224 also offers a slightly lower security level compared to Curve25519). For comparison, we also give some figures for the fastest Curve25519 implementation, as well as for the Galbraith-Lin-Scott implementation of a twisted Edwards curve over a field with $(2^{127} - 1)^2$ elements [9], as reported by the ECRYPT benchmarking suite SUPERCOP [11]. These implementations are, as far as we know, not constant-time.

From SUPERCOP, which reports performance on a variety of platforms, we chose the figures obtained from `boing`, a machine with a CPU identical to `ambrel`. Nevertheless, we stress that these are timings obtained via different benchmarking tools, on different machines, and as such, are only meant to give a very rough context to our results.

Finally, Bernstein et. al. also report extremely fast software for 192-bit modular arithmetic on 64-bit platforms [4]. Utilizing parallelism from hyperthreading on all 4 cores on an Intel Core 2 Quad, they are able to carry out over 100 million modular multiplications per second. Within our elliptic curve computation, we do about 10 million 224-bit modular multiplications, and another 10 million modular squarings per second on a single core—but due to the completely different setting, these results are not directly comparable.

5   Security Considerations

5.1   Ephemeral versus Fixed Keys

For (Elliptic Curve) Diffie-Hellman key exchange, TLS does not strictly mandate the use of ephemeral keys—in order to save computation, the server may reuse its Diffie-Hellman value for multiple connections. On one hand, we note that our implementation is resistant to timing-attacks and thus, we deem it safe to reuse the secret Diffie-Hellman value. On the other hand, as our implementation includes an optimization for fixed basepoints, computing a new Diffie-Hellman value is by far the cheapest of the three public key operations required in an ECDH-RSA handshake and thus, by reusing DH secrets, the application potentially stands to lose more security than it stands to gain in performance.

5.2   Latency Reduction Mechanisms and Forward Secrecy

A full SSL/TLS handshake takes two round trips between the server and the client. SSL/TLS includes several mechanisms for reducing this latency:

- **Session caching** keeps session information (including the session key) in server-side cache; clients can resume previous sessions by presenting the corresponding session ID.
- **TLS session tickets** [8] allow stateless session resumption: the session information is now sent to the client in a session ticket encrypted with the server's long-term key.
- **False Start** allows "optimistic" clients to start sending (encrypted) application data before the handshake is finished.

All these mechanisms cut the handshake latency down to one round trip. Yet care should be taken when using them in conjunction with DH ciphers. Both session caching and tickets conflict with perfect forward secrecy. In particular, session tickets invalidate any forward secrecy completely, as an adversary having control over the server's long-term private key can decrypt the ticket to obtain the session key. To facilitate forward secrecy, latest versions of OpenSSL allow to selectively disable session caching and tickets for forward-secure cipher suites.

In contrast, False Start is perfectly compatible with forward-secure ciphers. In fact, the False Start Internet-Draft [10] recommends that clients should *only* false start with forward-secure cipher suites, in order to avoid cipher suite downgrade attacks by rogue servers. Thus, we conclude that it is possible to maintain perfect forward secrecy without sacrificing communication latency.

The Source Code

This software will be released in OpenSSL 1.0.1, and is available in the latest snapshots at ftp://ftp.openssl.org/snapshot/. Please refer to the release notes to compile and test the implementation.

Acknowledgements. The author is grateful to Daniel J. Bernstein, Ian Goldberg, Adam Langley and Bodo Möller for their comments on the implementation.

References

1. Acıiçmez, O., Koç, Ç.K., Seifert, J.-P.: Predicting Secret Keys Via Branch Prediction. In: Abe, M. (ed.) CT-RSA 2007. LNCS, vol. 4377, pp. 225–242. Springer, Heidelberg (2006)
2. Bernstein, D.J.: A software implementation of NIST P-224 (2001), http://cr.yp.to/nistp224.html
3. Bernstein, D.J.: Curve25519: New Diffie-Hellman Speed Records. In: Yung, M., Dodis, Y., Kiayias, A., Malkin, T. (eds.) PKC 2006. LNCS, vol. 3958, pp. 207–228. Springer, Heidelberg (2006)
4. Bernstein, D.J., Chen, H.-C., Chen, M.-S., Cheng, C.-M., Hsiao, C.-H., Lange, T., Lin, Z.-C., Yang, B.-Y.: The billion-mulmod-per-second pc. In: Workshop record of SHARCS 2009: Special-purpose Hardware for Attacking Cryptographic Systems (2009)
5. Brown, M., Hankerson, D., López, J., Menezes, A.: Software Implementation of the NIST Elliptic Curves over Prime Fields. In: Naccache, D. (ed.) CT-RSA 2001. LNCS, vol. 2020, pp. 250–265. Springer, Heidelberg (2001)
6. Brumley, B.B., Hakala, R.M.: Cache-Timing Template Attacks. In: Matsui, M. (ed.) ASIACRYPT 2009. LNCS, vol. 5912, pp. 667–684. Springer, Heidelberg (2009)
7. Internet Engineering Task Force. Elliptic curve cryptography (ECC) cipher suites for transport layer security (TLS) (2006), http://www.ietf.org/rfc/rfc4492
8. Internet Engineering Task Force. Transport layer security (TLS) session resumption without server-side state (2008), http://www.ietf.org/rfc/rfc5077
9. Galbraith, S.D., Lin, X., Scott, M.: Endomorphisms for Faster Elliptic Curve Cryptography on a Large Class of Curves. In: Joux, A. (ed.) EUROCRYPT 2009. LNCS, vol. 5479, pp. 518–535. Springer, Heidelberg (2009)
10. TLS Working Group. Transport layer security (TLS) false start, https://tools.ietf.org/html/draft-bmoeller-tls-falsestart-00
11. ECRYPT II. eBACS: ECRYPT benchmarking of cryptographic systems, http://bench.cr.yp.to/supercop.html
12. ECRYPT II. Yearly report on algorithms and keysizes (2010), D.SPA.13 Rev. 1.0, ICT-2007-216676 (2010), http://www.ecrypt.eu.org/documents/D.SPA.13.pdf
13. Joye, M., Tunstall, M.: Exponent Recoding and Regular Exponentiation Algorithms. In: Preneel, B. (ed.) AFRICACRYPT 2009. LNCS, vol. 5580, pp. 334–349. Springer, Heidelberg (2009)
14. Kocher, P.C.: Timing Attacks on Implementations of Diffie-Hellman, RSA, DSS, and other Systems. In: Koblitz, N. (ed.) CRYPTO 1996. LNCS, vol. 1109, pp. 104–113. Springer, Heidelberg (1996)
15. Langley, A.: curve25519-donna: A 64-bit implementation of Curve25519, http://code.google.com/p/curve25519-donna/
16. Möller, B.: Algorithms for Multi-Exponentiation. In: Vaudenay, S., Youssef, A.M. (eds.) SAC 2001. LNCS, vol. 2259, pp. 165–180. Springer, Heidelberg (2001)

17. mozilla.org. Network Security Services,
    http://www.mozilla.org/projects/security/pki/nss/
18. NIST. Recommendation for key management, special publication 800-57 part 1
19. The OpenSSL project. OpenSSL—cryptography and SSL/TLS toolkit,
    http://www.openssl.org
20. Certicom Research. SEC 2: Recommended elliptic curve domain parameters (2010)
21. Ivan Ristic. Internet SSL survey. Technical report, Qualys, Black Hat USA (2010)

Cryptographic Treatment of Private User Profiles

Felix Günther, Mark Manulis, and Thorsten Strufe

TU Darmstadt & CASED, Germany
{guenther,strufe}@cs.tu-darmstadt.de, mark@manulis.eu

Abstract. The publication of private data in user profiles in a both secure and private way is a rising problem and of special interest in, e.g., online social networks that become more and more popular. Current approaches, especially for decentralized networks, often do not address this issue or impose large storage overhead. In this paper, we present a cryptographic approach to *Private Profile Management* that is seen as a building block for applications in which users maintain their own profiles, publish and retrieve data, and authorize other users to access different portions of data in their profiles. In this course, we provide: (i) formalization of *confidentiality* and *unlinkability* as two main security and privacy goals for the data which is kept in profiles and users who are authorized to retrieve this data, and (ii) specification, analysis, and comparison of two private profile management schemes based on different encryption techniques.

1 Introduction

Publishing personal profiles and other means of sharing private data are increasingly popular on the web. Online social networks (OSN) arguably are the most accepted network service, today. Facebook alone, serving a claimed base of over 500 Million active users[1], surpassed google, and currently enjoys the highest utilization duration by their users and one of the highest access frequencies of all web sites since January 2010[2]. Its users share 90 pieces of content per month on average, mainly consisting of personally identifiable information. Protecting this data against unauthorized access is of utmost importance, since users store private and sensitive data in their OSN profiles.

The *confidentiality* of published data, meant to be shared with only a chosen group of users, is already important in centralized services. Yet, it becomes even more pressing when establishing decentralized OSN, which have been proposed recently [8,4,13] in an attempt to avoid the centralized control and omnipotent access of commercial service providers. *Unlinkability* is the more subtle requirement of protecting the identity of users who are successively interact or access certain chunks of published data. It frequently is missed and only few general solutions achieve this privacy goal [2].

A serious corpus of solutions has been proposed to address these issues in the past. Yet, there so far exist no appropriate definitions for secure and private management of user profiles as we show in Section 2.

---

[1] http://www.facebook.com/press/info.php?statistics, Oct 2010.
[2] http://blog.nielsen.com/nielsenwire/, Oct 2010.

G. Danezis, S. Dietrich, and K. Sako (Eds.): FC 2011 Workshops, LNCS 7126, pp. 40–54, 2012.

Contributions. In this paper, we take a cryptographic approach to address the management of user profiles in a secure and privacy-friendly way. To this end, our first contribution is to come up with an appropriate formal model for private profile management aiming not only on *privacy of published data* (confidentiality) but also on *privacy of users* (unlinkability) who are allowed to access this data. We define and model several fundamental properties of a **Profile Management Scheme** (PMS). In particular, the ability of users (profile owners) to publish and remove data, as well as to grant, modify, and revoke access rights to the published data. We consider PMS as an independent building block, without relying on higher-level applications, network infrastructures, or any trusted third parties to perform its tasks.

Our second contribution are two provably secure PMS solutions based on different techniques: our first scheme PMS-SK combines symmetric encryption with shared keys that are then distributed amongst the authorized users. Our second scheme PMS-BE involves broadcast encryption techniques. As we will see, both solutions have their advantages and disadvantages with respect to their performance and privacy. In particular, PMS-SK provides confidentiality and perfect unlinkability, but imposes an overhead of keys linear in the number of attributes a user is allowed to access. PMS-BE reduces the key overhead to a constant value at the cost of lower privacy, expressed through the requirement of *anonymity*, which we also model and formally relate to the stronger notion of unlinkability. We further discuss the trade-off between privacy and efficiency by evaluating complexity of both approaches (in theory and practice based on statistics of some popular online communities) and suggest several optimizations that could further enhance their performance, while preserving their security and privacy guarantees.

Organization. In Section 2 we discuss drawbacks of previous cryptographic and non-cryptographic work on private management of user profiles. In Section 3, we introduce our formal model for such schemes and define two requirements: confidentiality of private data and unlinkability of users. In Sections 4 and 5 we specify our PMS-SK and PMS-BE solutions, evaluate their complexity (incl. possible optimizations) and formally address their security and privacy properties. In Section 6 we investigate the impact of our schemes on real-world communities such as Facebook, Twitter and Flickr.

2   Related Work

Substantial amount of work has been done in the field of secure and private publication of sensitive data in online social networks (OSNs), demonstrating threats and proposing countermeasures. For example, Gross et al. [14] and Zheleva et al. [24] studied how access patterns of users to the information stored in user profiles and how membership of users in different groups can be exploited for the disclosure of private data. Amongst the non-cryptographic solutions is the approach proposed by Carminati et al. [7], where access to private data is modeled using semantic rules taking into account the depth of social relationships and the amount of trust amongst the users. In addition to being semi-centralized, this approach requires synchronous communication — a significant limitation in our case. There exist several cryptographic approaches to improve confidentiality and privacy in existing, mostly centralized OSNs: Lucas et. al [17] presented *flyByNight*, an application to encrypt sensitive data in Facebook. Tootoonchian [21] proposed a system called *Lockr* to improve privacy in both centralized and decentralized social networks. Yet, both approaches are not able to keep security and/or privacy up under certain attacks: *flyByNight* trusts the Facebook server not to introduce malicious code or keys whilst in *Lockr* malicious users can reveal relationship keys or disclose relationship metadata for access control, compromising privacy properties of the system. Another cryptographic approach is *Scramble!* [19], a Firefox plugin that uses the OpenPGP standard [5] to encrypt data relying on its public-key infrastructure. Moreover, Scramble! tries to achieve recipient anonymity by omitting the public identifiers of recipients in the ciphertext and allows for data storage on third-party storage using "tiny URLs", thus reducing the size of ciphertexts. Nevertheless, the approach implies linear storage overhead and, as it relies on OpenPGP, is vulnerable to active attacks as shown by Barth et al. [2]. A number of solutions aim at fine-grained forms of access control to private data. For example, Graffi et al. [12] implemented an approach based on symmetric encryption of profile items with independent shared keys, yet without specifying or analyzing the desired security and privacy properties. OSN *Persona*, presented by Baden et al. [1], implements ciphertext-policy attribute-based encryption (CP-ABE) [3] for the enforcement of access rules to the encrypted profile data (e.g., " 'neighbor' AND 'football fan' "). Their approach aims at confidentiality of attributes but does not guarantee privacy. Similarly, *EASiER* [16] which in addition to CP-ABE requires a semi-trusted proxy for the update of decryption keys upon revocation events does not guarantee user privacy. Furthermore, the original CP-ABE scheme from [3] does not achieve adaptive CCA-security, which would be a necessary requirement in the OSN setting. Hence, neither *Persona* nor *EASiER* seem to offer confidentiality as modeled in our work and provided by our solutions. Recently, Zhu et al. [25] proposed a collaborative framework to enforce access control in OSNs. Their scheme is centralized and focuses on joint publication of data within communities, less on the individual users and protection of their own profiles and data. A somewhat more general construct for privacy-preserving distribution of encrypted content was proposed by Barth et al. [2] using public-key broadcast encryption. Of particular interest is their notion of *recipient privacy*, which is supposed to hide the identities of recipients of the broadcast content and can be applied for the private distribution of shared keys in our PMS-SK approach at the cost of linear storage overhead in the number of recipients.

3   Private User Profiles: Model and Definitions

3.1   Management of User Profiles

Users. Let $\mathcal{U}$ denote a set of at most N *users*. We do not distinguish between users and their identities but assume that each identity $U \in \mathcal{U}$ is unique. Furthermore, we assume that users can create authentic and, if necessary, confidential communication channels. This assumption is motivated by the fact that the profile management scheme will likely be deployed as a building block within an application, like an online social network, where users typically have other means of authentication. In this way we can focus on the core functionality of the profile management scheme, namely the management of and access to the profile data.

Profiles. A *profile* P is modeled as a set of pairs $(a, \bar{d}) \in \mathcal{I} \times \{0, 1\}^*$ where $\mathcal{I} \subseteq \{0, 1\}^*$ is the set of possible *attribute indices* a and $\bar{d}$ are corresponding *values* stored in P. We assume that within a profile P attribute indices are unique. Furthermore, we assume that each profile P is publicly accessible but is distributed in an authentic manner by its *owner* $U_P \in \mathcal{U}$. Also, every user U owns at most one profile and the profile owned by U is denoted P_U. The authenticity of profiles means that their content can only be manipulated by their respective owner who is in possession of the corresponding profile management key pmk. Since one of the goals will be to ensure confidentiality of attributes we assume that for each publicly accessible value $\bar{d}$ there exists an *attribute* d and that for any pair $(a, \bar{d}) \in P$ the profile owner U_P can implicitly retrieve this d as well as the group $\mathcal{G} \subseteq \mathcal{U}$ of users who are currently authorized to access d. By $\mathcal{G}^*_{a,P}$ we denote the set of users that have ever been authorized to access the attribute indexed by a within the profile P (we assume that $U_P \in \mathcal{G}^*_{a,P}$ for all attributes in P).

Definition 1 (Profile Management Scheme). *A profile management scheme PMS consists of the five algorithms* Init, Publish, Retrieve, Delete *and* ModifyAccess *defined as follows:*

Init(κ) : *On input the security parameter κ, this probabilistic algorithm initializes the scheme and outputs an empty profile P together with the private profile management key pmk.* Init *is executed by the owner U_P.*

Publish($pmk, P, (a, d), \mathcal{G}$) : *On input a profile management key pmk, a profile P, a pair $(a, d) \in \mathcal{I} \times \{0, 1\}^*$ (such that a is not yet in the profile), and a group of users $\mathcal{G}$, this probabilistic algorithm transforms the attribute d into value $\bar{d}$, adds $(a, \bar{d})$ to P, and $\mathcal{G}$ to $\mathcal{G}^*_{a,P}$. It outputs the modified P and a retrieval key rk_U for each $U \in \mathcal{G}$ (that may be newly generated or modified). Optionally, it updates pmk.* Publish *is executed by the owner U_P.*

Retrieve(rk_U, P, a) : *On input a retrieval key rk_U, a profile P, and an attribute index a, this deterministic algorithm checks whether $(a, \bar{d}) \in P$, and either outputs d or rejects with $\bot$.* Retrieve *can be executed by any user $U \in \mathcal{U}$ being in possession of the key for a in rk_U.*

Delete(pmk, P, a) : *On input a profile management key pmk, a profile P, and an attribute index a, this possibly probabilistic algorithm checks whether $(a, \bar{d}) \in P$, and if so outputs modified profile $P = P \setminus (a, \bar{d})$. Optionally, it updates pmk and rk_U of all $U \in \mathcal{G}$ where $\mathcal{G}$ denotes the set of users authorized to access the pair with index a at the end of the execution.* Delete *is executed by the owner U_P.*

ModifyAccess(pmk, P, a, U) : *On input a profile management key pmk, a profile P, an attribute index a, and some user $U \in \mathcal{U}$ this probabilistic algorithm checks whether $(a, \bar{d}) \in P$ for some $\bar{d}$, and if so finds the set $\mathcal{G}$ of users that are authorized to access the attribute d. The algorithm then proceeds according to the one of the following two cases:*
  - *If $U \in \mathcal{G}$ then it updates $\mathcal{G} = \mathcal{G} \setminus \{U\}$ (i.e., user U is removed from $\mathcal{G}$).*
  - *If $U \notin \mathcal{G}$ then it updates $\mathcal{G} = \mathcal{G} \cup \{U\}$ and $\mathcal{G}^*_{a,P} = \mathcal{G}^*_{a,P} \cup \{U\}$ (i.e., U is added to both $\mathcal{G}$ and $\mathcal{G}^*_{a,P}$).*

  Finally, the algorithm outputs the modified profile P. Optionally, it updates pmk and the retrieval keys rk_U of all $U \in \mathcal{G} \cup \{U\}$. ModifyAccess *is executed by the owner U_P.*

We remark that profile management schemes may include an additional algorithm ModifyAttribute allowing U_P to modify the attribute d behind some pair $(a, \bar{d}) \in P$. We model this functionality by a consecutive execution of Delete and Publish, which is sufficient from the formal security and privacy perspective.

3.2 Adversarial Model

In order to define security and privacy of a profile management scheme PMS we consider a PPT adversary $\mathcal{A}$ that knows all users in the system, i.e., the set $\mathcal{U}$ is assumed to be public, and interacts with them via the following set of queries:

Corrupt(U) : This corruption query gives $\mathcal{A}$ all secret keys known to U, including the profile management key pmk and all retrieval keys rk_U (with which U can access other users' profiles).
   U is added to the set of corrupted users that we denote by $\mathcal{C} \subseteq \mathcal{U}$.
Publish$(P, (a, d), \mathcal{G})$: In response, Publish$(pmk, P, (a, d), \mathcal{G})$ is executed using pmk of U_P. $\mathcal{A}$ is then given the modified profile P and all updated keys of corrupted users $U \in \mathcal{C}$.
Retrieve(P, a, U) : In response, Retrieve(rk_U, P, a) is executed using rk_U of U and its output is given back to $\mathcal{A}$.
Delete(P, a) : In response, Delete(pmk, P, a) is executed using pmk of U_P. $\mathcal{A}$ receives the updated profile P and all updated keys of corrupted users $U \in \mathcal{C}$.
ModifyAccess(P, a, U) : In response, ModifyAccess(pmk, P, a, U) is executed using pmk of U_P. $\mathcal{A}$ is then given the modified profile P and all updated keys belonging to corrupted users $U \in \mathcal{C}$.

3.3 Security and Privacy Requirements

We define two security and privacy requirements for a profile management scheme: (1) *confidentiality* that protects attributes d stored in a profile from unauthorized access, and (2) *unlinkability* that protects user privacy in the following sense: a profile management scheme should hide information on whether a user U has been authorized to access some attribute in a profile of another user U_P, and, moreover, it shouldn't leak information whether different attributes within a profile (or across different profiles) can be accessed by the same user, even if these attributes can be accessed by the adversary.

Confidentiality. We model *confidentiality* in Definition 2 through an indistinguishability game: It should be computationally infeasible for an adversary $\mathcal{A}$ to decide which attribute d is referenced by an index a. We stress that our definition assumes fully adaptive adversary that at any time can corrupt arbitrary users and reveal profile data. This behavior matches the reality, where (malicious) users can at any time join OSNs and access user profiles before mounting an attack.

Definition 2 (Confidentiality). *Let* PMS *be a profile management scheme from Definition 1 and $\mathcal{A}$ be a PPT adversary interacting with users via queries from Section 3.2 within the following game* $\text{Game}_{\mathcal{A},\text{PMS}}^{\text{conf}}$:

1. $\text{Init}(\kappa)$ *is executed for all users* $U \in \mathcal{U}$.
2. $\mathcal{A}$ *can execute arbitrary operations and ask queries. At some point it outputs* (a, d_0), $(a, d_1) \in \mathcal{I} \times \{0,1\}^*$, $\mathcal{G}_t \subset \mathcal{U}$, *and* $U_P \in \mathcal{U} \setminus \mathcal{G}_t$ *such that neither* U_P *nor any* $U \in \mathcal{G}_t$ *is corrupted (i.e.,* $(\{U_P\} \cup \mathcal{G}_t) \cap \mathcal{C} = \emptyset$*) and* $|d_0| = |d_1|$ *(i.e.,* d_0 *and* d_1 *have the same length).*
3. *Bit* $b \in_R \{0,1\}$ *is chosen uniformly,* $\text{Publish}(pmk, P, (a, d_b), \mathcal{G}_t)$ *with pmk of* U_P *is executed, and the modified* P *is given to* $\mathcal{A}$.
4. $\mathcal{A}$ *can execute arbitrary operations and ask queries. At some point it outputs bit* $b' \in \{0,1\}$.
5. $\mathcal{A}$ *wins, denoted by* $\text{Game}_{\mathcal{A},\text{PMS}}^{\text{conf}} = 1$, *if all of the following holds:*
   - $b' = b$,
   - $U_P \notin \mathcal{C}$,
   - $\mathcal{A}$ *did not query* $\text{Retrieve}(P, a, U)$ *with* $U \in \mathcal{G}_{a,P}^*$.
   - $\mathcal{G}_{a,P}^* \cap \mathcal{C} = \emptyset$ *(users that have ever been authorized to access the attribute indexed by* a *in* P *are not corrupted).*

The advantage probability of $\mathcal{A}$ *in winning the game* $\text{Game}_{\mathcal{A},\text{PMS}}^{\text{conf}}$ *is defined as*

$$\text{Adv}_{\mathcal{A},\text{PMS}}^{\text{conf}}(\kappa) := \left| \Pr\left[\text{Game}_{\mathcal{A},\text{PMS}}^{\text{conf}} = 1 \right] - \frac{1}{2} \right|$$

We say that PMS *provides* confidentiality *if for any PPT adversary* $\mathcal{A}$ *the advantage* $\text{Adv}_{\mathcal{A},\text{PMS}}^{\text{conf}}(\kappa)$ *is negligible.*

Unlinkability. We model *unlinkability* in Definition 3 using the indistinguishability game as well: $\mathcal{A}$ must decide which user, U_0 or U_1, has been authorized (via Publish or ModifyAccess) to access an attribute in a profile P even if $\mathcal{A}$ has access to P. Our definition implies access unlinkability of users across different profiles, e.g. P and P', since $\mathcal{A}$ can corrupt the owner of any other profile P' and learn all secrets that U_0 and U_1 might possess for P'.

Definition 3 (Unlinkability). *Let* PMS *be a profile management scheme from Definition 1 and* $\mathcal{A}$ *be a PPT adversary interacting with users via queries from Section 3.2 within the following game* $\text{Game}_{\mathcal{A},\text{PMS}}^{\text{unlink}}$:

1. $\text{Init}(\kappa)$ *is executed for all users* $U \in \mathcal{U}$.
2. $\mathcal{A}$ *can execute arbitrary operations and ask queries. At some point it outputs* U_0, U_1, (a, d), *and* U_P *(owner of some profile* P*).*
3. *Bit* $b \in_R \{0,1\}$ *is chosen uniformly and:*
   - *If* $(a, *) \notin P$ *then* $\text{Publish}(pmk, P, (a, d), \{U_b\})$ *with pmk of* U_P *is executed.*
   - *If* $(a, *) \in P$ *then* $\text{ModifyAccess}(pmk, P, a, \{U_b\})$ *with pmk of* U_P *is executed.*

   $\mathcal{A}$ *is given the modified* P *and the possibly updated retrieval keys* rk_U *for all* $U \in \mathcal{C}$.
4. $\mathcal{A}$ *can execute arbitrary operations and ask queries. At some point it outputs a bit* $b' \in \{0,1\}$.
5. $\mathcal{A}$ *wins, denoted by* $\text{Game}_{\mathcal{A},\text{PMS}}^{\text{unlink}} = 1$, *if all of the following holds:*

- $b' = b$,
- $\{U_0, U_1, U_P\} \cap \mathcal{C} = \emptyset$,
- $\mathcal{A}$ *neither queried* Retrieve(P, a, U_0) *nor* Retrieve(P, a, U_1).

The advantage probability of $\mathcal{A}$ *in winning the game* Game$^{\text{unlink}}_{\mathcal{A},\text{PMS}}$ *is defined as*

$$\text{Adv}^{\text{unlink}}_{\mathcal{A},\text{PMS}}(\kappa) := \left| \Pr\left[\text{Game}^{\text{unlink}}_{\mathcal{A},\text{PMS}} = 1 \right] - \frac{1}{2} \right|$$

We say that PMS *provides* unlinkability *if for any PPT adversary* $\mathcal{A}$ *the advantage* Adv$^{\text{unlink}}_{\mathcal{A},\text{PMS}}(\kappa)$ *is negligible.*

4 Private Profile Management with Shared Keys

Our first construction, called PMS-SK, is simple and uses *shared keys* to encrypt profile attributes for a group of authorized users. An independent symmetric key K_a is chosen by the owner of a profile P for each pair (a, d) and distributed to the group $\mathcal{G}$ of users that are authorized to access d. The key is updated on each modification of $\mathcal{G}$. We use a *symmetric encryption scheme* $SE = (SE.KGen, SE.Enc, SE.Dec)$ for which we assume classical indistinguishability against chosen-plaintext attacks (IND-CPA) and denote by $\text{Adv}^{\text{IND-CPA}}_{\mathcal{A},SE}(\kappa)$ the corresponding advantage of the adversary.

The distribution of K_a may be performed in two ways: K_a can be communicated to the authorized users online (over secure channels) or offline, e.g., by storing K_a securely (possibly using asymmetric encryption) either within the profile or at some centralized server. Our specification of PMS-SK leaves open how distribution of shared keys is done. In particular, the use of one or another technique may be constrained by the application that will use the scheme.

4.1 Specification of PMS-SK

In our constructions we implicitly assume that the uniqueness of indices a in a profile P is implicitly ensured or checked by corresponding algorithms.

Init(κ) : Output $P \leftarrow \emptyset$ and $pmk \leftarrow \emptyset$.

Publish$(pmk, P, (a, d), \mathcal{G})$: $K_a \leftarrow SE.KGen(1^\kappa)$, add $(a, SE.Enc(K_a, d))$ to P, K_a to rk_U for each $U \in \mathcal{G}$, and K_a to pmk.

Retrieve(rk_U, P, a) : Extract K_a from rk_U. If $(a, \bar{d}) \in P$ for some $\bar{d}$ then output $SE.Dec(K_a, \bar{d})$, else $\perp$.

Delete(pmk, P, a) : Delete $(a, \bar{d})$ from P. Delete K_a from pmk.

ModifyAccess(pmk, P, a, U) : If $U \in \mathcal{G}$ then remove U from $\mathcal{G}$, otherwise add U to $\mathcal{G}$. Execute Delete(pmk, P, a) followed by Publish$(pmk, P, (a, d), \mathcal{G})$ where d is the attribute indexed by a.

The description of ModifyAccess is kept general in the sense that it does not specify how the profile owner U_P reveals an attribute d indexed by a. Our scheme allows for different realizations: d can be stored by U_P locally (not as part of P) or it can be obtained through decryption of $\bar{d}$ using K_a which is part of pmk.

4.2 Complexity Analysis

PMS-SK requires each profile owner U_P to store one key per attribute $(a, \bar{d})$ currently stored in P. Additionally, each user has to store one key per attribute she is allowed to access in any profile. Assuming the worst case where all users in $\mathcal{U}$ have profiles with $|P|$ attributes that can be accessed by all other users, PMS-SK requires each $U \in \mathcal{U}$ to store $N \cdot |P|$ keys from which $|P|$ keys are stored in its pmk and $(N - 1) \cdot |P|$ in the retrieval keys rk_U for all others users' profiles. For each execution of Publish or ModifyAccess the profile owner needs further to perform one symmetric encryption.

4.3 Security and Privacy Analysis

In this section we prove that PMS-SK ensures confidentiality of attributes and provides unlinkability for the authorized users. (See [15] for our proof of Theorem 1.)

Theorem 1 (Confidentiality of PMS-SK). *If SE is IND-CPA secure, then* PMS-SK *provides confidentiality from Definition 2, and*

$$\mathsf{Adv}^{conf}_{\mathcal{A},\text{PMS-SK}}(\kappa) \leq (1 + q) \cdot \mathsf{Adv}^{IND-CPA}_{\mathcal{A}^*,SE}(\kappa)$$

with q being the number of invoked ModifyAccess *operations per attribute.*

Note that IND-CPA security of SE suffices here since each attribute is encrypted with an independent key and $\mathcal{A}$ is not allowed to retrieve d_b in the confidentiality game.

Theorem 2 (Unlinkability of PMS-SK). PMS-SK *provides perfect unlinkability as defined in Definition 3, i.e.,* $\mathsf{Adv}^{unlink}_{\mathcal{A},PMS-SK}(\kappa) = 0$.

Proof. The attribute keys K_a are statistically independent of the identities of users in $\mathcal{G}$ who have been authorized to access the attribute indexed by a. Therefore, $\mathcal{A}$ cannot win in Game$^{unlink}_{\mathcal{A},\text{PMS}}$ better than by a random guess, i.e., with probability $\frac{1}{2}$.   □

Remark 1. The perfect unlinkability property of our PMS-SK construction proven in the above theorem should be enjoyed with caution when it comes to the deployment of the scheme in practice. The reason is that PMS-SK does not specify how shared keys are distributed, leaving this to the application that will use the scheme. One approach to distribute keys in a privacy-preserving manner is given by Barth, Boneh, and Waters [2] and the *CCA recipient privacy* of their scheme, which however comes with storage overhead linear in the number of recipients and may be undesirable when encrypting small-sized attributes in social profiles. In any case it is clear that the distribution process will eventually have impact on the unlinkability property of the scheme, maybe to the point of ruling out its perfectness.

4.4 Further Optimizations

Regardless of the question, whether shared keys K_a are distributed by the application in an online or an offline fashion, there is a way to further optimize and further improve the actual management of these keys. In our specification of PMS-SK these keys are currently chosen fresh for each modification of the authorized group $\mathcal{G}$. However, by using *group key management schemes* that allow efficient update of group keys such as LKH [23,22] or OFT [6,20] with all the resulting efficiency differences, the overhead for the distribution can be further reduced. Another optimization concerns generation of shared keys K_a in case a profile owner U_P does not wish to store corresponding attributes d (outside of the profile). Instead of storing linear (in the number of attributes in P) many shared keys in pmk, the profile owner can derive each K_a using some pseudorandom function $f_s(a, i)$ where s is a seed used for all attributes, a is the unique attribute index, and i is a counter that is updated on each execution of ModifyAccess on a to account for possible repetitions of the authorized group $\mathcal{G}$ over the life time of the profile. This optimization allows to trade in the storage costs for pmk for the computation overhead for deriving K_a. We do not analyze the efficiency effects of the proposed optimizations in detail here, as the construction based on broadcast encryption presented in the next section has only a constant overhead of retrieval keys.

5   Private Profile Management with Broadcast Encryption

Our second generic construction of a profile management scheme, called PMS-BE, is based on an adaptively secure (identity-based) broadcast encryption scheme, e.g. [9].

Definition 4 (Broadcast Encryption Scheme [9]). *A broadcast encryption scheme $BE = (BE.Setup, BE.KGen, BE.Enc, BE.Dec)$ consists of the following algorithms:*

$BE.Setup(\kappa, n, \ell)$: *On input the security parameter κ, the number of receivers n, and the maximal size $\ell \leq n$ of the recipient group, this probabilistic algorithm outputs a public/secret key pair $\langle PK, SK \rangle$.*

$BE.KGen(i, SK)$: *On input an index $i \in \{1, \dots, n\}$ and the secret key SK, this probabilistic algorithm outputs a private (user) key sk_i.*

$BE.Enc(S, PK)$: *On input a subset $S \subseteq \{1, \dots, n\}$ with $|S| \leq \ell$ and a public key PK, this probabilistic algorithm outputs a pair $\langle Hdr, K \rangle$ where Hdr is called the header and $K \in \mathcal{K}$ is a message encryption key.*

$BE.Dec(S, i, sk_i, Hdr, PK)$: *On input a subset $S \subseteq \{1, \dots, n\}$ with $|S| \leq \ell$, an index $i \in \{1, \dots, n\}$, a private key sk_i, a header Hdr, and the public key PK, this deterministic algorithm outputs the message encryption key $K \in \mathcal{K}$.*

Correctness of BE requires that for all $S \subseteq \{1, \dots, n\}$ and all $i \in S$, if $\langle PK, SK \rangle \leftarrow_R BE.Setup(\kappa, n, \ell)$, $sk_i \leftarrow_R BE.KGen(i, SK)$, and $\langle Hdr, K \rangle \leftarrow_R BE.Enc(S, PK)$, then $BE.Dec(S, i, sk_i, Hdr, PK) = K$.

In Definition 5 we recall the adaptive CCA-security of a BE scheme [9]. The term "adaptive" means that $\mathcal{A}$ can corrupt users after the scheme is initialized, which is a more realistic setting for PMS applications where new (possibly malicious) users join the network as the time passes by.

Definition 5 (Adaptive CCA-Security of BE). *Let BE be a broadcast encryption scheme from Definition 4 and $\mathcal{A}$ be a PPT adversary in the following game, denoted $\mathsf{Game}_{\mathcal{A}, BE, n, \ell}^{\mathrm{ad-CCA}}(\kappa)$:*

1. $\langle PK, SK \rangle \leftarrow_R BE.Setup(\kappa, n, \ell)$. $\mathcal{A}$ is given PK *(together with n and ℓ).*
2. *$\mathcal{A}$ adaptively issues private key queries $BE.KGen(i)$ for $i \in \{1, \ldots, n\}$ and obtains corresponding sk_i. In addition, $\mathcal{A}$ is allowed to query $BE.Dec(S, i, Hdr, PK)$ to obtain message encryption keys K.*
3. *$\mathcal{A}$ outputs a challenge set of indices S^*, such that no $BE.KGen(i)$ with $i \in S^*$ was asked. Let $\langle Hdr^*, K_0 \rangle \leftarrow_R BE.Enc(S^*, PK)$ and $K_1 \in_R \mathcal{K}$. Bit $b \in_R \{0, 1\}$ is chosen uniformly and $\mathcal{A}$ is given (Hdr^*, K^*) with $K^* = K_b$.*
4. *$\mathcal{A}$ is allowed to query $BE.Dec(S, i, Hdr, PK)$, except on inputs of the form $\langle S^*, i, Hdr^*, PK \rangle$, $i \in S^*$.*
5. *$\mathcal{A}$ outputs bit $b' \in \{0, 1\}$ and wins the game, denoted $\mathsf{Game}^{\mathsf{ad-CCA}}_{\mathcal{A}, BE, n, \ell}(\kappa) = 1$, if $b' = b$.*

We define $\mathcal{A}$'s advantage against the adaptive CCA-security of BE as

$$\mathsf{Adv}^{\mathsf{ad-CCA}}_{\mathcal{A}, BE, n, \ell}(\kappa) = \left| \Pr\left[\mathsf{Game}^{\mathsf{ad-CCA}}_{\mathcal{A}, BE, n, \ell}(\kappa) = 1 \right] - \frac{1}{2} \right|$$

We say that BE is adaptively CCA-secure *if for all PPT adversaries $\mathcal{A}$ the advantage $\mathsf{Adv}^{\mathsf{ad-CCA}}_{\mathcal{A}, BE, n, \ell}(\kappa)$ is negligible.*

Remark 2. Our analysis shows that BE must be adaptively CCA-secure when used to obtain confidentiality in user profiles. This requirement also applies to CP-ABE schemes when used for the same purpose. Therefore, neither *Persona* [1] nor *Easier* [16] seem to guarantee our notion of confidentiality since they rely on the CP-ABE scheme from [3] that does not provide the required level of security.

5.1 Specification of PMS-BE

The main idea behind our PMS-BE is that each profile owner U_P manages independently its own instance of the BE scheme, that is: U_P assigns fresh indices i, which we call *pseudonyms*, to the users from $\mathcal{U}$ (upon their first admission to P) and gives them corresponding private (user) keys sk_i. In order to publish an attribute d for some authorized group $\mathcal{G}$, the owner encrypts d using the BE scheme and the set of indices assigned to the users in $\mathcal{G}$. This process allows for very efficient modification of the authorized group $\mathcal{G}$: In order to admit or remove a member U with regard to d the profile owner simply adjusts $\mathcal{G}$ and re-encrypts d. In particular, there is no need to distribute new decryption keys. However, this flexibility comes at the price of a somewhat weaker privacy, since BE schemes include indices i into ciphertext headers, which in turn allows for linkability of an authorized user U across multiple attributes within P. Yet, the use of pseudonyms still allows us to show that PMS-BE satisfies the weaker goal of *anonymity*, which we discuss in Section 5.4.

$\mathtt{Init}(\kappa)$: Execute $\langle PK, SK \rangle \leftarrow BE.Setup(\kappa, n, \ell)$ with $n = \ell = N$ [3]. Output $P \leftarrow \emptyset$ and $pmk \leftarrow \{PK, SK\}$. Additionally, PK is made public.

---

[3] We use this upper bound for simplicity here. One may cut down both on n and ℓ to improve the efficiency of BE.

Publish($pmk, P, (a, d), \mathcal{G}$) : For every $U \in \mathcal{G}$ without pseudonym for P pick an un-
   used pseudonym i at random from $[1, n]$, extract $sk_i \leftarrow BE.KGen(i, SK)$, and
   define new $rk_U \leftarrow \langle i, sk_i \rangle$. For every $U \in \mathcal{G}$ add the corresponding pseudonyms to
   the set S. Compute $\langle Hdr, K_a \rangle \leftarrow BE.Enc(S, PK)$, $\hat{d} \leftarrow SE.Enc(K_a, d)$, and
   $\bar{d} \leftarrow \langle Hdr, S, \hat{d} \rangle$. Add $(a, \bar{d})$ to P and K_a to pmk. Output P, all new rk_U, and
   pmk.

Retrieve(rk_U, P, a) : Extract $(a, \bar{d})$ from P. Parse $\bar{d}$ as $\langle Hdr, S, \hat{d} \rangle$. Extract $\langle i, sk_i \rangle$
   from rk_U. Set $K_a \leftarrow BE.Dec(S, i, sk_i, Hdr, PK)$ and output $SE.Dec(K_a, \hat{d})$.

Delete(pmk, P, a) : Delete $(a, \bar{d})$ from P. Delete K_a from pmk.

ModifyAccess(pmk, P, a, U) : If $U \in \mathcal{G}$ remove U from $\mathcal{G}$; otherwise add U to $\mathcal{G}$.
   Execute Delete(pmk, P, a) followed by Publish($pmk, P, (a, d), \mathcal{G}$), where d is
   the attribute indexed by a.

5.2 Complexity Analysis

PMS-BE requires each profile owner U_P to store one key per index-attribute pair $(a, \bar{d})$
currently published in P and the key pair $\langle PK, SK \rangle$. For each profile containing at
least one attribute a user U is allowed to access, U has to store its secret key $\langle i, sk_i \rangle$
contained in rk_U. Assuming the worst case where all users in $\mathcal{U}$ have profiles contain-
ing $|P|$ attributes that can be accessed by all other users, PMS-BE requires each $U \in \mathcal{U}$
to store $|P| + N + 1$ keys from which $|P| + 2$ keys are stored in pmk and $N - 1$
secret keys $\langle i, sk_i \rangle$ are stored in the retrieval keys rk_U of all others users' profiles. For
each execution of Publish or ModifyAccess the profile owner performs one broad-
cast encryption $BE.Enc$ and one symmetric encryption. The storage overhead may be
reduced by omitting the storage of attribute keys K_a in pmk as the profile owner is able
to reconstruct K_a by executing $sk_i \leftarrow BE.KGen(i, SK)$ for any index i in the set of
authorized indices S for a. With the authorized user's secret key sk_i, the profile owner
is able to execute $BE.Dec$, receiving K_a. That way, the total number of stored keys is
reduced by $|P|$ to $N + 1$, traded in for a higher computation overhead when executing
ModifyAccess. Obviously, the main advantage of the PMS-BE construction over the
PMS-SK approach is the constant number of keys that have to be stored in rk_U. Yet, this
efficiency benefit comes at the cost of a weaker user privacy, as we discuss below.

5.3 Confidentiality of PMS-BE

We first analyze the confidentiality property of the PMS-BE scheme. (See [15] for our
proof of Theorem 3.)

Theorem 3 (Confidentiality of PMS-BE). *If SE is IND-CPA secure and BE is adaptively CCA-secure, PMS-BE provides confidentiality from Definition 2, and*

$$\mathsf{Adv}^{\mathsf{conf}}_{\mathcal{A}, \mathrm{PMS\text{-}BE}}(\kappa) \leq (1 + q) \cdot \left(\mathsf{Adv}^{\mathsf{IND\text{-}CPA}}_{\mathcal{B}_1, SE}(\kappa) + N \cdot \mathsf{Adv}^{\mathsf{ad\text{-}CCA}}_{\mathcal{B}_2, BE, n, \ell}(\kappa) \right)$$

with q being a number of invoked ModifyAccess operations per attribute.

5.4   Privacy of PMS-BE

Our PMS-BE construction does *not* provide unlinkability as defined in Definition 3 since the indices of users are linkable across different published attributes. The attack is simple: After initialization of PMS-BE, unlinkability adversary $\mathcal{A}$ outputs two arbitrary users U_0, U_1, some pair (a, d) and a profile owner U_P. Then, $\mathcal{A}$ executes Publish$(P, (a', d'), \{U_0\})$ for an arbitrary pair (a', d') and extracts the two pairs $(a, \bar{d})$ and $(a', \bar{d}')$ from P such that $\bar{d} = \langle Hdr, S, \hat{d} \rangle$ and $\bar{d}' = \langle Hdr', S', \hat{d}' \rangle$. If $S = S'$, $\mathcal{A}$ outputs 0, otherwise 1.

Since PMS-BE has simpler management and distribution of retrieval keys it would be nice to see whether it can satisfy some weaker, yet still meaningful privacy property. It turns out that PMS-BE is still able to provide *anonymity* of users that are members of different authorized groups $\mathcal{G}$ within the same profile, even in the presence of an adversary in these groups. We formalize anonymity by modifying the unlinkability game based on the following intuition: An anonymity adversary shall not be able to decide the identity of some user $U_b \in \{U_0, U_1\}$ in the setting where the adversary is restricted to publish attributes or modify access to them either by simultaneously including both U_0 and U_1 into the authorized group or none of them. This definition rules out linkability of users based on their pseudonyms, while keeping all other privacy properties of the unlinkability definition. Finally, we can prove that PMS-BE provides *perfect anonymity* using similar arguments as we used for the perfect unlinkability of the PMS-SK scheme. We still observe that our discussion in Remark 1 regarding the potential loss of perfectness for the unlinkability of PMS-SK when deployed in the concrete application applies to PMS-BE as well, due to the distribution of private user keys sk_i. (See [15] for our formal definition of anonymity and for the proofs that unlinkability is strictly stronger than anonymity and that PMS-BE is perfectly anonymous.)

6   Analysis and Discussion for Real-World Social Communities

We analyze the impact imposed by PMS-SK and PMS-BE schemes on the most representative online social community *Facebook* as well as the two well-known services *Twitter* and *Flickr*, and focus on the main complexity difference between both approaches, namely on the average overhead for the storage of private keys.

Being a very general platform for social networking, Facebook users share data with a high amount of contacts. Facebook's own statistics[4] indicates an average of 130 contacts per user, while Golder et al. [11] found a mean of about 180. According to Facebook's statistics, about 500 million active users share more than 30 billion pieces of content (e.g., web links, blog posts, photo albums, etc.) each month. Assuming a rather short lifetime of only three months per item, each user stores on average about 180 pieces of content, i.e., attributes in our profile management scheme. For an average of 150 contacts per user and 180 attributes per profile we obtain 332 keys that have to be stored by each user when using PMS-BE in contrast to over 27000 keys that would be required by PMS-SK. Considering a key length of 192 bits for the private (decryption) key as a basis, this results in a storage overhead of about 8 KB for PMS-BE,

---
[4] http://www.facebook.com/press/info.php?statistics, Oct 2010.

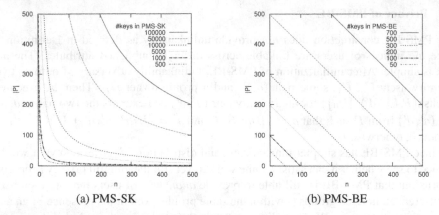

(a) PMS-SK   (b) PMS-BE

Fig. 1. Plots of the number of keys each user has to store in PMS-SK resp. PMS-BE, depending on the average number of contacts n and the average number of attributes per profile $|P|$.

compared to about 650 KB for PMS-SK. Regarding the microblogging service Twitter, where users have on average approximately 50 contacts ("followers") and publish about 60 attributes ("tweets") per month[5], the number of stored keys per user is 232 in PMS-BE and over 9000 in PMS-SK, resulting in about 6 KB respectively 220 KB storage overhead (assuming again a lifetime of three months). Flickr, an online community for image and video hosting, has a very low average of only 12 contacts ("friends") per user according to a study of Mislove et al. [18] in 2007. Assuming the limit of 200 images for a "free account"[6] as average number of attributes per profile, the number of keys each Flickr user has to store would be 214 in the PMS-BE construction and 2600 in PMS-SK, which yields a storage overhead of about 5 KB respectively 62 KB.

We observe that in these average settings the absolute difference of both approaches in storage overhead is not very high. Although relatively differing by a factor of roughly 100, the absolute storage overhead for the assumed average parameters remains below 1 MB in all three networks. We observe that these costs are practical not only for desktop computers but also for modern smart phones. Hence, in practice the two constructions PMS-SK and PMS-BE would allow for a trade-off between minimization of the storage overhead and maximization of privacy (as PMS-BE only provides anonymity, but not unlinkability). On the other hand, when applied to very large profiles (with more contacts and attributes than assumed above) the difference in storage overhead increases rapidly as illustrated in Figure 1. For example, a profile with 300 contacts[7] and 2000 attributes leads to the overhead of about 15 MB in PMS-SK compared to only 55 KB in PMS-BE. Therefore, using PMS-BE is advisable in this case.

---

[5] http://www.website-monitoring.com/blog/2010/05/04/twitter-facts-and-figures-history-statistics/, Oct 2010.

[6] http://www.flickr.com/help/limits/, Oct 2010.

[7] More than 10% of the Facebook users have more than 300 contacts [10].

7 Conclusion and Future Work

Privacy preserving publication of personal data in user profiles is a valuable building block that can be used to boot-strap various collaborative and social data sharing applications. So far, security and privacy of user profiles was addressed in an "ad-hoc" fashion, resulting in several implementations without clearly specified privacy goals. In this work, we applied cryptographic methodology and introduced the first formal model for profile management, capturing two fundamental privacy goals, namely confidentiality of profile data and privacy of users who are allowed to retrieve this data. Our model enables independent design and analysis of private profile management schemes that are then usable in different social applications and both centralized and distributed environments. We also proposed and analyzed two private profile management schemes, PMS-SK and PMS-BE, based on symmetric and broadcast encryption techniques, respectively. Both schemes provide confidentiality of profile data against adaptive adversaries, yet differ in their privacy guarantees: PMS-SK offers unlinkability, whereas PMS-BE only guarantees anonymity, while being more scalable and efficient. Of particular interest for future work are the following questions:

- Can unlinkability of users being authorized to access different attributes within a profile be achieved with a sub-linear overhead?
- How concrete implementations of PMS-SK and PMS-BE do behave regarding the imposed overhead for retrieval key distribution? This will obviously depend on the used distribution mechanism, which seems more complex in case of PMS-SK.

Acknowledgements. Mark Manulis was supported in part through the German Science Foundation (DFG) project PRIMAKE (MA 4957), DAAD project PACU (PPP 50743263), and BMBF project POC (AUS 10/046).

References

1. Baden, R., Bender, A., Spring, N., Bhattacharjee, B., Starin, D.: Persona: an online social network with user-defined privacy. In: ACM SIGCOMM Conference on Applications, Technologies, Architectures, and Protocols for Computer Communications, pp. 135–146 (2009)
2. Barth, A., Boneh, D., Waters, B.: Privacy in Encrypted Content Distribution using Private Broadcast Encryption. In: Di Crescenzo, G., Rubin, A. (eds.) FC 2006. LNCS, vol. 4107, pp. 52–64. Springer, Heidelberg (2006)
3. Bethencourt, J., Sahai, A., Waters, B.: Ciphertext-policy attribute-based encryption. In: IEEE Symposium on Security and Privacy (S&P 2007), pp. 321–334 (2007)
4. Buchegger, S., Schiöberg, D., Vu, L.-H., Datta, A.: PeerSoN: P2P social networking: early experiences and insights. In: ACM EuroSys Workshop on Social Network Systems (SNS 2009), pp. 46–52 (2009)
5. Callas, J., Donnerhacke, L., Finney, H., Shaw, D., Thayer, R.: OpenPGP Message Format. RFC 4880, Informational (2007)
6. Canetti, R., Garay, J.A., Itkis, G., Micciancio, D., Naor, M., Pinkas, B.: Multicast security: A taxonomy and some efficient constructions. In: INFOCOM 1999, pp. 708–716 (1999)
7. Carminati, B., Ferrari, E., Perego, A.: Enforcing access control in web-based social networks. ACM Transactions on Information and System Security 13(1) (2009)

8. Cutillo, L.A., Molva, R., Strufe, T.: Safebook: A privacy-preserving online social network leveraging on real-life trust. IEEE Communications Magazine 47(12) (2009); Consumer Communications and Networking Series
9. Gentry, C., Waters, B.: Adaptive Security in Broadcast Encryption Systems (with Short Ciphertexts). In: Joux, A. (ed.) EUROCRYPT 2009. LNCS, vol. 5479, pp. 171–188. Springer, Heidelberg (2009)
10. Gjoka, M., Kurant, M., Butts, C.T., Markopoulou, A.: Walking in Facebook: A Case Study of Unbiased Sampling of OSNs. In: INFOCOM 2010, pp. 2498–2506 (2010)
11. Golder, S.A., Wilkinson, D.M., Huberman, B.A.: Rhythms of social interaction: Messaging within a massive online network. In: Communities and Technologies 2007, pp. 41–66 (2007)
12. Graffi, K., Mukherjee, P., Menges, B., Hartung, D., Kovacevic, A., Steinmetz, R.: Practical security in p2p-based social networks. In: Annual IEEE Conference on Local Computer Networks (LCN 2009), pp. 269–272 (2009)
13. Graffi, K., Podrajanski, S., Mukherjee, P., Kovacevic, A., Steinmetz, R.: A distributed platform for multimedia communities. In: IEEE International Symposium on Multimedia (ISM 2008), pp. 208–213 (2008)
14. Gross, R., Acquisti, A.: Information revelation and privacy in online social networks. In: ACM Workshop on Privacy in the Electronic Society (WPES 2005), pp. 71–80 (2005)
15. Günther, F., Manulis, M., Strufe, T.: Cryptographic Treatment of Private User Profiles. Cryptology ePrint Archive, Report 2011/064 (2011),
   http://eprint.iacr.org/2011/064
16. Jahid, S., Mittal, P., Borisov, N.: EASiER: Encryption-based access control in social networks with efficient revocation. In: ACM Symposium on Information, Computer and Communications Security (ASIACCS 2011), pp. 411–415 (2011)
17. Lucas, M.M., Borisov, N.: flyByNight: mitigating the privacy risks of social networking. In: Symposium on Usable Privacy and Security, SOUPS 2009 (2009)
18. Mislove, A., Marcon, M., Gummadi, P.K., Druschel, P., Bhattacharjee, B.: Measurement and analysis of online social networks. In: ACM SIGCOMM Conference on Internet Measurement 2007, pp. 29–42 (2007)
19. PrimeLife. Scramble! (September 2010),
   http://www.primelife.eu/results/opensource/65-scramble
20. Sherman, A.T., McGrew, D.A.: Key Establishment in Large Dynamic Groups Using One-Way Function Trees. IEEE Transactions on Software Engineering 29(5), 444–458 (2003)
21. Tootoonchian, A., Saroiu, S., Ganjali, Y., Wolman, A.: Lockr: better privacy for social networks. In: ACM International Conference on Emerging Networking Experiments and Technologies (CoNEXT 2009), pp. 169–180 (2009)
22. Wallner, D., Harder, E., Agee, R.: Key Management for Multicast: Issues and Architectures. RFC 2627, Informational (1999)
23. Wong, C.K., Gouda, M.G., Lam, S.S.: Secure group communications using key graphs. In: ACM SIGCOMM Conference on Applications, Technologies, Architectures, and Protocols for Computer Communications 1998, pp. 68–79 (1998)
24. Zheleva, E., Getoor, L.: To join or not to join: the illusion of privacy in social networks with mixed public and private user profiles. In: International Conference on World Wide Web (WWW 2009), pp. 531–540 (2009)
25. Zhu, Y., Hu, Z., Wang, H., Hu, H., Ahn, G.-J.: A Collaborative Framework for Privacy Protection in Online Social Networks. In: International Conference on Collaborative Computing (CollaborateCom 2010) (2010)

An Introspection-Based Memory Scraper Attack against Virtualized Point of Sale Systems

Jennia Hizver and Tzi-cker Chiueh

Department of Computer Science, Stony Brook University,
Stony Brook, USA

Abstract. Retail industry Point of Sale (POS) computer systems are
frequently targeted by hackers for credit/debit card data. Faced with increasing security threats, new security standards requiring encryption for
card data storage and transmission were introduced making harvesting
card data more difficult. Encryption can be circumvented by extracting
unencrypted card data from the volatile memory of POS systems. One
scenario investigated in this empirical study is the introspection-based
memory scraping attack. Vulnerability of nine commercial POS applications running on a virtual machine was assessed with a novel tool, which
exploited the virtual machine state introspection capabilities supported
by modern hypervisors to automatically extract card data from the POS
virtual machines. The tool efficiently extracted 100% of the credit/debit
card data from all POS applications. This is the first detailed description of an introspection-based memory scraping attack on virtualized
POS systems.

1 Introduction

One of the most vulnerable links in the payment operations chain is the Point of
Sale (POS) system deployed at physical locations where sales transactions and
payment authorization take place (such as retail and hospitality businesses). The
majority of POS systems are Windows-based computers running POS applications. Therefore, securing these systems is no different than securing any other
Windows host. However, POS systems represent high-value targets for attackers
who are financially motivated because they contain valuable card data that could
be sold on black markets to reap considerable monetary gains. Negligence in securing POS systems carries a high risk as illustrated by a number of high-profile
POS system breaches that have occurred recently. These successful attacks targeted at POS systems whose underlying hosts were not properly secured and
eventually caused loss of tens of millions of credit card account information from
merchants and credit card processors [1].

To improve security in payment processing systems, the Payment Card Industry (PCI) Security Standards Council developed and released two security standards: the Payment Card Industry Security Standard (PCI-DSS) and Payment

G. Danezis, S. Dietrich, and K. Sako (Eds.): FC 2011 Workshops, LNCS 7126, pp. 55–69, 2012.

Application Data Security Standard (PA-DSS) [2]. The PCI-DSS and PA-DSS standards established stringent security requirements to safeguarding sensitive card data. The current version of the PCI-DSS specifies 12 major requirement areas for compliance with over 200 individual control tests. All entities that store, process, or transmit card data are required to comply with the PCI-DSS to ensure that their computer systems are better protected from unauthorized exposure. Noncompliant entities receive monthly fines and lose their ability to process credit card payments. The PA-DSS was derived from the PCI-DSS and was intended specifically to deal with secure POS software development life-cycle. The PCI Security Standards Council requires merchants to use PA-DSS compliant POS applications for credit and debit card transactions. The most important security requirement of these two standards is to prohibit storage of unencrypted card data. As a result, simply breaching a payment processing system and downloading card data stored on its disks is no longer a viable option. However, attackers have developed new attack techniques to obtain card data from the volatile memory of POS processes. In these attacks known as RAM scrapers, following infiltration of a POS system the attacker sets up a persistent operating system service designed to dump a POS process's virtual memory at specified time intervals and use regular expressions to parse the memory dump to extract card data. Attackers typically focus only on a POS process's virtual memory, rather than the whole system's physical memory. This strategy allows for fast processing and avoids excessive disk usage, which may be flagged as a malicious activity. Because the card data of a transaction commonly resides in unencrypted form in the volatile memory of a POS process when it processes the transaction, the memory scrapper attack is relatively easy to construct as compared with vulnerability-based exploit code.

One of the first RAM scraper attack incidents was reported in late 2008 [3]. In the 2009 Data Breach Investigation Report, Verizon reported 15 most prevalent threats and their frequency [4]. RAM scrapers surpassed phishing attacks and were ranked #14 among cyber security cases investigated by Verizon's Investigative Response team. In the 2010 Data Breach Investigation Report, Verizon reported that the use of RAM Scrapers to capture sensitive data continued to increase [5].

As virtualization technology becomes prevalent in enterprise data centers, POS systems also start to run on virtual machines hosted on virtualized physical servers [6-8]. These virtualized POS systems enable new forms of memory scraper attacks. This paper describes a study that aims to develop techniques that automate memory scraper attacks against commercial POS applications running inside virtual machines, and measure the effectiveness of such memory scraper attacks against commercial POS applications. We expect these attacks to emerge as a serious threat once virtualization technology takes hold in the POS market because the aggregate trusted computing base (TCB) of typically virtualized servers, which includes the hypervisor and a privileged domain (e.g. Dom0 in Xen), is too large to be free of security vulnerabilities.

A memory scraper attack on a POS virtual machine may originate completely outside of the virtual machine, and is thus more difficult to detect. This is possible because of virtual machine (VM) state introspection capabilities provided by modern hypervisors, such as Xen and VMware's ESX. VM state introspection mechanisms allow one to examine a VM's state from another VM running on the same physical server, and are mainly used in security tools implementations, such as intrusion detection/prevention systems and malware detection applications [9-11]. VM state introspection enables security tools to actively monitor a VM's run-time state and events in a way that cannot be affected by the OS and applications running in the monitored VM making the security tools isolated from attack code as powerful as kernel rootkits.

This paper describes the design and implementation of an introspection-based RAM scraper called V-RAM scraper, which is designed to extract card data from POS applications running on Windows-based VMs hosted on a Xen-based virtualized server. We have applied V-RAM scraper against nine commercial POS applications, and were able to extract card data from every payment processing transaction that passed through each application. To the best of our knowledge, this is the first successful demonstration of an introspection-based RAM scraper attack on virtualized POS systems.

2   Background

A traditional POS network contains a central payment processing server and a number of POS application terminals connected using standard client-server architecture. After a credit card is used at the POS terminal, the terminal connects to the central payment processing server in the merchant's corporate environment, which, in turn, provides payment card authorization (Figure 1).

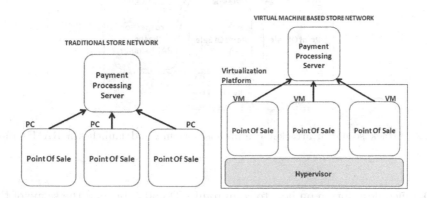

Fig. 1. (Left) In the traditional POS network setup, each POS system is hosted on a separate platform in the store. The payment processing server is located in the corporate environment. (Right) In a VM-based POS network setup, all POS systems are hosted on the same physical host.

Use of virtualization technology enables consolidation of the POS application hosts into a smaller number of physical machines, forcing POS applications to run inside virtual machines, as shown in Figure 1. One example of such virtualization technology is Xen [12]. Xen was used in this study due to two important advantages: 1) it is an open-source hypervisor, and 2) it is capable of supporting multiple types of guest operating systems, including Windows and Linux. In Xen and similar virtual environments, out-of-VM RAM scraping attacks become even more powerful because if they could extract card data from one VM, they will be able to do so on all VMs running on the same physical server.

In Xen, the first VM, which boots automatically after the hypervisor is loaded, is called Dom0 domain. By default, Dom0 is granted special privileges for controlling other VMs including access to the raw memory of other VMs known as DomU domains. If an attacker could compromise Dom0 domain, she could then launch a RAM scraper attacker on virtual machines that run POS applications on the same physical server, as shown in Figure 2. Such an attack is possible because Dom0 is given the privilege to view the raw memory of all VMs on the same physical machine. Likewise, it is possible to mount a RAM scraper attack from a DomU domain if sufficient privileges are given to that domain to perform memory monitoring. For our implementation, we conduct the RAM scraper attack from within Dom0 because it already has the necessary privileges to view the raw memory of other VMs.

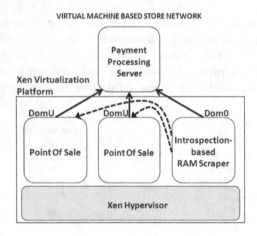

Fig. 2. Attack scenario: attacker compromises Dom0 and launches a RAM scraper attack

Detailed description on how to compromise Dom0 is beyond the scope of this article. However, some of the common POS vulnerabilities are likely to exist on Dom0 in a virtualized POS environment because Dom0 domain is essentially a virtual machine running a full-blown operating system. There are several possible ways to gain access to Dom0 without proper authorization. Briefly, the top vulnerabilities contributing to POS, and, potentially, Dom0 compromises include missing or outdated security patches, use of default settings and passwords, unnecessary and vulnerable services on servers, and use of improperly configured remote access management tools. These vulnerabilities were commonly encountered and exploited by hackers in real life attacks against retail and hospitality businesses to obtain payment card data [5, 13, 14]. Exploitation of a vulnerable service running inside Dom0 could lead to a compromise and control of Dom0. As more and more functionalities are introduced to the Dom0 domain, the probability of such a compromise also increases. Another potential attack on Dom0 is through misuse of insecure remote management tools creating a "back door" in the system. Yet another possibility is to gain local access on one of the unprivileged VMs and from there to launch an attack on a service in the Dom0 domain. For example, a known vulnerability in code running in Dom0, CVE-2007-4993 [15], may be exploited from an unprivileged VM with the end result of this exploit is to execute chosen privileged commands in Dom0. Accordingly, this study's assumption was that the access on Dom0 had been already gained by the attacker using one of the methods briefly described above.

Compromise of Dom0 and subsequent access to a VM's raw memory would not immediately compromise all payment data processed by the system. Only one card number is received per transaction, and as found by this study, it often exists in a POS process memory only a few seconds (sometimes milliseconds) before it is erased or overwritten upon completion of the transaction. Given the short data lifetime, an attacker has to acquire frequent VM memory images to ensure that all data entering the system is captured. Capturing full system memory images is not only time consuming, but may also increase the disk space usage alerting a system administrator of a suspicious activity, especially if numerous full memory snapshots from a number of VMs are taken concurrently.

Conversely, by looking only at the most probable segments of the memory that contain the data, the attacker could significantly reduce the memory search space and the hard disk usage and avoid false positives because number strings that look like payment card numbers but appear outside POS processes would be ignored. Therefore, if the attacker could fetch POS process memory pages exclusively, only small memory regions (as opposed to full system memory images) need to be searched for card data. However, determining which memory regions belong to the POS process may present a challenge. If a RAM scraper attack is conducted on the machine locally, the attacker has explicit access to high-level objects, such as processes, and can gather the required information. In a VM-based attack scenario, large amount of unstructured memory necessitates POS process identification before proceeding with payment data extraction. This study demonstrated that this challenge can be circumvented by leveraging VM introspection technique. The approach presented in this article effectively solved the problem of POS process identification significantly simplifying card data extraction.

3 The V-RAM Scraper Attack Tool

There are three steps in the V-RAM scraper tool. First, the tool maps the physical memory pages of the virtual machine on which the target POS application runs to its virtual address space, so that it can inspect and analyze their contents. Second, it identifies the portion of the mapped physical memory space that belongs to the target POS process or processes, so that it can focus on that portion only. Third, it searches the memory-resident portion of the target POS application process's virtual address space for possible payment card data.

3.1 Step 1: Mapping the Target VM's Physical Memory Pages

The Xen distribution provides a Xen Control library (libxc) for a Dom0 process to act on the DomU virtual machines, including pausing a DomU VM, resuming a paused DomU VM, reading a DomU VM's physical memory page, modifying a DomU's physical memory page, etc. Specifically, libxc provides a xc_map_foreign_range() function that is designed to map the physical memory space of a target DomU VM into a Dom0 process's virtual address space so that the latter can easily manipulate the target VM's physical memory. The V-RAM scraper leverages this API function to map the physical memory pages of the VM on which the target POS application runs.

Because libxc is supported by the Xen hypervisor, neither the target VM nor the hypervisor require modification. Moreover, the target VM's physical memory space mapping to a Dom0 is transparent to the operating system or any user-level processes in the target VM, including the POS application. This means that it is difficult for a POS application running inside a VM to resist such memory mapping procedures.

3.2 Step 2: POS Process Identification

Instead of scanning the entire physical memory image of the target VM, the V-RAM scraper attempts to identify the user-level process running the target POS application, and scans only that process's physical memory pages for card data. Given a VM's physical memory mapped in the above step, the V-RAM scraper needs to apply VM state introspection [6] to make sense of it, particularly the high-level data structures embedded in the physical memory pages. This requires intimate knowledge of the target VM's operating system structure in order to bridge the so-called semantic gap [10, 11, 16] between the low-level memory pages and high-level kernel data structures, such as process list, page directories and tables, etc. It is non-trivial to reverse-engineer these guest OS-specific constructs, especially for a closed-source operating system such as Windows XP, which is the target of this project. Fortunately, a large body of knowledge about the Windows kernel's internal structure has been accumulated and documented by both black hats and white hats over the years. We leverage this knowledge and effectively solve the problem of POS process identification.

In Windows OS, the EPROCESS in-memory data structures are used to keep information about running processes [17]. To uncover the list of all running processes inside a VM, the V-RAM scraper extracts all the EPROCESS data structures by parsing the VM's physical memory pages mapped in the previous step. From an EPROCESS data structure, one can derive the corresponding process's attributes, such as the process' name and memory pages. All EPROCESS data structures are connected together in a double-linked-list and are stored in the address space of the System process. By recognizing the EPROCESS data structure of the System process and following the links embedded there, one could locate all other EPROCESS data structures.

The simplified representation of the EPROCESS data structure in Windows XP is shown in Figure 3. To discover the System process's EPROCESS data structure, one searches the physical memory pages for the known values of its 'DirectoryTableBase' and 'ImageFileName' fields. For instance, in Windows XP the System process' physical address of its Page Directory is always at 0x39000, which is recorded in the 'DirectoryTableBase' field, which is located at the 0x018 offset. The 'ImageFileName' field, which is located at the 0x174 offset, contains the value 'System'. Hence, the System EPROCESS data structure can be discovered by searching for byte strings of '00039000' and 'System' that are 0x15C bytes apart. Once the System process' EPROCESS data structure is known, all other EPROCESS data structures are readily available, as shown in Figure 3. Another well-known approach to locate the EPROCESS list is to search for the special PsInitialSystemProcess symbol exported by the Windows kernel.

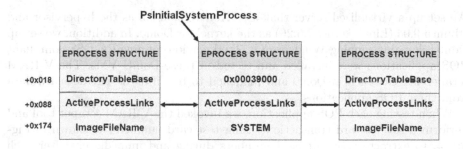

Fig. 3. The linked list of EPROCESS data structures. Each EPROCESS data structure has multiple data fields, which are located at pre-defined offsets with respect to the base of the structure.

Once the EPROCESS data structures are available, the V-RAM scraper identifies the target POS process by examining the name field of these EPROCESS structures. To identify the list of physical memory pages associated with the POS process, the V-RAM scraper first leverages the information in the 'DirectoryTableBase' field, which gives the base of the POS process's page directory, and then traverses the POS process's page directory and page table to find all the physical memory pages owned by the POS process.

The V-RAM scraper examines the target VM's physical memory pages using the user-space library XenAccess [18] that is specifically designed to facilitate VM state inspection.

3.3   Step 3: Card Data Extraction

Once the target POS process's memory pages are identified, the V-RAM scraper routinely searches them for card data using the following patterns. Payment card numbers are sequences of 13 to 16 digits. The card issuer is identified by a few digits at the start of these sequences. For instance, Visa card numbers have a length of 16 and a prefix value of 4. MasterCard numbers have a length of 16 and a prefix value of 51-55. Discover card numbers have a length of 16 and a prefix value of 6011. Finally, American Express numbers have a length of 15 and a prefix value of 34 or 37. Therefore, finding these card numbers in memory can be accomplished by searching for ASCII strings that match the following regular expression: $((4\backslash d\{3\})|(5[1\text{-}5]\backslash d\{2\})|(6011))\text{-?}\backslash d\{4\}\text{-?}\{4\}\text{-?}\backslash d\{4\}|3[4,7]\backslash d\{13\}$.

However, sequences of 13 to 16 digits with proper prefix values are not always card numbers. Each potential card number obtained by the above search procedure has to be further verified using the Luhn algorithm [19], which is a simple checksum formula that is commonly used to validate the integrity of a wide variety of identification numbers.

4   Testing Results and Analysis

We set up a virtualized server that uses Xen version 3.3 as the hypervisor and Ubuntu 9.04 (Linux kernel 2.6.26) as the kernel for Dom0. In addition, we set up DomU domains running Windows XP. Trial versions of nine PA-DSS compliant POS applications were installed and tested in these DomU VMs. The V-RAM scraper was installed in Dom0 and launched to test if it can extract card data from these POS applications.

When testing each POS application, we invoked the V-RAM scraper tool and performed several card transactions using test card numbers, as shown in Figure 4, to extract these test card numbers during and immediately after each transaction using the tool. Because we are mainly interested in how effectively these POS applications hide card data when they perform transactions involving card numbers, a small number of test transactions are sufficient to expose their behaviors in this regard. Following each card transaction, the V-RAM scraper captures a snapshot of the test POS process's physical memory pages every second, while letting the POS application continue to run as the memory snapshot is being taken. The performance overhead of memory snapshotting is largely unnoticeable. For each captured snapshot, the V-RAM scraper searches for any credit card number patterns.

As expected, the V-RAM scraper was able to successfully identify all test card numbers in the memory snapshots of all test POS applications when the transactions are being processed, as shown in Figure 5. Moreover, the V-RAM scraper is able to identify other card related information including the card expiration date, CVV number, and the card holder's name within the same memory segment as the corresponding card number.

Based on the timings and the portions of the snapshots from which card data are extracted, we classify each card data extraction instance into four categories:

1. Transient/Stack: The card data are uncovered from a stack region while the associated transaction is being processed.
2. Persistent/Stack: The card data are uncovered from a stack region after the associated transaction is completed.
3. Transient/Heap: The card data are uncovered from a heap region while the associated transaction is being processed.
4. Persistent/Heap: The card data are uncovered from a heap region after the associated transaction is completed.

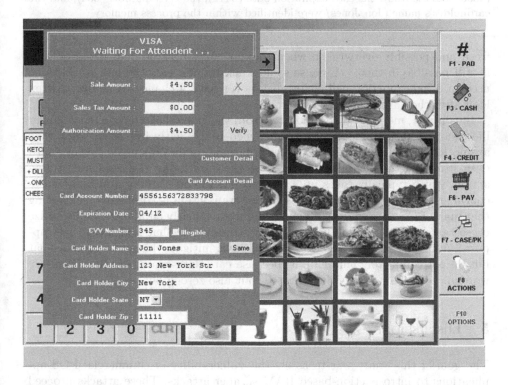

Fig. 4. We ran several card transactions against each POS application by entering transaction-specific information, such as sale amount, card number, expiration date, CVV number, card holder name etc.

The successful card data extractions the V-RAM scraper is able to perform against the nine test POS applications fall into category (1), (3) and (4). Category (2) is rare because memory words allocated on the stack are automatically

```
00CA7910   00 00 00 00 00 00 00 00   00 00 00 00 00 00 00 00   ...............
00CA7920   00 00 00 00 00 00 00 00   00 00 00 00 00 00 00 00   ...............
00CA7930   00 00 00 00 00 00 00 00   00 00 00 00 00 00 00 00   ...............
00CA7940   00 00 00 00 00 00 00 00   00 00 00 00 00 00 00 00   ...............
00CA7950   34 35 35 36 31 35 36 33   37 32 38 33 33 37 39 38   4556156372833798
00CA7960   00 00 00 00 30 34 31 32   00 00 00 00 34 35 30 2E   ....0412....450.
00CA7970   30 30 00 00 00 00 00 00   00 00 00 00 00 00 00 00   00.............
00CA7980   00 00 00 00 00 00 00 00   00 00 00 00 00 00 00 00   ...............
00CA7990   00 00 00 00 00 00 00 00   00 00 00 00 00 00 00 00   ...............
00CA79A0   00 43 56 56 32 20 47 4F   4F 44 20 4D 41 54 43 48   .CVV2 GOOD MATCH
00CA79B0   00 00 00 00 00 00 00 00   00 00 00 00 00 00 00 00   ...............
00CA79C0   33 35 34 00 00 00 00 00   00 00 00 00 00 00 00 00   354............
00CA79D0   00 00 00 00 00 00 00 00   00 00 00 00 00 00 00 00   ...............
00CA79E0   00 00 00 00 00 00 00 00   00 00 00 00 00 00 00 00   ...............
00CA79F0   00 00 00 4A 6F 6E 20 4A   6F 6E 65 73 00 00 00 00   ...Jon Jones....
00CA7A00   00 00 00 00 00 00 00 00   00 00 00 00 00 00 00 00   ...............
```

Fig. 5. Detailed information uncovered about a test card, including the card number (4556156372833798), the card expiration date (0412), the CVV number (354), and the cardholder's name (Jon Jones) were identified within the process memory

freed and possibly overwritten when they are no longer needed. However, this is still possible in theory, because some stack frames, e.g., the last stack frame used in a long function call chain, may never have a chance to be overwritten long after they are freed.

In contrast, memory words allocated from the global heap have a much longer life time, because application programs need to explicitly free them when they are no longer needed, but application programs rarely do so. As a result, card data stored on the heap exist for at least the duration of the associated transaction, which typically takes up a few seconds to complete, and in many cases continue to exist even after the associated transaction is completed, suggesting that many POS application developers did not explicitly de-allocate and sanitize these card data-containing heap memory words. Note that languages that support automatic garbage collection, such as Java, mitigate this problem somewhat but do not completely eliminate it, because card data-containing heap memory words need to be not only de-allocated, but also zeroed out.

5   Discussions

The goal of this study was to assess the vulnerability of commercial POS applications to introspection-based RAM scraper attacks. These attacks proceed in a way that is completely transparent to the attacked POS system and thus represent a very attractive option for an attacker to quickly extract sensitive information from a large number of POS instances.

The test results demonstrated that the V-RAM scraper prototype could successfully extract all card data from the volatile memory of POS processes in fast, efficient, and un-intrusive manner while the card transactions are in progress. Card data capture was possible because the data were stored in an unencrypted form in memory and therefore susceptible to a window of vulnerability exploited by the memory scraper tool during the time when transactions were being processed.

One cause of this vulnerability is POS application developers failing to follow secure coding techniques. After a payment transaction is completed, it is mandatory to clean up all occurrences of unencrypted card data stored in stack and heap memory. However, this coding practice is not always followed in practice. In idle POS systems, this coding error leads to card data persistence in volatile memory for as long as several days greatly increasing the risk of card data exposure. Even when the software developers follow secure coding technique, it is still possible for the attack tools such as the V-RAM scraper described in this study to extract card data from running POS applications. This is possible because card data need to be present on the stack while a card transaction is being processed, which may easily take several seconds providing enough time for the V-RAM scraper to extract card data from a monitored POS VM.

Although Xen was used as the virtualization platform for this study, the V-RAM scraper attack tool is expected to be equally effective on any other virtualization platform supporting VM introspection capabilities. For example, VMware's ESX provides a VMsafe API with similar functionalities to the Xen Control library. While VM state introspection allows for good visibility and enables deployment of security solutions that are immune to tampering by malicious software inside monitored VMs, the same introspection capability also creates the threat of high precision attacks and opens new avenues for attackers to obtain payment data without breaching the POS application hosts with the attack tool described in this article as one example.

This security threat associated with VM introspection is not addressed by the current version of the industry security standard (PCI DSS). Adoption and inclusion of VM introspection capabilities into POS environments should be reassessed in light of the feasibility demonstrated by the V-RAM scraper attack tool developed in this study.

Potential solutions to V-RAM scraper attacks are outside the scope of this paper. Nevertheless, there are several promising venues. One possibility is a programming system allowing a developer to annotate a piece of data structure as sensitive and for the compiler to automatically encrypt it when stored on the stack or heap. With this approach, it would be more difficult to detect sensitive data using plaintext-based scanning and matching. Another possibility is to introduce fine-grain access control mechanisms to control inter-VM communications (including VM introspection requests) according to a security policy manipulable only by the hypervisor [20]. Reduction in data persistence and information leakage can be also achieved by asking developers to follow privacy-protecting coding practices. One simple coding practice involves zeroing out heap memory locations that contain sensitive data before they are marked for de-allocation. Finally, a VM should be able to protect itself through detection of VM introspection [21].

6   Related Work

Previous studies on attacks targeting sensitive in-memory data and originating outside the host mainly focused on developing techniques for locating crypto-graphic keys within large blobs of memory, such as full system memory images. Shamir and Someren [22] described visual and statistical methods to efficiently search and identify encryption keys from system memory where the attacker required physical access to the system. Petterson [23] reviewed key recovery techniques from full-system memory images of Linux systems using the knowledge of encryption key holding data structures of open source crypto applications. While the research demonstrates that keys can be successfully located by guessing in-memory values of the variables surrounding the key, in attacks on closed source software, the attacker will not have access to the application source code and thus, can not apply the method. Halderman et al., [24] presented several attack scenarios exploiting DRAM remanence effects through acquisition of full system memory images to extract cryptographic key material. This attack also required physical access to the system. Ristenpart et al., [25] investigated the problem of confidential information leakage via side channels in a cross-VM attack, which neither required physical access to the system nor full-system memory acquisitions. Although in non-virtualized multi-process environment side channel attacks based on inter-process leakage have been shown to enable extraction of secret keys [26, 27], the cross-VM attacks presented in [25] were more coarse-grained than those required to extract cryptographic keys. In addition, the authors were not aware of any published extensions of these attacks to the virtual machine environment.

The attack scenario investigated in this study differed from the above examples because it did not require either physical access to the host or acquisition of full-system memory images. Moreover, the attack targeted short-lived transient data, unique per each transaction, and therefore, required frequent and efficient interactions with the system memory to capture all the data passing through the system. This efficiency requirement was accomplished by leveraging the virtual machine introspection technique.

The term "'virtual machine introspection"' was introduced by Garfinkel and Rosenblum to describe the operation of a Livewire host-based intrusion detection system for virtual machines [9]. Subsequently, several other systems, such as Lares and VMwatcher applied VM introspection to monitor hosts running in virtual machines by reconstructing the semantics of the internal state within the VM with the goal of detecting malicious activity [10, 11]. Only limited details were given regarding the implementation of the introspection mechanisms employed in those systems. Conversely, XenAccess was the first open source project that described the introspection implementation in detail [28]. It also provided access to the programming APIs, therefore enhancing experimental research in IDS/IPS and malware detection.

Advances in VM introspection gave rise to its application in digital forensic analysis. Using VM introspection, unobtrusive live system analysis may be performed on the target virtual machine without changing the system state during the data acquisition process. The research on this topic is still ongoing, but there are several interesting techniques that have been developed for analyzing volatile memory in Linux virtual machines using VM introspection [29]. Despite the fact that most research has been conducted in Linux OS, analogous Windows OS based techniques can be developed utilizing methods borrowed from forensic analysis in non-virtualized systems. Our tool utilized these methods to generate a list of active processes, extract information relating to a specific process, and reconstruct the virtual address space of a process [30-32].

7   Conclusions

Payment card data processed by POS systems have been a covetous target for financially motivated attackers. Recognizing this threat, the payment card industry has issued multiple security standards to tighten the security requirements on POS systems. Although a step forward, these standards cannot prevent all possible attacks against the POS systems in the field. Memory scraping attack, in which the attacker scans the physical memory of POS application processes to extract payment card information, is particularly noteworthy because it aims directly at the most valuable data touched by POS systems. As POS systems start to run on virtualized platforms, newer forms of memory scraping attack become possible. This paper successfully demonstrates an introspection-based memory scraping attack that leverages VM state introspection capabilities offered by modern hypervisors such as Xen and VMware's ESX to extract payment card data from POS processes running inside VMs that execute on the same physical machine. The attack tool was applied against nine commercial POS applications resulting in extraction of 100% of card data. Although the proposed attack is contingent upon a successful break-in into the TCB of a POS virtualized server, the fact that such breaches have been reported previously suggests that this attack is not theoretical presenting a real threat.

Because the vulnerability exploited by the proposed memory scraper attack is a programming error, a compiler that can automatically encrypt payment card data and destroy them when the associated memory words are de-allocated, appears to be the best solution to this problem.

References

1. Chronology of Data Breaches,
   http://www.privacyrights.org/ar/ChronDataBreaches.htm
2. PCI Security Standards Council,
   https://www.pcisecuritystandards.org/
3. Evolution of Malware: Targeting Credit Card Data in Memory,
   https://www.trustwave.com/downloads/whitepapers/Trustwave_WP_Evolution
   _of_Malware_.pdf
4. Data Breach Investigations Supplemental Report (2009),
   http://www.verizonbusiness.com/resources/security/reports/rp_2009-data
   -breach-investigations-supplemental-report_en_xg.pdf

5. Data Breach Investigation Report (2010),
   http://www.verizonbusiness.com/resources/reports/rp_2010-data-breach-report_en_xg.pdf
6. Restaurant Chain Upgrades Systems and Cuts 2,000 Servers Using Virtual Machines,
   http://download.microsoft.com/documents/customerevidence/7146_jack_in_the_box_cs.doc
7. Bringing virtualization and thin computing technology to POS,
   http://www.pippard.com/pdf/virtualized_pos_whitepaper.pdf
8. MICROS Systems, Inc. Announces Deployment of MICROS 9700 HMS at M Resort Spa Casino in Las Vegas,
   http://www.micros.com/NR/rdonlyres/3E357BE8-70DB-468D-B9AB-68F0E784527F/2296/MResort.pdf
9. Garfinkel, T., Rosenblum, M.: A virtual machine introspection based architecture for intrusion detection. In: Proceedings of the 10th Annual Symposium on Network and Distributed System Security, pp. 191–206 (2003)
10. Payne, B.D., Carbone, M., Sharif, M., Lee, W.: Lares: an architecture for secure active monitoring using virtualization. In: Proceedings of the IEEE Symposium on Security and Privacy, pp. 233–247 (2008)
11. Jiang, X., Wang, A., Xu, D.: Stealthy Malware Detection Through VMM-Based "'Out-of-the-Box"' Semantic View Reconstruction. In: Proceedings of the 14th ACM Conference on Computer and Communications Security, pp. 128–138 (2007)
12. What is Xen?, http://www.xen.org/
13. Critical Vulnerabilities Identified to Alert Payment System Participants of Data Compromise Trends,
    http://usa.visa.com/download/merchants/bulletin_critical_vulnerabiliti es_041509.pdf
14. Top Five Data Security Vulnerabilities Identified to Promote Merchant Awareness,
    http://usa.visa.com/download/merchants/Cisp_alert_082906_Top5Vulnerabil ities.pdf
15. Common Vulnerabilities and Exposures: CVE-2007-4993,
    http://cve.mitre.org/cgi-bin/cvename.cgi?name=CVE-2007-4993
16. Jones, S.T., Arpaci-Dusseau, A.C., Arpaci-Dusseau, R.H.: Antfarm: tracking processes in a virtual machine environment. In: Proceedings of the 2006 USENIX Annual Technical Conference (2006)
17. Russinovich M.E., Solomon, D.A.: Microsoft Windows Internals. Microsoft Press (2005)
18. XenAccess Documentation, http://doc.xenaccess.org/
19. Luhn, H. P.: Computer For Verifying Numbers. In: Office, U. S. P., USA (1954)
20. Sailer, R., Jaeger, T., Valdez, E., Caceres, R., Perez, R., Berger, S., Griffin, J.L., Van Doorn, L.: Building a MAC-Based Security Architecture for the Xen Open-Source Hypervisor. In: Proceedings of the 21st Annual Computer Security Applications Conference, pp. 276–285 (2005)
21. Nance, K., Bishop, M., Hay, B.: Investigating the Implications of Virtual Machine Introspection for Digital Forensics. In: 2009 International Conference on Availability, Reliability and Security (2009)
22. Shamir, A., van Someren, N.: Playing Hide and Seek with Stored Keys. In: Franklin, M.K. (ed.) FC 1999. LNCS, vol. 1648, pp. 118–124. Springer, Heidelberg (1999)
23. Petterson, T.: Cryptographic key recovery from Linux memory dumps. In: Chaos Communication Camp (2007)

24. Halderman, J., Schoen, S., Heningen, N., Clarkson, W., Paul, W., Calandrino, J., Feldman, A., Appelbaum, J., Felten, E.: Lest we remember: cold boot attacks on encryption keys (2008)
25. Ristenpart, T., Tromer, E., Shacham, H., Savage, S.: Hey, You, Get Off of My Cloud: Exploring Information Leakage in Third-Party Compute Clouds. In: Conference on Computer and Communications Security, pp. 199–212 (2009)
26. Percival, C.: Cache missing for fun and profit. BSDCan, Ottawa (2005)
27. Osvik, D.A., Shamir, A., Tromer, E.: Cache Attacks and Countermeasures: the Case of AES. In: Pointcheval, D. (ed.) CT-RSA 2006. LNCS, vol. 3860, pp. 1–20. Springer, Heidelberg (2006)
28. Payne, B., Carbone, M., Lee, W.: Secure and Flexible Monitoring of Virtual Machines. In: Proceedings of the Annual Computer Security Applications Conference (2007)
29. Hay, B., Nance, K.: Forensics examination of volatile system data using virtual introspection. SIGOPS Operating Systems Review 42(3), 75–83 (2008)
30. Schuster, A.: Searching for processes and threads in Microsoft Windows memory dumps. In: Proceedings of the 6th Annual Digital Forensic Research Workshop, pp. 10–16 (2006)
31. Memparser analysis tool,
    http://www.dfrws.org/2005/challenge/memparser.shtml
32. An Introduction to Windows memory forensic,
    http://forensic.seccure.net/pdf/introduction_to_windows_memory_forensic.pdf

A Study on Computational Formal Verification for Practical Cryptographic Protocol: The Case of Synchronous RFID Authentication

Yoshikazu Hanatani[1,2], Miyako Ohkubo[3], Shin'ichiro Matsuo[3], Kazuo Sakiyama[2], and Kazuo Ohta[2]

[1] Toshiba Corporation, Komukai Toshiba-cho 1, Saiwai-ku, Kawasaki-shi, Kanagawa 212-8582, Japan
yoshikazu.hanatani@toshiba.co.jp
[2] The University of Electro-Communications, Chofugaoka 1-5-1, Chofu-shi, Tokyo 182-8585, Japan
{saki,ota}@inf.uec.ac.jp
[3] The National Institute of Information and Communications Technology, 4-2-1 Nukui-Kitamachi, Koganei, Tokyo 184-8795, Japan
{m.ohkubo,smatsuo}@nict.go.jp

Abstract. Formal verification of cryptographic protocols has a long history with a great number of successful verification tools created. Recent progress in formal verification theory has brought more powerful tools capable of handling computational assumption, which leads to more reliable verification results for information systems.

In this paper, we introduce an effective scheme and studies on applying computational formal verification toward a practical cryptographic protocol. As a target protocol, we reconsider a security model for RFID authentication with a man-in-the-middle adversary and communication fault. We define three model and security proofs via a game-based approach that, in a computational sense, makes our security models compatible with formal security analysis tools. Then we show the combination of using a computational formal verification tool and handwritten verification to overcome the computational tool's limitations. We show that the target RFID authentication protocol is robust against the above-mentioned attacks, and then provide game-based (handwritten) proofs and their verification via CryptoVerif.

Keywords: RFID, Authentication, Privacy, Formal proofs, Light weight, Desynchronization.

1 Introduction

1.1 Background

Cryptographic protocols are widely used in real-life information systems, and serve as significant components in fulfilling systems' complicated security requirements. To put a system into use, it must be demonstrated to have security

G. Danezis, S. Dietrich, and K. Sako (Eds.): FC 2011 Workshops, LNCS 7126, pp. 70–87, 2012.

sufficient to satisfy the fundamental security requirements. Formal verification theory and tools provide a good method to meet this challenge, and many attempts have been made in their development over the last 30 years. As the use of such theory and tools becomes more common, the framework for reliably using them is being standardized in ISO/IEC 29128. In the standardizing process of ISO/IEC 29128, the use and limitations of computational verification tools, which offer superior power and reliability, become a major issue [15]. Thus, we need much experiences in applying computational verification tool to real-life cryptographic protocols.

For example real-life protocol, a great number of low-power devices called RFID tags, which communicate over wireless channels, have entered into everyday use by executing cryptographic protocols. In most cases, RFID tags are used for identifying goods, authenticating parties' legitimacy, detecting fakes, and billing for services; applications that demand secure authentication of each tag. If a tag's output is fixed or related to a different type of authentication, privacy issues also arise in the sense that an adversary can trace the tag and the activity of the owner. Therefore, most research on RFID authentication protocols realizes the importance of tag-unforgeability and forward privacy. To verify the security and privacy of an RFID-authentication protocol, we must consider two aspects, security on wireless communication channels and computational security.

Though a large number of proposed secure protocols assume wired networks, the next consideration is how to deal with issues caused via wireless networks. In wireless network environments where RFID is used, the adversary has opportunities to conduct, for instance, man-in-the-middle or relay attacks. Connections are less stable than in a wired setting, so we have to consider robustness against communication errors. Formal verification is a good approach for dealing with such communication-related security issues, and its recent progress in cryptographic protocols helps achieve rigorous verification, even for the computational security of cryptographic building blocks. This rigor is needed to foster a high level of trust in actual RFID authentication protocols. However, for this application we do not have results that cover both communication-related issues and computational security. We also need to construct a security model and definition, secure protocol, and security proofs for such situations in order to reveal the security strength in actual use.

Two types of cryptographic protocol security exist. Symbolic security, e.g., Dolev-Yao model [10], assumes that cryptographic primitives that construct the cryptographic protocol are ideally secure. Some symbolic security can be automatically checked using formal verification tools such as ProVerif [6]. However, the symbolic security might not correspond to the real system's security. On the other hand, in computational security, the vulnerability of cryptographic primitives is considered. Computational security expresses the security of the real system compared with symbolic security. Recently, some frameworks that verify computational security have been proposed, and formal verification tools such as CryptoVerif [7,8] were developed.

1.2   Our Contribution

In this paper, we show how we can apply computational verification theory and tool to real-life cryptographic protocol. The target protocol of this work is robust RFID-authentication protocol, which is tolerant against communication errors. The paper's main contributions are in two areas. (1) We provide a formal security model and definitions that deal with man-in-the-middle adversaries and communication faults. This model is similar to key exchange protocol security models and suitable for rigorously estimating the success probability of attacks. (2) We prove the security and privacy of a robust RFID authentication protocol that satisfies the above model. We choose a hash-based scheme due to the extremely high computation cost in a public key-based scheme. The protocol is based on the OSK protocol [17] , which can provide forward privacy. Because OSK protocol is not free from desynchronization problem caused from communication errors, we combine a mechanism that synchronizes the internal status of the tag and reader with OSK protocol to overcome it. We prove the security of our proposed scheme using CryptoVerif formal verification tool. There are limitations in formalizing of security notion of cryptographic protocols which are practical and useful in real-life setting. For example, though desynchronization and forward privacy are needed for practical sense for cryptographic protocols, we cannot easily formalize this environment. To solve this limitation, we combine the CryptoVerif and handwritten proof. We give formalizations of security notions without forward privacy and a simplified proposed protocol for CryptoVerif, and by using CryptoVerif we also show that the protocol satisfies them. Next, By handwritten proof, we show the proposed protocol satisfies security notions with forward privacy if the simplified proposed protocol satisfies the security notions with forward privacy. This is evidently the first work in the RFID arena that defines the security notion and in a computational sense shows the security via a formal verification tool. This is one practical direction for application of computational formal verification.

1.3   Related Works

Many schemes exist for secure RFID authentication that protects privacy; and these are summarized in [1]. For security models for RFID authentication, Juels and Weis first proposed the privacy model [13]. Vaudenay then proposed a classification of security concepts for privacy regarding tag-authentication [19]. Paise and Vaudenay presented a classification of security concepts for mutual-authentication with privacy [18]. Hancke and Kuhn introduced a type of RFID authentication scheme that is robust against replay attacks and wireless settings using the distance-bounding protocol [11]. Because this protocol needs many rounds of communication we chose another construction.

A major contribution of this paper is proving the security of our scheme by using a formal verification tool. Security verification using formal methods has a long history dating back to the 1980s. Formal verification of privacy for RFID systems has been discussed [9,4]. Brusò et al. [9] gave a formal model for

RFID privacy, expressing unlinkability and forward privacy as equivalences in the applied pi calculus [2], and showed on privacy issues of the original OSK protocol [17] using Proverif, which can conduct formal verification by assuming cryptographic building blocks as *ideal*. Only the work in [9,4] discussed symbolic security. Recently, combining *computational difficulty*, a major concept in cryptography, and *automated verification*, a prime benefit of the formal method, has become the subject of mainstream research in this area. Adabi and Rogaway pioneered work on the gap [3], and many works have subsequently been proposed. Practical tools such as CryptoVerif [7,8], which we use in this paper, have also been proposed. Our result uses a game-based approach for representing the proof of a cryptographic protocol, and then uses a formal method to verify the handwritten proof.

2   Security Model and Definitions

2.1   RFID System

First we show informal descriptions for a general RFID system.

Communication: Communication between servers and clients is provided via a wireless network, upon which third parties can easily eavesdrop, and which can be cut or disturbed.

Client: We assume small devices like passive RFID tags as clients, called a set of "tags". Clients are only provided a poor level of electronic power by servers and can only perform light calculations. Memory in the client is not resilient against tamper attacks.

Server: We assume PCs and devices readers as servers. Generally, an RFID system tag communicates with readers over wireless channels, and the readers then communicate with servers over secure channels. We assume that the communication between reader and server is secure by using ordinal cryptographic techniques such as secure socket layer (SSL) and virtual private network (VPN). We therefore describe the communications in an RFID system using two players, client and server.

2.2   Adversary Model

An adversary can acquire information by eavesdropping or accessing a tag. Let such information be given to the adversary by the oracles.

The server, tag and random oracles are used for modeling an adversary against a mutual authentication algorithm. All of the information from the output of a tag is described in outputs of tag oracle $\mathcal{T}$, and all of the information from the output of a server is described in outputs of server oracle $\mathcal{S}$. All calculation results of functions are described in output of random oracle $\mathcal{R}$. So all of the information, that adversary can obtain by attacking, can be described by using oracle $\mathcal{T}$, $\mathcal{S}$, and $\mathcal{R}$. I.e., information that adversary can obtain are given by oracles.

Server oracle S: This gives the adversary the same outputs as an honest server's output in the regular process of a mutual authentication algorithm. The adversary is allowed to request *Send* queries from the server oracle S. If S receives a *Send* query, $Send(*)$, the same processes as the regular processes of an honest server are performed upon receiving a request $(*)$, and it then returns the output as an answer to the adversary. In the database S-List of S, all pairs of *sid* and I/O of S, $(sid, Inputdata, Outputdata)$, are recorded.

Tag oracle T: This gives the adversary the same outputs as an honest tag's output in the regular process of a mutual authentication algorithm. The adversary is allowed to request *Send* queries from and *Reveal* queries to the tag oracle T. If T receives a *Send* query, $Send(*)$, the same processes as the regular processes of an honest tag are performed when it receives the request $(*)$, and it then returns the output as an answer to the adversary. If T receives a *Reveal* query, it returns the session's key $sk_{ID,sid}$, and then all statuses of the sessions which are executed after the revealed session are set as *Revealed*. In the database T-List of T, all pairs of *sid* and I/O of T, $(sid, Inputdata, Outputdata)$, are recorded.
Random Oracle: Ideal Hash Functions. (Our proposed mutual authentication algorithm needs three hash functions: $\mathcal{H}_0$, $\mathcal{H}_1$, and $\mathcal{H}_2$)

We add information regarding electricity to the input of a tag in order to describe a situation in which a device uses external power to perform processes, such as with an RFID passive tag. In the model tag processes depend on the information on the external electricity. If a tag is given enough electricity, it processes completely and outputs a result. Otherwise, it processes as much as possible depending on the amount of external electricity and then cuts off.

2.3   Required Properties

There are some security requirements for secure mutual authentication using lightweight devices like RFID tags.

First, the basic properties are identification, authentication, and privacy, and then forward security and synchronization are extended properties. There are two perspectives on privacy issues. One is that, if a party identifies the ID there are risks of breaching the privacy of products or people connected to tags. Another is that if the output of a tag can be identified, the tag can be used as a tracing tool. For instance, a tagged person (or an item such as a book, glasses, and a bag) can be traced by tracing the tag output. From these two standpoints, indistinguishability is required; i.e., a tag's output must be indistinguishable from random values. For authentication requirements, there are two as for directions, client authentication and server authentication. Mutual authentication should satisfy both requirements. Since low cost is a requirement of small devices such as RFID tags many are unable to satisfy the further requirement of tamper resistance. This gives an adversary the chance to acquire the secret key in these devices by tampering, which poses the risk of the tag's past output being traced, identified, and/or forged i.e., client privacy and/or authenticity are breached. To protect the history in tampered devices, the property of forward security is required. Synchronization is another important requirement since small devices such as RFID tags and readers communicate wirelessly and wireless communication is easily lost. Therefore when desynchronization occurs, a state-full protocol requires the property of self-synchronization.

2.4   Security Definitions

In this section we show security requirements for mutual authentication using lightweight devices. Note that κ : is a security parameter: i.e., a key length of hash functions.

Definition 1. (*Forward-secure Client Indistinguishability*) : *The simulator selects $b \in \{0, 1\}$ randomly, exceeds the Key Generation Algorithm, and then gives the generated security parameter and secret key to S and T. Adversary $\mathcal{A}_{FI}$ is allowed to access S and T in no particular order. in the case of a random oracle model, the adversary is also allowed to access the random oracle in no particular order. $\mathcal{A}_{FI}$ can at any time send a Test query with sid* to T^{sid}. A coin is flipped. If $b = 0$, T performs regular processes of the algorithm and returns the result to $\mathcal{A}_{FI}$. Otherwise, i.e., $b = 1$, T selects a random value in the output space, and returns that random value to $\mathcal{A}_{FI}$. After $\mathcal{A}_{FI}$ sends a Test query, $\mathcal{A}_{FI}$ is again allowed to access S and T in no particular order. At the end, $\mathcal{A}_{FI}$ outputs $\tilde{b} \in \{0, 1\}$, and then stops. $\mathcal{A}_{FI}$ wins if $\tilde{b} = b$ and the status of T at sid*, T_{sid*}, is not Revealed.*

$$\mathsf{AdvCIND}_{\mathcal{A}} = \Pr\left[\tilde{b} = b \wedge T_{sid} \text{ is not revealed} \big| b \xleftarrow{R} \{0, 1\}, \tilde{b} \leftarrow \mathcal{A}_{FI}^{S,T}\right]$$

The mutual authentication algorithm satisfies Forward-secure Client Indistinguishability if $|\mathsf{AdvCIND}_{\mathcal{A}} - \frac{1}{2}|$ is negligible.

The above requirement provides the property of the tag's untraceability. Note that if the adversary cuts all responses from server to tag, the secret key in the tag cannot be updated. In such a case, if the tag is tampered, the tag can be traced. The above tag's tracing can be avoided by updating secret key each session whether previous session is finished or not. However, the maximum number of key updating must be set for verification and calculation cost for verification should be increased since there are several participants as session keys for a tag. Additionally, Dos-like attack presented in [14] can be applied. Therefore, in the paper traceability when key updating is obstructed is out of scope. As a practical matter, obstructing key updating of a target tag is not so easy, if tag's output seems random value and is changed every session like the proposed protocol. While, we care about *untraceability* for secret key updating. Roughly speaking, untraceability defined above is satisfied, if it is indistinguishable between (Tag/Server) outputs before key updating and after key updating. We can construct a protocol that satisfy this property with no limitation of the maximum number of key updating and small cost for verification. Moreover, Dos-like attack can not be applied.

Definition 2. (*Forward-secure Client Unforgeability*) : *The simulator selects* $b \in \{0,1\}$ *randomly, exceeds the Key Generation Algorithm, and then gives the generated security parameter and secret key to* S *and* T. *Adversary* $\mathcal{A}_{FU}$ *is allowed to access* S *and* T *in no particular order. (For a random oracle model, the adversary is also allowed to access the random oracle in no particular order.)* $\mathcal{A}_{FU}$ *can at any time send a* Test *query with* sid^* *to* S^{sid}. S *normally processes the algorithm and communicates with* $\mathcal{A}_{FU}$. $\mathcal{A}_{FU}$ *wins if the status of* S *at* sid^*, S_{sid^*}, *is Accepted and the status of* T *at* sid^*, T_{sid^*}, *is not Revealed, and the output of* S^{sid} *has not been requested from* T^{sid}.

$$\mathsf{AdvCUF}_{\mathcal{A}} = \Pr \left[\begin{array}{l} \mathsf{S_{sid}} is\ accepted \wedge \mathsf{T_{sid}}\ is\ not\ revealed \\ \wedge\ Output\ of\ S^{sid} \notin T\text{-}List \end{array} \middle| test(sid) \leftarrow \mathcal{A}^{S,T}_{CU} \right]$$

The mutual authentication algorithm satisfies Forward-secure Client Unforgeability if $\mathsf{AdvCUF}_{\mathcal{A}}$ *is negligible.*

The above requirement provides the property of impossibility of the tag's impersonation.

Definition 3. (*Forward-secure Server Unforgeability*) : *The simulator selects* $b \in \{0,1\}$ *randomly, exceeds the Key Generation Algorithm, and then gives the generated security parameter and secret key to* S *and* T. *Adversary* $\mathcal{A}_{FU}$ *is allowed to access* S *and* T *in no particular order. in the case of a random oracle model, the adversary is also allowed to access the random oracle in no particular order.* $\mathcal{A}_{FU}$ *can at any time send a* Test *query with* sid^* *to* T^{sid}. T *normally processes the algorithm and communicates with* $\mathcal{A}_{FU}$. $\mathcal{A}_{FU}$ *wins if the status of* T *at* sid^*, T_{sid^*}, *is Accepted and the status of* T *at* sid^*, T_{sid^*}, *is not Revealed, and the output of* T^{sid} *has not been requested from* S^{sid}.

$$\mathsf{AdvSUF}_{\mathcal{A}} = \Pr \left[\begin{array}{l} \mathsf{T_{sid}} is\ accepted \wedge \mathsf{T_{sid}} is\ not\ revealed \\ \wedge\ Output\ of\ T^{sid} \notin S\text{-}List \end{array} \middle| test(sid) \leftarrow \mathcal{A}^{S,T}_{SU} \right]$$

The mutual authentication algorithm satisfies Forward-secure Server Unforgeability if $\mathsf{AdvFCSF}_{\mathcal{A}}$ *is negligible.*

The above requirement provides the property of impossibility of the server's impersonation.

Definition 4. (*Resiliency of Desynchronization*) *A mutual authentication between an honest server and tag succeeds with overwhelming probability, independent of the result of previous sessions.*

The above requirement provides the resistance property against DOS-like attacks, as presented by Juels [12].

3 Construction

In this section, we show a proposed mutual authentication scheme for lightweight devices like RFID tags.

3.1 Proposed Protocol and Its Design Concepts

Our proposed protocol meets the security requirements set out in section 2. [1] The details of the protocol are shown in Fig. 1. In the figure, a lightweight device is described as an RFID-tag. Additionally, i is the times of key updating events in Server; i.e., counts of key updating in Server. $sk_{ID,i}$ is the i-th secret key of a tag. ID is the tag's ID. i' is the times of key updating events in Tag; i.e., counts of key updating in Tag. Data generated in a tag are described with quotation mark, for example, Y'. [2]

The basic concept is combining the OSK protocol and key update mechanism from mutual authentication. Let H_0 and H_2 be hash functions (random oracles). H_0 and H_2 work in the same manner as the output function and key update function in the OSK protocol, respectively. In this protocol, the tag executes as follows. First, the client (i.e., tag) is requested from the server, a secret key is then input, which is recorded in the tag's memory, to H_2. The output is then input to H_0. At the end, the tag outputs the calculated results of H_0 to the server. The server receives the tag's output and then searches its database for the relevant secret key, which is shared with, and is unique data for each tag, to H_2 and then inputs the output to H_0 using the same processes.

To accomplish key updates in both the RFID tag and the server, we must cope with the problem of desynchronization. If only one side of the party updates its secret key, the protocol fails upon further authentication attempts. Such desynchronization not only causes failure of authentication, but also risks breaching privacy. We prevent desynchronization by using a key update in the mutual authentication which consists of two challenge-response protocols via hash functions. Key update is allowed just only if the result of verification is OK, AND the verified secret keys between tag and server are getting into synchronization. First, the server sends a random challenge, and then the tag calculates a response with H_0. The second challenge-response is initiated by the tag. The tag sends the challenge with the calculated response in Y'. The server calculates the response by using H_1 with the current secret or previous (old) secret. Note that the server stores both the current and previous secret key and which secret key is used depends on which one the server detects to calculate the received Y'. The server only calculates the value with the previous secret key if it detects that the received Y' is calculated using it, and, likewise, calculates the value with the current updated secret key if it detects that the received Y' is calculated using it. This mechanism deals with desynchronization by communication

---

[1] You can find e-print version in [16]. Formally our protocol is published in this paper.

[2] This figure put being easy to understand above optimization of a process. We will show the description putting a top priority on optimization of a process before very long.

error. After that, the server sends the (second) response to the tag. Only when the tag confirms the response will it update the secret key. The basic security requirements are fulfilled with OSK-like construction, and desynchronization is solved by mutual authentication holding two secret keys, current and previous, on the server side.

3.2   Strong Points of the Proposed Scheme

Synchronization: The secret key is updated by both servers and clients, and if desynchronization occurs, the server can distinguish it and follow to the client's current state in the next session. This protocol can therefore solve the desynchronization problem. *Resiliency against DOS-like attack*: Juels and Weis discussed the requirements of RFID protocols in [14]. They introduced the attack against a hash-chain-based scheme like a DOS-like attack against a server via the Internet. In the proposed scheme, the event in which the secret key updated in the tag proceeds only when the verification check is OK; and therefore a DOS-like attack cannot be applied to this scheme.

Saving computational cost of server: Generally, hash-based identification schemes like [17] require many server calculations in order to identify a tag (i.e., a client), and the server must compute $2m$ hash calculations for each tag, where m is a maximum number of updates of the secret key. In the proposed scheme, a server and a tag can share the current state of the common secret key; therefore a server only needs to compute two hash calculations for each tag, and the server's huge computational cost can thereby be saved.

Resiliency against replay attack: In the proposed scheme, fresh randomnesses chosen by both a server and a tag are used; therefore a replay attack cannot be applied to it.

4   Security Verification Using CryptoVerif and Security Proofs

In this section, we show the security proof of the proposed protocol using CryptoVerif verification results. We introduce formal models for unlinkability (Client indistinguishability) and mutual authenticity (Client unforgeability and Server unforgeability) of the proposed protocol without key update functionality by the probabilistic polynomial-time process calculus, and prove its computational security using CryptoVerif. This is evidently the first paper to show RFID system computational security by using a formal verification tool. Moreover, by manually using the formal verification results we prove froward privacy and forward mutual authenticity of the proposed protocol with key update functionality.

4.1   Formalization of Proposed Protocol

Since indexes of alignment cannot be controlled in CryptoVerif, the key update property in the proposed protocol cannot be described. Therefore we omit the

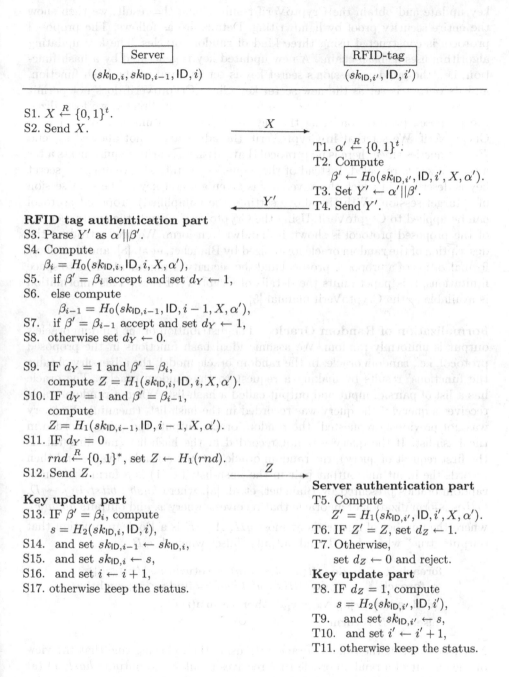

S1. $X \xleftarrow{R} \{0,1\}^t$.
S2. Send X.

$\xrightarrow{\quad X \quad}$

T1. $\alpha' \xleftarrow{R} \{0,1\}^t$.
T2. Compute
   $\beta' \leftarrow H_0(sk_{\text{ID},i'}, \text{ID}, i', X, \alpha')$.
T3. Set $Y' \leftarrow \alpha' \| \beta'$.
T4. Send Y'.

$\xleftarrow{\quad Y' \quad}$

RFID tag authentication part
S3. Parse Y' as $\alpha' \| \beta'$.
S4. Compute
   $\beta_i = H_0(sk_{\text{ID},i}, \text{ID}, i, X, \alpha')$,
S5.   if $\beta' = \beta_i$ accept and set $d_Y \leftarrow 1$,
S6.   else compute
   $\beta_{i-1} = H_0(sk_{\text{ID},i-1}, \text{ID}, i-1, X, \alpha')$,
S7.   if $\beta' = \beta_{i-1}$ accept and set $d_Y \leftarrow 1$,
S8. otherwise set $d_Y \leftarrow 0$.

S9. IF $d_Y = 1$ and $\beta' = \beta_i$,
   compute $Z = H_1(sk_{\text{ID},i}, \text{ID}, i, X, \alpha')$.
S10. IF $d_Y = 1$ and $\beta' = \beta_{i-1}$,
   compute
   $Z = H_1(sk_{\text{ID},i-1}, \text{ID}, i-1, X, \alpha')$.
S11. IF $d_Y = 0$
   $rnd \xleftarrow{R} \{0,1\}^*$, set $Z \leftarrow H_1(rnd)$.
S12. Send Z.

$\xrightarrow{\quad Z \quad}$

Server authentication part
T5. Compute
   $Z' = H_1(sk_{\text{ID},i'}, \text{ID}, i', X, \alpha')$.
T6. IF $Z' = Z$, set $d_Z \leftarrow 1$.
T7. Otherwise,
   set $d_Z \leftarrow 0$ and reject.

Key update part
S13. IF $\beta' = \beta_i$, compute
   $s = H_2(sk_{\text{ID},i}, \text{ID}, i)$,
S14.   and set $sk_{\text{ID},i-1} \leftarrow sk_{\text{ID},i}$,
S15.   and set $sk_{\text{ID},i} \leftarrow s$,
S16.   and set $i \leftarrow i+1$,
S17. otherwise keep the status.

Key update part
T8. IF $d_Z = 1$, compute
   $s = H_2(sk_{\text{ID},i'}, \text{ID}, i')$,
T9.   and set $sk_{\text{ID},i'} \leftarrow s$,
T10.   and set $i' \leftarrow i'+1$,
T11. otherwise keep the status.

Fig. 1. Proposed protocol

key update and obtain the CryptoVerif result. Using the result, we then show the entire security proof by handwriting. Details are as follows. The proposed protocol is constructed using three kind of random oracles. The key updating algorithm uses a "hash-chain." A new updated key is generated by a hash function, i.e., the previous session's secret key is set as input of the hash function, and its output is set as the new secret key. Since CryptoVerif does not permit control of indexes of a list of the hash function's output directly, we formalized the proposed protocol omitting the key updating algorithm and applied it to CryptoVerif. We set that in CryptoVerif, the adversary is not allowed to send *Reveal* queries since there is no protocol that satisfies security requirements after a session key is revealed. Instead of these queries, a state of revealing the secret key is described in which the adversary is given a secret key of the next session of a target session. With the above setting, the (simplified) proposed protocol can be applied to CryptoVerif. Using the CryptoVerif output, the entire security of the proposed protocol is shown in handwritten form. We first introduce the description of the random oracle formalized by Blanchet, et al. [8], and then show formalization of a proposed protocol and the security requirements. Due to space limitations, this paper omits the details of CryptoVerif rules. This information is available in the CryptoVerif manual [5].

Formalization of Random Oracles. The distribution of the random oracle's output is uniformly random. We assume ideal hash functions in the proposed protocol, i.e., random oracle. In the random oracle model, the adversary obtains the functions' results by making a request to the random oracles. The oracle has a list of pairs of input and output called a hash-list. When a random oracle receives a query, if the query was recorded in the hash-list, (meaning the query was not previously requested) the random oracle outputs the value recorded in the hash-list. If the query was not recorded in the hash-list (meaning this is the first request of query), the random oracle outputs a random value and then records the input and output pair in the hash-list. Eq.(1) is a formalization of random oracles presented by Blanchet, et al. [8], where $hash : bitstring \rightarrow D$. OH is a formalization of an oracle that receives a query x, and outputs $hash(x)$, where the number of queries is at most qH. $A \overset{?}{=} B$ is a Boolean function that outputs "true" when $A = B$, and outputs "false" when $A \neq B$.

$$
\begin{aligned}
&\textbf{foreach } i_h \leq n_h \textbf{ do } OH(x : bitstring) := \textbf{return}(hash(x)) \text{ [all]} \\
&\approx_0 \textbf{foreach } i_h \leq n_h \textbf{ do } OH(x : bitstring) := \textbf{find } u \leq n_h \textbf{ suchthat} \\
&\quad (\textbf{defined}(x[u], r[u]) \wedge x \overset{?}{=} x[u]) \textbf{ then return}(r[u]) \\
&\textbf{else } r \overset{R}{\leftarrow} D; \textbf{return}(r)
\end{aligned}
\tag{1}
$$

Next, we describe the random oracle OH using the following rule that the view of the output of a random oracle that receives input x and outputs $hash(x)$ (at most q_H times), is the same as that of a random oracle, that receives input x and, if there is $x = x[u]$ in its list, outputs $r[u]$, otherwise it chooses a random value r and outputs it. All inputs and chosen r are recorded as alignments in CryptoVerif. This means that if the oracle receives the i-th input x and randomly chooses a value r uniformly, the value of x is assigned to $x[i]$, and the value of r is assigned to $r[i]$. In Eq.(1), a pair of $(x[i], r[i])$, of which index i is the same, means a pair of input and output of the random oracle. As above, functions of a random oracle are described as alignments of $x[]$ $r[]$. In the proposed protocol, the following three random oracles are used. $H_0 : key \times IDs \times index \times nonce \times nonce \rightarrow h_0$, $H_1 : key \times IDs \times index \times nonce \times nonce \rightarrow h_1$, $H_2 : key \times IDs \times index \rightarrow key$. OH_0, OH_1, OH_2 are processes that receive input and send output of a random oracle, where key is a group of session keys, IDs is a group of ID, $index$ is a group of indexes of session keys, and $nonce$ is a group of t-bit random values.

Formalization of Attack Games. Attack games consist of three processes Server, Tag, and Challenge and random oracles H_0, H_1, H_2. The processes Server and Tag are a formalization of a server and tag in the proposed protocol. Challenge is a formalization of the attacker's target, and depends on security requirements and that is the verifier. The following are descriptions of the Server, Tag, and attack model. First we define functions $test1, test2, test3$. $test1 : bool \times nonce \times nonce \rightarrow nonce$, $test2 : bool \times h_0 \times h_0 \rightarrow h_0$, $test3 : bool \times h_1 \times h_1 \rightarrow h_1$. $test1(b, A, B)$ is a function for which if b is $true$, outputs A, if b is $false$, outputs B for any $A, B \in nonce$, In the function, the view of the process in which if input is $b : bool$, chooses $A, B \xleftarrow{R} nonce$ and outputs $test(b, A, B)$, is same as that of the process in which if input is $b : bool$, outputs $C \xleftarrow{R} nonce$. The property is formalized as Eq.(2). $test2$ and $test3$ are defined in the same way.

$$\textbf{foreach } i_t \leq n_t \textbf{ do } test1(b : bool) := A, B \xleftarrow{R} nonce; \textbf{return}(test1(b, A, B))[all]$$
$$\approx_0 \textbf{foreach } i_t \leq n_t \textbf{ do } test1(b : bool) := C \xleftarrow{R} nonce; \textbf{return}(C) \tag{2}$$

Next, we formalize the processes of Server and Tag, as Eq.(3) and Eq. (4) respectively, where "yield" indicates a process of stopping and doing nothing.

$$\textbf{foreach } i_p \leq n_p \textbf{ do } Server := \textbf{input}(); X_s \xleftarrow{R} nonce; \textbf{return}(X_s);$$
$$\textbf{input}(\alpha_s : nonce, \beta_s : h_0); \textbf{if } \beta_s \stackrel{?}{=} H_0(SK0, ID, i_0, X_s, \alpha_s) \textbf{ then}$$
$$\textbf{return}(H_1(SK0, ID, i_0, X_s, \alpha_s)) \tag{3}$$
$$\textbf{else } Z_{rnd} \xleftarrow{R} h_1; Z_s \leftarrow H_1(SK1, ID, i_1, X_s, \alpha_s);$$
$$b_s : bool \leftarrow (\beta_s \stackrel{?}{=} H_0(SK1, ID, i_1, X_s, \alpha_s)); \textbf{return}(test3(b_s, Z_s, Z_{rnd})).$$

$$\textbf{foreach } i_p \leq n_p \textbf{ do } Tag := \textbf{input}(X_t : nonce); \alpha_t \xleftarrow{R} nonce;$$
$$\beta_t \leftarrow H_0(SK1, ID, i_1, X_t, \alpha_t); \textbf{return}(\alpha_t, \beta_t); \tag{4}$$
$$\textbf{input}(Z_t : h1); \textbf{if } Z_t \stackrel{?}{=} H_1(SK1, ID, i_1, X_t, \alpha_t) \textbf{ then yield}.$$

By using the above processes, an attack game is formalized as Eq.(5).

$$OH_1|OH_2|OH_3|(\textbf{input}(i_0 : index, i_1 : index, i_2 : index); ID \xleftarrow{R} IDs;$$
$$seed \xleftarrow{R} key; SK0 \leftarrow H_2(seed, ID, i_0); SK1 \leftarrow H_2(SK0, ID, i_1); \tag{5}$$
$$SK2 \leftarrow H_2(SK1, ID, i_2); \textbf{return}(ID, SK2)|(Server|Tag|Challenge)).$$

Formalization of Client Indistinguishability Game. *Challenge* on the Client indistinguishability game is formalized as Eq.(6).

$$Challenge := \mathbf{input}(X^* : nonce); \; b^* \xleftarrow{R} \{true, false\}; \alpha^* \xleftarrow{R} nonce;$$
$$\beta^* \leftarrow H_0(SK1, ID, i_1, X^*, \alpha^*); \alpha_{rnd} \xleftarrow{R} nonce; \; \beta_{rnd} \xleftarrow{R} h_0; \tag{6}$$
$$\mathbf{return}(test1(b, \alpha^*, \alpha_{rnd}), test2(b, \beta^*, \beta_{rnd}));$$

In the above attack game, if *secrecy* is shown when b is chosen in *Challenge*, in the proposed protocol, the adversary cannot distinguish between Tag's output and random values. In this case, we can say that the protocol satisfies the property of Client indistinguishability.

Formalization of Client Unforgeability Game. *Challenge* on the Client unforgeability game is formalized as Eq.(7).

$$Challenge := \mathbf{input}(); \; X^* \xleftarrow{R} nonce; \mathbf{return}(X^*);$$
$$\mathbf{input}(\alpha^* : nonce, \beta^* : nonce); \mathbf{if} \; \beta^* \stackrel{?}{=} H_0(SK0, ID, i_0, X^*, \alpha^*) \; \mathbf{then}$$
$$\mathbf{find} \; u \le n_p \; \mathbf{suchthat} \; (\mathbf{defined}(X_t[u]) \wedge X^* \stackrel{?}{=} X_t[u]) \; \mathbf{then} \; \mathrm{yield}$$
$$\mathbf{else} \; \text{event bad} \tag{7}$$
$$\mathbf{else} \; \mathbf{if} \; \beta^* \stackrel{?}{=} H_0(SK1, ID, i_1, X^*, \alpha^*) \; \mathbf{then}$$
$$\mathbf{find} \; u \le n_p \; \mathbf{suchthat} \; (\mathbf{defined}(X_t[u]) \wedge X^* \stackrel{?}{=} X_t[u]) \; \mathbf{then} \; \; \mathrm{yield}$$
$$\mathbf{else} \; \text{event bad}.$$

The event "event bad" has occurred, only when α^*, β^* received by *Challenge* is accepted and X^* given to the adversary by *Challenge* have not been requested to the Tag oracle. This means that the adversary successfully forges the Tag's output only when "event bad" occurs. Tag unforgeability is satisfied if the probability of "event bad" is negligible.

Formalization of Server Unforgeability Game. *Challenge* on Server unforgeability game is formalized as Eq.(8).

$$Challenge := \mathbf{input}(X^* : nonce); \; \alpha^* \xleftarrow{R} nonce; \beta^* \leftarrow H_0(SK1, ID, i_1, X^*, \alpha^*);$$
$$\mathbf{return}(\alpha^*, \beta^*);$$
$$\mathbf{input}(Z^* : h_1); \mathbf{if} \; Z^* \stackrel{?}{=} H_1(SK1, ID, i_1, X^*, \alpha^*) \; \mathbf{then} \tag{8}$$
$$\mathbf{find} \; u \le n_p \; \mathbf{suchthat} \; (\mathbf{defined}(\alpha_s[u], \beta_s[u]) \wedge \alpha^* \stackrel{?}{=} \alpha_s[u] \wedge \beta^* \stackrel{?}{=} \beta_s[u])$$
$$\mathbf{then} \; \mathrm{yield} \; \mathbf{else} \; \text{event bad}$$

The event "event bad" occurs, only when Z^* received by *Challenge* is accepted and, α^*, β^* given to the adversary by *Challenge* have not been requested to the Server oracle. This means that the adversary successfully forges server's output only when "event bad" occurs. Server unforgeability is satisfied if the probability of "event bad" is negligible.

4.2 Theorems

In section 2, we defined security notions to achieve not only basic but also extended properties. As a result, the following theorems can be proven by using CryptoVerif.

Theorem 1. Forward-secure Indistinguishability
The proposed scheme is Forward-secure Indistinguishable, if hash functions H_0, H_1, and H_2 are random oracles.

Theorem 2. Forward-secure Client Unforgeability
The proposed scheme is Forward-secure Client Unforgeable if hash functions H_0, H_1, and H_2 are random oracles.

Theorem 3. Forward-secure Server Unforgeability
The proposed scheme is Forward-secure Server Unforgeable if hash functions H_0, H_1, and H_2 are random oracles.

4.3   Output of Verification on CryptoVerif

Following are the result of CryptoVerif verification. We use a PC as follows, Intel(R) Core(TM)2 Duo CPU U9300 @ 1.20GHz, RAM 2.85GB. CryptoVerif is version 1.10pl1.

Client Indistinguishability Game Result. The adversary has an advantage in this game, which can be shown to be negligible by applying the following commands: auto, simplify, remove_assign all, auto, and transforming the game 34 times. Running time is about 45 seconds. The result is as follows.

RESULT Proved secrecy of b with probability $2.*n_{H0}/|key|+3.*n_{H1}/|key|+7.*n_{H2}/|key|+n_p*n_{H0}/|key|+3.*n_p/|h_0|+n_p*n_{H0}/|nonce|+4.*n_p*n_p/|nonce|+n_{H0}/|nonce|+5.*n_p/|nonce|+6.*1./|key|$

$|key|, |h_0|, |nonce|$[3] are exponent functions of the security parameter, n_p, n_{H0}, n_{H1}, n_{H2} are polynomial functions of the security parameter. From the above results, we can say that the advantage of breaking the secrecy of b is negligible.

Client Unforgeability Game Result. The adversary has an advantage in this game, which can be shown to be negligible by applying the following commands: auto, simplify, auto, and transforming the game 14 times. Running time is about 40 seconds. The result is as follows.

RESULT Proved event bad $==> false$ with probability $3. * n_{H0}/|key| + 3. * n_{H1}/|key| + 7. * n_{H2}/|key| + n_p * n_{H0}/|key| + 3. * n_p/|h_0| + n_p * n_{H0}/|nonce| + 3. * n_p/|nonce| + 4. * n_p * n_p/|nonce| + 2. * 1./|h_0| + 6. * 1./|key|$

$|key|, |h_0|, |nonce|$ are exponent functions of the security parameter, n_p, n_{H0}, n_{H1}, n_{H2} are polynomial functions of the security parameter. From the above results, we can say that the probability of "event bad" is negligible.

Server Unforgeability Game Result. The adversary has an advantage in this game, which can be shown to be negligible by applying the following commands: auto and transforming the game 13 times. Running time is about 15 seconds. The result as the follows.

---

[3] $|A|$ is an element number of a group A.

RESULT Proved event bad $==> false$ with probability $2. * n_{H0}/|key| + 2. * n_p * n_{H0}/|key| + n_{H1}/|key| + 7. * n_{H2}/|key| + n_p/|h_0| + n_p * n_{H0}/|nonce| + 2. * n_p * n_p/|nonce| + n_{H0}/|nonce| + 4. * n_p/|nonce| + 1./|h_1| + 6. * 1./|key|$

$|key|, |h_0|, |h_1|, |nonce|$ are exponent functions of the security parameter, n_p, $n_{H_0}, n_{H_1}, n_{H_2}$ are polynomial functions of the security parameter. As above results, we can say that the probability of "event bad" is negligible.

4.4   Proof Sketch

If there is an adversary $\mathcal{A}$, that can break the proposed protocol, there is an adversary $\mathcal{B}$ that breaks the knocked-down one shown in the above session. We can show that the proposed protocol is secure by showing the above proof. $\mathcal{A}$ is allowed to access server oracle $\mathcal{S}_A$ at most n times, and is also allowed to access tag oracle $\mathcal{T}_A$ at most n times, and in total is allowed to access the random oracles at most q_H times. Mutual authentications between tag and server succeed at most n times; therefore the variations of session keys are at most n. $\mathcal{B}$ is allowed to access the server oracle $\mathcal{S}_B$ at most n times, and also is allowed to access the tag oracle $\mathcal{T}_B$ at most n times, and totally is allowed to access the random oracles at most q_H times. We first show how to construct with $\mathcal{B}$. Fig.2

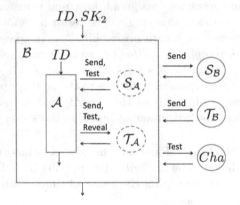

Fig. 2. Rough construction of $\mathcal{B}$ by using $\mathcal{A}$

is a rough construction of $\mathcal{B}$ by using $\mathcal{A}$. $\mathcal{B}$ executes the following, when given target ID and the next session key $SK2$ of the target session, $\mathcal{B}$ guesses $i \xleftarrow{R} [1, n]$ that is the number of the session key that $\mathcal{A}$ uses for its attack, sets the session key as $SK_{i+1} \leftarrow SK2$, and then sends a query to random oracle H_2 with the $SK_{i+1} \leftarrow SK2$ and acquires $SK_{i+2}, \ldots SK_n$. Next, $\mathcal{B}$ gives ID to $\mathcal{A}$ and runs $\mathcal{A}$. $\mathcal{B}$ simulates $\mathcal{S}_A^{sid}$ and $\mathcal{T}_A^{sid}$ as follows, letting $sid = j||ssid$. $\mathcal{B}$ transfers all queries to the random oracles from $\mathcal{A}$ to the random oracles for $\mathcal{B}$, and receives output from the random oracles for $\mathcal{B}$ and transfers the value to $\mathcal{A}$.

- If $j < i$,
  - $\mathcal{S}_A^{sid}$: If he
    * receives (), chooses $X_{sid} \xleftarrow{R} \{0,1\}^t$, then outputs X_{sid}.
    * receives $\alpha_{sid}, \beta_{sid}$, chooses $Z_{sid} \xleftarrow{R} h_1$, then outputs Z_{sid}.
    * receives a *Test* query, stop the simulation.
  - $\mathcal{T}_A^{sid}$: If he
    * receives X'_{sid}, chooses $\alpha_{sid} \xleftarrow{R} \{0,1\}^t, \beta_{sid} \xleftarrow{R} h_0$, then outputs $(\alpha_{sid}, \beta_{sid})$.
    * receives Z'_{sid}, outputs ().
    * receives *Revealed* queries, stop the simulation.
    * receives a *Test* query, stop the simulation.

- If $j = i$,
  - $\mathcal{S}_A^{sid}$: If he
    * receives (), send () to $\mathcal{S}_B$ and receives X_{sid}, then outputs X_{sid}.
    * receives $\alpha_{sid}, \beta_{sid}$, send $\alpha_{sid}, \beta_{sid}$ to $\mathcal{S}_B$ and receives Z_{sid}, then outputs Z_{sid}.
    * receives a *Test* query, transfer the query to *Challenge*, and receives a value, then outputs the received value.
  - $\mathcal{T}_A^{sid}$: If he
    * receives X'_{sid}, send X'_{sid} to $\mathcal{T}_B$, receives $(\alpha_{sid}, \beta_{sid})$, then outputs $(\alpha_{sid}, \beta_{sid})$.
    * receives Z'_{sid}, send Z'_{sid} to $\mathcal{T}_B$, receives (), then outputs the ().
    * receives a *Revealed* query, stop the simulation.
    * receives a *Test* query, transfer the query to *Challenge* oracle, and receives a value, then outputs the value.

- If $j > i$,
  - $\mathcal{S}_A^{sid}$: If he
    * receives (), chooses $X_{sid} \xleftarrow{R} \{0,1\}^t$, then outputs X_{sid}.
    * receives $\alpha_{sid}, \beta_{sid}$, calculate Z_{sid} using SK_j along the protocol, and outputs the calculated result.
    * receives a *Test* query, stop the simulation.
  - $\mathcal{T}_A^{sid}$: If he
    * receives X'_{sid}, calculate $(\alpha_{sid}, \beta_{sid})$ using SK_j along the protocol, then outputs the calculated $(\alpha_{sid}, \beta_{sid})$.
    * receives Z'_{sid}, executes using SK_j along the protocol, then outputs ().
    * receives a *Revealed* query, outputs SK_j.
    * receives a *Test* query, stop the simulation.

If the guessed i is correct, $\mathcal{B}$ can set the target problem as a problem of $\mathcal{A}$'s target. Therefore if there exists an adversary $\mathcal{A}$ that successfully attacks with non-negligible probability, there exists an adversary $\mathcal{B}$ that successfully attacks with non-negligible probability at least for the guessed i. (This is because if the success probability of adversary $\mathcal{B}$ at the guessed i is negligible, the success probability of adversary $\mathcal{A}$ is also negligible. It is $1/n$ at least that the probability that the i guessed by $\mathcal{B}$ is correct. Since the upper bound of queries, n, is a polynomial function of the security parameter, the above proof means that if there is an adversary $\mathcal{A}$, there is an adversary $\mathcal{B}$ that can succeed with non-negligible probability.

4.5 Note

The proposed protocol satisfies the resiliency of desynchronization (Def.4) against an adversary that can only control the communicated data, because the proposed protocol satisfies the mutual authenticity. If the adversary can control not only the communicated data but also the number of steps that tag executes, the proposed protocol cannot satisfy the property of resiliency of desynchronization. If, however, the proposed protocol can satisfy this property by modifying it as follows, i.e., when the server receives Y from a tag, check the following formula with $sk_{\mathsf{ID},i'}$ and $i'-1$, $\beta' \overset{?}{=} H_0(sk_{\mathsf{ID},i'}, \mathsf{ID}, i'-1, X, \alpha')$ as well as the verifications in the original proposed protocol. By this modification, the server can detect the desynchronization of a session ID i. Proof against such an adversary as that above is a topic for future work.

5   Conclusion

This paper proposed a formal security model and definitions for an RFID authentication protocol that is robust against a man-in-the-middle adversary. An RFID authentication protocol from the OSK protocol and synchronization mechanism was then put forth. The security of the protocol was proved by combining a handwritten proof and CryptoVerif results as well as by using a manual proof method in a game-based approach.

References

1. RFID security & privacy lounge, http://www.avoine.net/rfid/
2. Abadi, M., Fournet, C.: Mobile values, new names, and secure communication. In: POPL, pp. 104–115 (2001)
3. Abadi, M., Rogaway, P.: Reconciling Two Views of Cryptography (The Computational Soundness of Formal Encryption). In: Watanabe, O., Hagiya, M., Ito, T., van Leeuwen, J., Mosses, P.D. (eds.) TCS 2000. LNCS, vol. 1872, pp. 3–22. Springer, Heidelberg (2000)
4. Arapinis, M., Chothia, T., Ritter, E., Ryan, M.: Analysing unlinkability and anonymity using the applied pi calculus. In: CSF, pp. 107–121 (2010)
5. Blanchet, B.: CryptoVerif computationally sound, automatic cryptographic protocol verifier user manual, http://www.cryptoverif.ens.fr/
6. Blanchet, B.: An Efficient Cryptographic Protocol Verifier Based on Prolog Rules. In: 14th IEEE Computer Security Foundations Workshop (CSFW-14), Cape Breton, Nova Scotia, Canada, pp. 82–96. IEEE Computer Society (2001)
7. Blanchet, B.: A computationally sound mechanized prover for security protocols. In: IEEE Symposium on Security and Privacy, Oakland, California, pp. 140–154 (May 2006)
8. Blanchet, B., Pointcheval, D.: Automated Security Proofs with Sequences of Games. In: Dwork, C. (ed.) CRYPTO 2006. LNCS, vol. 4117, pp. 537–554. Springer, Heidelberg (2006)
9. Brusò, M., Chatzikokolakis, K., den Hartog, J.: Formal verification of privacy for RFID systems. In: CSF, pp. 75–88 (2010)

10. Dolev, D., Yao, A.C.-C.: On the Security of Public Key Protocols. In: FOCS 1981, pp. 350–357 (1981)
11. Hancke, G., Kuhn, M.: An RFID Distance Bounding Protocol. In: Conference on Security and Privacy for Emerging Areas in Communication Networks – SecureComm 2005, Athens, Greece, pp. 67–73. IEEE Computer Society (2005)
12. Juels, A.: RFID security and privacy: A research survey (September 2005) (manuscript)
13. Juels, A., Weis, S.: Defining strong privacy for RFID. Cryptology ePrint Archive, Report 2006/137 (2006)
14. Juels, A., Weis, S.: Defining Strong Privacy for RFID. In: International Conference on Pervasive Computing and Communications – PerCom 2007, New York City, New York, USA, pp. 342–347. IEEE Computer Society Press (2007)
15. Matsuo, S., Miyazaki, K., Otsuka, A., Basin, D.: How to Evaluate the Security of Real-Life Cryptographic Protocols? - The Cases of ISO/IEC 29128 and CRYPTREC. In: Sion, R., Curtmola, R., Dietrich, S., Kiayias, A., Miret, J.M., Sako, K., Sebé, F. (eds.) RLCPS, WECSR, and WLC 2010. LNCS, vol. 6054, pp. 182–194. Springer, Heidelberg (2010), http://www.springerlink.com/content/05t7653287066880/
16. Ohkubo, M., Matsuo, S., Hanatani, Y., Sakiyama, K., Ohta, K.: Robust RFID authentication protocol with formal proof and its feasibility. Cryptology ePrint Archive, Report 2010/345 (2010)
17. Ohkubo, M., Suzuki, K., Kinoshita, S.: Cryptographic approach to "privacy-friendly" tags. In: RFID Privacy Workshop. MIT, MA (2003)
18. Radu-Ioan, P., Vaudenay, S.: Mutual Authentication in RFID: Security and Privacy. In: Proceedings of the 3rd ACM Symposium on Information, Computer and Communications Security – ASIACCS 2008, Tokyo, Japan, pp. 292–299. ACM Press (2008)
19. Vaudenay, S.: On Privacy Models for RFID. In: Kurosawa, K. (ed.) ASIACRYPT 2007. LNCS, vol. 4833, pp. 68–87. Springer, Heidelberg (2007)

Biometric Transaction Authentication Protocol: Formal Model Verification and "Four-Eyes" Principle Extension

Daniel Hartung and Christoph Busch

Norwegian Information Security laboratory
Faculty for Computer Science and Media Technology
Gjøvik University College
Teknologivn. 22, N-2802 Gjøvik, Norway
{daniel.hartung,christoph.busch}@hig.no

Abstract. The BTA protocol for biometric authentication of online banking transactions is extended to allow for multiple person authenticated transactions. In addition a formal specification is given, the protocol is modelled in the applied pi calculus and the security properties of data and person authentication as well as non-repudiation are verified using the tool ProVerif.

Keywords: Online Banking, Transaction Authentication, Payment Scheme, Non-Repudiation of Origin, ProVerif, Applied Pi Calculus, Biometric Systems, Template Protection.

1 Introduction

The need for secure authentication methods is evident when looking at the assets transferred over the Internet, the level of interconnectedness and the posed threats: a recent example of malware affecting vital, well-protected infrastructures is the Stuxnet computer worm. And even more, badly protected client computers are exposed to threats: malware on clients endanger especially online banking transactions, whose manipulation promise rapid financial gain to attackers. This has to be prevented. However from a service providers view, not only the integrity of the data, but also its origin is to be guaranteed, which will be referred to as data and person authentication throughout the paper. Until now, no method for online banking transactions features non-repudiation of origin (natural person). One reasonable solution to this problem is the use of biometric systems, but not without raising threats to the users privacy.

In [5] a protocol was proposed that addresses the aforementioned problems, it uses a system for biometric person authentication using so called Privacy Enhancing Technologies (PETs) or Template Protection to authenticate online banking transactions without revealing the sensitive biometric data. At the same time the transaction data has to be authentic in order to get executed by the banking server side. These properties hold true even if the client is considered to be insecure and possibly controlled by an attacker.

G. Danezis, S. Dietrich, and K. Sako (Eds.): FC 2011 Workshops, LNCS 7126, pp. 88–103, 2012.

The BTA protocol – Biometric Transaction Authentication Protocol – is summarized in the next section. It is modelled in section 3 using the applied pi calculus [6] and its security properties are verified using the tool ProVerif [3] in section 4. Before concluding the paper, an extension of the protocol, enabling multi-user, multi-modal as well as multi-factor authentication of single transactions, is given in section 6.

2   BTAP Wrap-Up

The goal of BTAP [5] is to enable data and person authentic online banking transactions on insecure client computer environments. To reach this goal a biometric subsystem has to be combined with classic cryptographic functionality. The critical transaction authentication is sourced out on a tamper-proof biometric transaction device (BTD) with limited functionality that can be certified using information technology security evaluations. The other different parties that communicate in the protocol are shown in figure 1: the customer using a potentially insecure client computer running a banking software (BSW) and a trusted online banking server (OBS).

Within the first phase of the protocol, the user is enrolled on the BTD using a biometric identifier and a pre-shared secret key (SBV). The user can afterwards conveniently initiate a transaction on the client as it is done nowadays using e.g. the online portal of the bank. The transaction information is then shared with the OBS and the BTD. On the BTD the information is displayed within the trusted environment, the user has to check and verify the data by presenting his or her biometric trait(s) to the sensor of the BTD. A seal TOS' is created within the BTD over the transaction data using the pre-shared key, that is released by the biometric sample. This seal is sent to the OBS, which can then check the authenticity of the transaction data as well as the authenticity of the transaction initiator – only in the case of a successful verification of the seal, the transaction is confirmed and executed.

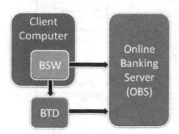

Fig. 1. Threat scenario: online banking SW (BSW) resides on possible malware controlled client environment and communicates with trusted online banking server (OBS) as well as with a secure biometric transaction device (BTD)

2.1 Information Flow Enrolment and Verification

The protocol involves more complex procedures inside the building blocks. Within the *BTD* the biometric subsystem is found, it covers the process of enrolment and verification that are inspired by the Helper-Data-Scheme [8] for privacy protection, which performs a fuzzy commitment. For the enrolment, a biometric sensor inside the *BTD* captures the biometric sample multiple times, extracts a fixed-length bit feature vector, which is then analyzed for reliable positions. The resulting reliable bit vector (RBV) is fused using the XOR-function ($\oplus$) with an error-encoded version of a pre-shared key (CBV = ECC(SBV)) that has the same length. Correcting errors using the decoding DEC of the ECC makes it possible to cope with the noise caused by the variability in the biometric information. The information stored on the *BTD* are not revealing any sensitive biometric information: pseudo identifier PI = hash(SBV), auxiliary data $AD1$ = indexes of reliable positions in the feature vector, auxiliary data

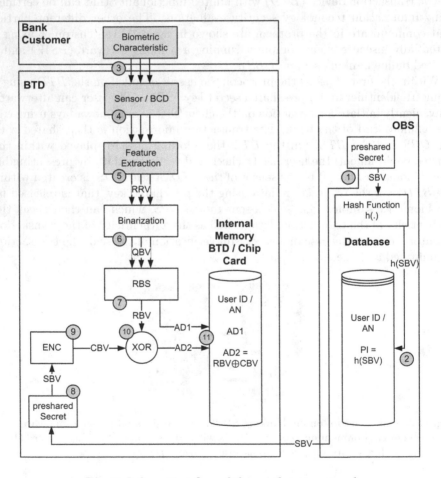

Fig. 2. Information flow of the enrolment protocol

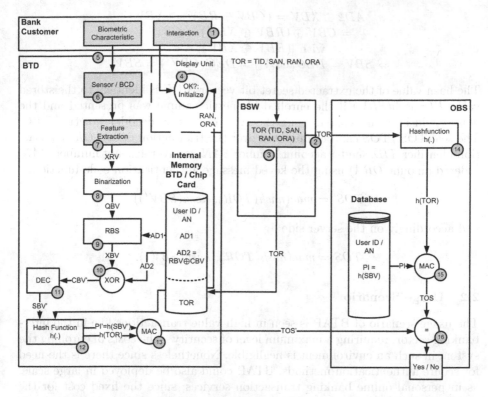

Fig. 3. Information flow of the transaction verification protocol in the core BTAP

$AD2 = CBV \oplus RBV$. Figure 2 depicts the enrolment process of binding an identity to a pre-shared secret key, this process is modelled in a simplified way as described in section 3.6. Note that the pseudo identifier can be renewed or exchanged to enable revocation in a biometric system, which is not possible if the biometric information itself was used for the verification of identity. Furthermore no cross matching of different template protected biometric databases can succeed if the secret SBV is chosen independent from each other. Potentially sensitive biometric data is never stored or decrypted for comparison in its original form.

After this step, transactions can be authenticated as shown in Figure 3. Inverting the enrolment process is releasing the hash value of the pre-shared secret: the data subject presents the biometric trait, a biometric sample is generated, features are extracted. The helper data is loaded, so the system is able to extract the bits of the fixed-length feature vector at positions that should be reliable for the enrolled data subject. The resulting reliable bit vector XBV is releasing the key if the error correction capabilities ϵ (in bits) of the used code is higher than the amount of single bit errors $|(XBV \oplus RBV)|$ occurred during the feature extraction step:

$$AD2 \oplus XBV = (CBV \oplus RBV) \oplus XBV$$
$$= CBV \oplus (RBV \oplus XBV) = CBV'$$
$$\text{with } |(RBV \oplus XBV)| < \epsilon$$
$$\Rightarrow SBV = DEC(CBV) = DEC(CBV') = SBV'$$

The hash value of the extracted secret bit vector SBV' is identical to the stored value $PI=$hash(SBV) if the enrolled biometric sample was presented and the noise could be compensated using the error correction decoder function DEC. The seal TOS'/TOS can be computed over the transaction data TOR (transaction identifier TID, sender account number SAN, receiver account number RAN, ordered amount ORA) using the keyed message authentication code function:

$$TOS' = mac(hash(TOR), \, hash(SBV'))$$

and accordingly on the server side

$$TOS = mac(hash(TOR), \, hash(SBV)).$$

2.2   Usage Scenario

The usage scenario of BTAP is seen in high value transactions like in the inter-banking sector, requiring a maximum level of security – the costs of enrolling the system in such an environment is negligible. Nonetheless since there is the need for secure authentication methods, BTAP could also be deployed in large scale, as in personal online banking transaction services, since the fixed cost for the BTD and the infrastructure would amortize considering the loss due to malware triggered false transactions over time.

3   Formal Model

This section describes the formal method that was used to model BTAP and to analyse its security properties. The considered attacker model is sketched, the intended security properties are defined. Then the protocol is described using the exchanged messages as well as the applied pi calculus. The verification process based on the formal model is given in the end of this section.

3.1   Applied Pi Calculus and ProVerif

The applied pi calculus is a generalized version of the spi calculus [1], which itself is an extension of the pi calculus [6]. The pi calculus is a process calculus with the goal to formally describe concurrent systems, whose configuration may change during execution. Its variants are specifically designed to analyse and verify security properties of cryptographic protocols. The tool ProVerif was developed by Blanchet et al. [3] and it supports automated reasoning for applied pi calculus processes. It translates the protocol description into Horn clauses and acts upon them as a resolution prover. ProVerif fully automatically tries to prove security properties, its outcome can be either one of the following: robust safety can be proven, an attack as counter example is found, or it can neither prove or disprove robust safety according to the property. The protocol is modelled and verified using ProVerif, one advantage of using the tool: the Dolev-Yao attacker model, which is described in the next section, is specified and can be used directly.

3.2   Attacker Model

We assume the Dolev-Yao attacker model [4], which uses idealizations about the cryptographic primitives: an attacker can not learn from encrypted messages without the knowledge of the keys used for encryption. Changing an encrypted message without the knowledge of the key is detectable. Keys can not be guessed or learned from encrypted messages, also random numbers can not be guessed. Hash functions are collision free one-way functions. The attacker has full control over the communication channels, specifically he can: eavesdrop, inject and redirect messages. Furthermore he can generate keys and random numbers, as well as apply cryptographic primitives on what he learned.

3.3   Intended Security Properties

The intended properties of the BTA protocol are:

- *Authentication*: of the transaction data (integrity), the transaction initiator (proof of identity).
- *Non-Repudiation of Origin*: a valid transaction can not be repudiated by the initiator.
- *Secrecy*: the pre-shared secret and the sensitive biometric information stay secret.

Note: secrecy of the transaction data itself can not be assured if the client computer is compromised, and is therefore not covered in the core protocol. Additionally the internal *BTD* process is not modelled according to the applied pi calculus. Using the security assumptions, we model an idealized version of it.

3.4   Security Assumptions

The security assumptions for the verification of BTAP are listed below:

- *BTD* (in the model *B*) is tamper proof: no malware infection or manipulation of the processes and the storage of the *BTD* are possible (Note the advantages of using the privacy enhancing technology: revocation is enabled, the templates are protected additionally, only nonsensitive data is stored, storage capacity is negligible, efficient processing of the bitstrings, no hill climbing attacks possible). *BTD* supports secure I/O.
- Biometric subsystem: the biometric sensor can only be spoofed with unreasonable effort (suitable for unsupervised authentication). Biometric traits are unique and can not be replicated. The feature extraction system is able to extract a feature vector close to the enrolled sample, in a way that the shared key is released correctly (see section 2.1).

- Enrolment phase is completed by the authentic person, the process is not tampered.
- Helper-Data-Scheme (HDS) is not leaking private information about the extracted biometric feature vector nor the pre-shared secret. The biometric entropy is high enough to enable reasonable long pre-shared secrets to avoid brute force attacks.
- Online banking server *OBS*, or short *S* in the model: trusted and secure environment. Its public key *pkEncS* for encryption and pkSignS for signatures are publicly available.
- Client computer is considered untrusted and can be manipulated by malware.
- Secret keys are secret: pre-shared key *SBV* is shared[1] between server *OBS* and *BTD*, extracted biometric feature vector is also secret.
- Computational limitations are: none for the client and server, no public-key crypto for *BTD*.
- Communication channel between server *S* and client *C* (running the banking software *BSW*), unidirectional channels from *C* to the *BTD* and from *BTD* to the server.

3.5   BTAP: Message Sequence

Informally a protocol can be described by the messages that are exchanged, the core message sequence for BTAP [5] is given below, where {} indicate an encryption with a symmetric key Kxy, a public key pkEncX from X for encryption, or a signature using the private key prSignX from X. X->Y stands for a message from X to Y. The four parties are client C, server S, biometric transaction device B and user U:

```
Message 1: C->S: {(Nonce1, AN, ORA, RAN)}pkEncS
Message 2: S->C: {(Nonce1, Nonce2, AN, ORA, RAN)}prSignS
Message 3: C->B: (Nonce2, AN, ORA, RAN)
Message 4: U->B: (Ok)
Message 5: B->S: (mac(hash(Nonce2, AN, ORA, RAN), hash(SBV')))
Message 6: S->C: {hash(true, Nonce2, AN, ORA, RAN)}prSignS
```

The transaction information consists of the sender account number *AN*, ordered amount of money to be transferred *ORA*, and the receiver account number *RAN*. Nonces are random numbers that are used only once for proof of freshness. *Nonce1* in message 1 and 2 serve as server authentication, only the owner of the private signature key *prSignS* (server *S*) can decrypt message 1 and reply the correct *Nonce1* (*Nonce1* should include a simple time stamp besides the random part, that has to be checked for freshness on the server side before sending message 2). Message 1 is encrypted with the public encryption key of the server. *Nonce2* is included for the freshness of the transaction data, to avoid

---

[1] In a real-life scenario the key could be shared using a secure independent channel. Personalized confidential (physical) mails or credentials could serve as a direct input to the *BTD*.

replay attacks and to limit the validity using a timestamp part. The transaction data received by the server as well as *Nonce1* and *Nonce2* are signed and send back to the client as message 2. The client forwards the information in message 3 to the *BTD*. The user has to check and verify the transaction data displayed on the *BTD* with his or her biometric trait(s), which is modelled simplified as message 4. The pre-shared key *SBV* is released and used to create a seal *TOS'=mac(hash(Nonce2, AN, ORA, RAN), hash(SBV'))* using a message authentication code (MAC) mechanism in message 5 with *hash(Nonce2, AN, ORA, RAN)* as the message and *hash(SBV')* as the secret key. The server confirms the transaction in message 6 only if the seal from message 5 is identical to the seal *TOS* that can be created on the server side with the information from message 1, *Nonce2*, and the pre-shared key *SBV'.*

3.6   BTAP: Model in the Applied Pi Calculus

The internal processes of the biometric key release inside the *BTD* are not modelled here, since we are assuming a secure and tamper-proof environment and an idealized biometric subsystem. An attacker has no access per definition on the internal variables and processes. In order to model the process of checking and verification of the authentic transaction data by the user, we use the following approximation: the authentic transaction data is modelled as data signed with the secret key (the reliable biometric information *XBV* or equivalently *RBV* (see section 3.4)) of a "public-key biometric" system only known to the user and verifiable by, among others, the *BTD*.

The attacker can create an arbitrary number of transaction information, which is modelled as *evilRAN* and *evilORA*. As we will see in section 4, this is interesting for proving if such transaction information can be falsely authenticated.

All other protocol steps are modelled straightforward according to the message sequence shown in Sec. 3.5. The ProVerif code for the definition of functions, reductions and free names is given below. The number behind a function name is its cardinality. As primitives we need the hash-, mac-function as well as public-key crypto in this model, the destructors describe the behaviour of the abstract functions:

```
(* Constants *)
data true/0.

(* Functions *)
fun hash/1.
fun mac/2. (* with destructor checkmac/2. *)

(* Asymmetric Encryption *)
fun pencrypt/2. (* with destructor pdecrypt/2 *)
fun prv/1. (* private part of a key pair *)
fun pub/1. (* public part of a key pair *)

(* Reductions *)
reduc   pdecrypt(pencrypt(x, prv(y)), pub(y)) = x;
```

pdecrypt(pencrypt(x, pub(y)), prv(y)) = x.
reduc   checkmac(mac(y, x), x) = y.

(* Security Assumptions *)
(* Public Channels / Free Names *)
free c, cs, sb, cb, ub, uc, ORA, RAN, m, m2, m3.

The core of the protocol model are the processes, which define the behaviour of the communicating parties using the applied pi calculus. The processes are behaving like the user (processU), the client (processC), the server (processS), the *BTD* (processB) as well as the attacker (processAttacker). If a message is not as expected, the 0.-process is executed (process stops).

ProcessC receives a message *m* on the open channel *uc*. *m* is expected to have the form of a 2-tuple, the two elements are defined as *ORA* and *RAN* in the rest of the process. A nonce (*Nonce1*) is created and send on the open channel *cs* (to the server) with the transaction data received in *m* as well as the fixed account number, all encrypted with public encryption key of *S*. A reply is expected on *cs* in the form of a 5-tuple. The values received should be signed with the private signature key of the server, and they are expected to be equal to *Nonce1*, *AN*, *ORA* and *RAN*. On the second position a new nonce is received, which is defined *Nonce2*. The new nonce (used as a transaction identifier) as well as the transaction data is send on the open channel *cb* (also to the *BTD B*). The last line indicates the process to be waiting for the decision of the server (without function in the model, for the notification if a transaction was successful):

let *processC* =
  in(uc, m); *(* user interaction: transaction data generated *)*
  let (ORA, RAN) = m **in**
    (**new** *Nonce1*;
    out(cs, pencrypt((*Nonce1*, *AN*, ORA, RAN), pub(*secretEncS*))); *(* Message 1 *)*
    in(cs, *reply*); *(* Message 2 *)*
    let (= *Nonce1*, *Nonce2*, = *AN*, = ORA, = RAN) = pdecrypt(*reply*, pub(*secretSignS*)) **in**
      (**out**(cb, (*Nonce2*, *AN*, ORA, RAN)); *(* Message 3 *)*
      in(cs, *decision*))).

ProcessS describes the server behaviour. It receives a message on channel *cs*, which is encrypted with the public encryption key of *S*. Its decrypted form is expected to be a 4-tuple (*Nonce1*, *SAN*, *ORA*, *RAN*). If *Nonce1* is fresh (was not received before) and its timestamp is valid, a fresh and random number is generated (*Nonce2*) and send on *cs* with *Nonce1* as proof of authenticity as well as *SAN*, *ORA* and *RAN*, all signed with the private signature key from *S*. Note: in the model the freshness check of *Nonce1* is not performed due to limitations in the abstraction of memory in the applied pi calculus. The next expected message is the seal sent on channel *sb* (from the *BTD B*). If the MAC was created using the secret pre-shared key *hash(SBV)* and using the transaction data received earlier in *m*, then the server accepts the transaction and creates a signed authentication reply over the transaction data including the nonce.

let *processS* =
  in(cs, m);
  let (*Nonce1*, *SAN*, ORA, RAN) = pdecrypt(m, prv(*secretEncS*)) **in** *(* Message 1 *)*
    (**new** *Nonce2*;

```
out(cs, pencrypt((Nonce1, Nonce2, SAN, ORA, RAN), prv(secretSignS)));  (* Message 2 *)
in(sb, m2);  (* Message 5 *)
if checkmac(m2, hash(SBV)) = hash((Nonce2, SAN, ORA, RAN)) then
  (* Message 6 *)
  out(cs, pencrypt(hash((true, Nonce2, SAN, ORA, RAN)), prv(secretSignS)))).
```

ProcessB describes the biometric transaction device (*BTD*, here short: *B*). It receives message *m3* on channel *ub* (from the user). The message is expected to be a signed hash value of the authentic transaction data, only the party in possession of the private signature key can sign. This is a simplified model of the biometric subsystem. Message 3 is received from the (possibly malware infected) client *C*. Only if the hash of this transaction data is equal to the received signed hash, the seal (keyed MAC) is created over the message *m*:

```
let processB =
  (* reliable and authentic RAN, ORA from the user *)
  in(ub, m3);
  let hashvalue = pdecrypt(m3, pub(XBV)) in
    (* possibly UNreliable and UNauthentic RAN, ORA from the client *)
    (in(cb, m);  (* Message 3 *)
    (let (Nonce, = AN, ORAin, RANin) = m in
      (if hashvalue = hash((ORAin, RANin)) then
        out(sb, mac(hash(m), hash(SBV)))))).  (* Message 5 *)
```

ProcessU models the user, which is creating new authentic ordered amount and receiver account numbers (a new transaction). It signs these values with the secret private key (check and verify with biometric trait) and sends it on channel *ub*. The transaction data is not considered to be private (guessable + insecure client) and needs to be submitted to the client *C*, so it is made available on channel *uc*:

```
let processU =
  (* user creates new transaction *)
  new authORA;
  new authRAN;
  (* user checks and verifies authentic transaction data *)
  out(ub, pencrypt(hash((authORA, authRAN)), prv(XBV)));
  out(uc, (authORA, authRAN)).
```

The last process, the attacker, is simply creating evil (non-authentic) transaction information and makes it available on channel *c*. The idea behind this is to check later, if non-signed transaction data can be authenticated:

```
let processAttacker =
    new evilORA;
    new evilRAN;
    out(c, (evilORA, evilRAN)).
```

The following steps are modelled in the main process that is executed initially: create a new secret biometric feature vector *XBV* and make its public part available for verification. This is for the simulation of the checked and verified transaction data. A new secret pre-shared key *SBV* is created, as well as a sender account number AN, which is made public. *secretEncS* and *secretSignS* are the secrets for generating the servers key-pairs, again, the public keys are made available to all parties on channel c. The last part describes the processes that can run after this initialization in parallel. Note: an unlimited number of processes is indicated by !*process*. A parallel execution of two processes X and Y is defined by $(processX) \mid (processY)$. That means any number of process instances of the user $(processU)$, the client $(processC)$, the server $(processS)$, the BTD $(processB)$ and the attacker $(processAttacker)$ can run in parallel. The client and server are running by purpose with an unbound number of instances in this model, this may be counter intuitive but can be understood when looking at the specific processes:

process
  new XBV;
  out(c, pub(XBV));
  new SBV;
  new AN;
  out(c, AN);
  new *secretEncS*;
  new *secretSignS*;
  out(c, pub(*secretEncS*));
  out(c, pub(*secretSignS*));

  $(((!processAttacker) \mid (!processU) \mid (!processC) \mid (!processS) \mid (!processB))$.

4   Verification of Security Properties

In order to verify security properties, queries have to be formalized that are checked by ProVerif. A query of the form **query** *attacker:x.*, checks if the attacker gets to know x during the execution of the processes. The attacker model is set to active.

(* Queries *)
(* Query 1: reliable bit vector extracted from biometric trait(s) *)
query *attacker:XBV*.
(* Query 2: modelled as public-key system *)
query *attacker:*prv(XBV).
(* Query 3: pre-shared secret key *)
query *attacker:SBV*.
(* Query 4: *)
query *attacker:*hash(SBV).
(* Query 5: encryption secret for public-key server construction *)
query *attacker:secretEncS*.
(* Query 6: private encryption server key *)
query *attacker:*prv(*secretEncS*).
(* Query 7: signature secret for public-key server construction *)
query *attacker:secretSignS*.
(* Query 8: private signature server key *)
query *attacker:*prv(*secretSignS*).
(* Query 9: seal over authentic transaction data *)
query *attacker:*mac(hash(($Nonce2, AN, authORA, authRAN$)), hash($SBV$)).

(* Query 10: seal over arbitrary transaction data *)
query *attacker*:mac(hash(($Nonce2, AN, evilORA, evilRAN$)), hash($SBV$)).
(* Query 11: server reply over authentic transaction data *)
query *attacker*:pencrypt(hash((true, $Nonce2, AN, authORA, authRAN$)), prv($secretSignS$)).
(* Query 12: server reply over arbitrary transaction data *)
query *attacker*:pencrypt(hash((true, $Nonce2, AN, evilORA, evilRAN$)), prv($secretSignS$)).

Execution of the queries in ProVerif shows: query 9 (authentic seal) and query 11 (authentic reply from the server) are true. That means, the attacker gets to know information that is available on the channels after a successful run of the transaction authentication protocol using authentic transaction data on the server as well as in the *BTD*. The fresh nonce with limited time validity inside the seal and the server reply avoid replay and delayed-play attacks, therefore the information can not be used to authenticate another transaction.

To wrap up the ProVerif simulation we could show, that the attacker does not get knowledge about the secret keys and the biometric feature vector. Non-authentic transaction data does not get sealed because of the process of checking and verifying inside the secure environment. If the integrity of a verified transaction is compromised, the two generated seals, the one inside the *BTD* and the one inside the server will differ, in this case the transaction is dropped. Non-repudiation of origin is ensured using the biometric subsystem, which only releases the key that is used to generate the seal, if the enrolled person is verifying the transaction. The private server keys stay secret, therefore the authenticity of the server towards C is guaranteed in the protocol, since only the owner of the private encryption key can respond with the correct nonce from message 1 (S only responds to message 1 if *Nonce1* is fresh). Attacks on availability are possible in our model if the attacker drops messages from the channels.

The security properties from section 3.3 hold if the security assumptions from section 3.4 hold true. Especially the assumption, that the authentic user is completing the enrolment phase correctly, is necessary for the non-repudiation of origin property. In a real-life scenario the enrolment of a user could be performed under controlled conditions to satisfy the assumption.

A drawback of the core protocol is that the user is incapable of deciding if the transaction was successfully executed, since a malware infected client can compromise / drop the result from the server, this issue and new features are addressed in the next section.

5   BTAP Extension: Secret Message Exchange

Even though an attacker can not gain information from the seal, it is desirable to encrypt all exchanged messages to ensure privacy of the banking information. Note that the seal in message 5 does not need to be encrypted, since an attacker can not get any information about the key, nor the message from the MAC value. The best known forgery attacks for an MAC based on iterated keyed hash functions are birthday attacks, that are also used to find collisions in hash functions [2,7]. Note also that the property of secrecy of the messages can not hold when the client is compromised, since for convenience reasons the client is still used to generate the transactions and to communicate with the server.

```
Message 1: C->S: {(Nonce1, Ksc, AN, ORA, RAN)}pkEncS
Message 2: S->C: {{(Nonce1,Nonce2,Nonce3,AN,ORA,RAN, ...
                 {((Nonce2, AN, ORA, RAN)}Kbs))}prSignS}Ksc
Message 3: C->B: (Nonce3,AN,ORA,RAN,{(Nonce2, AN, ORA, RAN)}Kbs)
Message 4: U->B: (Ok)
Message 5: B->S: {(mac(hash(Nonce2, AN, ORA, RAN), hash(SBV)))}Kbs
Message 6: S->C: {{hash(true, Nonce2, AN, ORA, RAN), ...
                 ({hash(true, Nonce2, AN, ORA, RAN)}Kbs)}prSignS}Ksc
Message 7: C->B: {hash(true, Nonce2, AN, ORA, RAN)}Kbs
```

Message 1 carries a symmetric session key Ksc, encrypted with the server's public encryption key pkEncS for an encrypted communication between S and C (PKI key verification required). Another symmetric session key, derived from the pre-shared secret SBV, is securing the communication for message 5, 6 and 7:

$$Kbs = onewayfunction((hash(Nonce3), hash(SBV))).$$

Since hash(SBV) is known to S and B, Kbs can only be computed within the two parties (on B after the enrolled user presents his or her biometric trait to release SBV).

After releasing Kbs on the *BTD*, it is ensured to the device, that S has received the information (Nonce2, AN, ORA, RAN), since it is forwarded encrypted with Kbs in message 3 from the client. The *BTD* can check if the same transaction information was also send from the client and displayed to the user. Only if the two sets are identical, the transaction seal is created, otherwise a warning is shown on the secure display. When receiving message 7, it is proven to the *BTD*, that the server executed the transaction encoded in the authentic transaction data. On the secure display of the *BTD* the decision can be shown to the user.

The extended protocol does not send any transaction data in an unencrypted form over the channels, without the need for public-key crypto on the *BTD*. This extension ensures that the transaction data stays private and that the execution of the authentic transaction can be verified.

6   BTAP Extension: Online Banking Transactions Using the "Four-Eyes" Principle

Authentication of transaction data through multiple persons might be part of a policy if the ordered amount succeeds the liability of a single person or role. This procedure might help to prevent financial frauds. BTAP is extendible without much effort to comply with this requirement. Three different scenarios of a multiple-person authentication are identified, the pros and cons are discussed thereafter: 1.) one local *BTD*, one shared secret, 2.) one local *BTD*, multiple shared secrets, 3.) multiple remote *BTDs*, multiple shared secrets.

6.1   One Local BTD, One Shared Secret

The enrolment process of the Helper-Data-Scheme subsystem (Fig. 2) has to be adapted, the shared secret has to be binded to n different data subjects.

Therefore n different auxiliary-data-1 $(AD1)$ sets have to be generated that define the reliable positions in the fixed length biometric feature vectors of each biometric trait. The pseudo identifier is created as in the original enrolment: $PI = hash(SBV)$. Only one auxiliary-data-2 $(AD2)$ is generated during the process using the following formula for the error correction encoded pre-shared secret $CBV = ECC(SBV)$ and the data subjects reliable boolean biometric feature vectors RBV_i for $i = 2...n$ and $n \geq 2$:

$$AD2 = CBV \oplus (\bigoplus_{i=1...n} RBV_i)$$

The result of this adapted enrolment: the shared secret can only be released and therefore the transaction seal can only be generated over the transaction data, if all enrolled biometric feature vectors RBV_i can be extracted during the authentication phase. This means, every enrolled person must verify the transaction data locally with his or her biometric trait. Advantage: the order of presenting the biometric traits is negligible since the XOR-operation is commutative (still $AD1$ is person specific and therefore an ID claim like a token is needed); a data subject k could be revoked, by just presenting the biometric trait (where RBV_k can be extracted from), $AD2$ could be updated accordingly:

$$AD2' = AD2 \oplus RBV_k$$
$$= CBV \oplus (\bigoplus_{i=1...n} RBV_i) \oplus RBV_k$$
$$= CBV \oplus (\bigoplus_{i=1...(k-1),(k+1)...n} RBV_i) \oplus (RBV_k \oplus RBV_k)$$
$$= CBV \oplus (\bigoplus_{i=1...(k-1),(k+1)...n} RBV_i)$$

The drawback in this operation mode is that the amount of bit errors that can be corrected stays limited – only CBV carries the error-correction code. Evenly distributed bit errors in the feature vectors RBV_i would affect all positions of the codeword.

Alternatively the XOR-operation is applied to the concatenation of all RBV_i vectors and CBV. The entropy of the concatenated feature vector will be increased compared to a single feature vector, a longer key SBV and a longer resulting CBV could be used for high security demands:

$$AD2 = CBV \oplus (RBV_1, ... RBV_k, ..., RBV_n)$$

Advantage: Higher level of security against brute force attacks on the secret SBV. Disadvantage: the system is inflexible, a re-enrolment is needed if data subject k is not allowed to authenticate online banking transactions anymore.

6.2   One Local BTD, Multiple Shared Secrets

When using multiple shared secrets, again an ID claim like a token is needed to distinguish between the enrolled data subjects. A binding of a pre-shared secret key and each extracted reliable boolean biometric feature vector (RBV_i) has to be conducted. This relates to n different enrolments on the same biometric transaction device (BTD) as described in the core BTAP. In this scenario, it is possible to create n different transaction order seals (TOS_i) over the same transaction order record $TOR = (TID, SAN, RAN, ORA)$ using a keyed MAC-function:

$$TOS_i = mac(hash(TOR), hash(SBV_i))$$

The seals are send independently from each other to the server, which knows all the enrolled subject for a specific banking account. Advantage: Flexible solution for the user enrolment; Fine-grained policies on the server side enable different levels of security and flexible requirements (number of seals, seals from specific persons) for a transaction based on the ordered amount or the receiver account number, or other metadata. And the non-repudiation property is hold in this scenario, since a unique pre-shared key is bind to a natural person.

6.3   Multiple Remote BTDs, Multiple Shared Secrets

As seen in the previous case, a flexible system could be constructed using multiple shared secrets and one local $BTDs$. The same description applies to this case, with the difference that different $BTDs$ could be used independent from each other, no ID claim is needed if every data subject is enrolled on a different BTD using a different pre-shared secret. This case enables time-shifted transaction authentication but it requires the distribution of pending transactions to the client, which could be done by using the online banking portal, simple e-mail transfer or a dedicated software.

6.4   Additional Authentication Factors and Multiple Biometric Modalities

BTAP can be extended to a multiple factor authentication system, adding possession as well as knowledge authentication factors that are given as input to the BTD. Including this information, which is shared with the server side, the transaction seal TOS would be computed as:

$$TOS = mac(hash(TOR), (hash(SBV), hash(Password), hash(TokenSecret)))$$

with the keyed mac-function. Adding additional authentication factors would strengthen the BTAP even more.

Extracted reliable biometric feature vectors RBV_i originating from multiple biometric modalities M_i with $i = 2...n$ and $n \geq 2$ of the same person, like e.g. fingerprint and fingervein data, can be used to generate a concatenated biometric feature vector $RBV' = (RBV_1, ..., RBV_n)$ that is used to release the pre-shared key in the BTA protocol.

7   Conclusions

The proposed security properties could be proven using a formal model of the core BTA protocol message exchanges and the protocol verification tool ProVerif. The protocol enables non-repudiable person and data authentic online banking transaction. The extensions enable privacy of the transaction data and in addition new security features: transactions can be sealed by multiple individuals to comply with restrictive policies. BTAP supports multiple biometric modalities and can be extended for multi-factor authentication as well. In the near future the pi-calculus must be extended in order to be able to deal with noisy biometric data as part of security protocols – then also the internal processes of the biometric transaction device could be modelled and verified.

References

1. Abadi, M., Gordon, A.D.: A Calculus for Cryptographic Protocols: the Spi Calculus. In: CCS 1997: Proceedings of the 4th ACM Conference on Computer and Communications Security, pp. 36–47. ACM, New York (1997)
2. Bellare, M., Canetti, R., Krawczyk, H.: Pseudorandom Functions Revisited: the Cascade Construction and its Concrete Security. In: Annual IEEE Symposium on Foundations of Computer Science, p. 514 (1996)
3. Blanchet, B.: An Efficient Cryptographic Protocol Verifier Based on Prolog Rules. In: 14th IEEE Computer Security Foundations Workshop (CSFW-14), pp. 82–96. IEEE Computer Society, Cape Breton (2001)
4. Dolev, D., Yao, A.C.: On the Security of Public Key Protocols. In: SFCS 1981: Proceedings of the 22nd Annual Symposium on Foundations of Computer Science, pp. 350–357. IEEE Computer Society, Washington, DC, USA (1981)
5. Hartung, D., Busch, C.: Biometric Transaction Authentication Protocol. In: The International Conference on Emerging Security Information, Systems and Technologies, vol. 4 (2010)
6. Milner, R., Parrow, J., Walker, D.: A Calculus of Mobile Processes, i. Information and Computation 100(1), 1–40 (1992)
7. Preneel, B., van Oorschot, P.C.: MDx-MAC and Building Fast MACs from Hash Functions. In: Coppersmith, D. (ed.) CRYPTO 1995. LNCS, vol. 963, pp. 1–14. Springer, Heidelberg (1995)
8. Tuyls, P., Goseling, J.: Capacity and Examples of Template-Protecting Biometric Authentication Systems. In: Maltoni, D., Jain, A.K. (eds.) BioAW 2004. LNCS, vol. 3087, pp. 158–170. Springer, Heidelberg (2004)

Exploration and Field Study of a Password Manager Using Icon-Based Passwords

Kemal Bicakci[1], Nart Bedin Atalay[2], Mustafa Yuceel[1], and P.C. van Oorschot[3]

[1] TOBB University of Economics and Technology, Turkey
[2] Selcuk University, Turkey
[3] School of Computer Science, Carleton University, Canada

Abstract. We carry out a hybrid lab and field study of a password manager program, and report on usability and security. Our study explores iPMAN, a browser-based password manager that in addition uses a graphical password scheme for the master password. We present our findings as a set of observations and insights expected to be of interest both to those exploring password managers, and graphical passwords.

Keywords: password managers, graphical passwords, field study, security and usability.

1 Introduction

Despite continuing status as the default method for Internet authentication, passwords have well known deficiencies. They are often highly predictable, not well protected, and have many usability issues. Seriously complicating this, users must remember not just one, but multitudes of passwords. Given the growing number of web sites users have passwords for [10], it is almost impossible to avoid the poor practice of re-using a password across several accounts, with obvious negative security implications [6, p.3]. On the other hand, using distinct passwords increases the occurrence of forgetting, or mis-matching passwords across sites.

Password managers offer to ease usability problems related to a multiplicity of passwords, by reducing the memory burden to a single master password. They may be implemented as standalone programs or extensions to web browsers. The latter is more convenient for Internet applications, relieving users from the task of starting up a separate program, and providing protection against phishing attacks [26].

We carry out a hybrid lab and field study to explore the usability of a browser-based password manager, including user perception of acceptability. While many password managers exist (see §2), their usability has received surprisingly little attention. A few preliminary lab studies have considered usability [26,8,5], but to our knowledge, no field study of password manager programs has been reported in the literature,[1] leaving a gap in understanding usability and security issues

---

[1] An informal test for PassPet reported preliminary information about results [31].

G. Danezis, S. Dietrich, and K. Sako (Eds.): FC 2011 Workshops, LNCS 7126, pp. 104–118, 2012.

in natural environments—which is amplified by the challenge of emulating, with high ecological validity, factors related to password managers, especially those involving *changes in user behavior*. For example, users may access all accounts by entering a master password to the manager program, rather than site-specific passwords; in actual practice, will they choose to do so?

Our field study is further distinguished by exploring graphical passwords for the master password of a password manager. A motivating factor is their claim to offer several advantages over text passwords [17] but also of special interest in our work, they may help to reduce the likelihood of inducing insecure behavior [5,8]. The graphical scheme we use is GPI [3], wherein user passwords involve recognizing a sequence of icons from a large displayed set. Around the password interface of GPI, we design and implement a password manager program called *iPMAN* (**i**con-based **P**assword **MAN**ager).

Beyond reporting on the hybrid study of iPMAN, we present our observations and insights from an evaluation of the resulting data. Some lessons generalize to other password manager tools, while others apply to stand-alone graphical passwords. The study also provides additional insight on the GPI scheme itself. The selection of weak (graphical) master passwords by many participants motivated a further contribution to protect against password guessing attacks, of independent interest beyond password managers and graphical passwords: a new salt generation method which avoids the long user wait time of earlier work [15]. For space reasons we defer discussion of this to an extended version [4].

2   Background and Related Work

The numerous graphical password (gp) schemes proposed in recent years can be classified into three types according to the memory task involved: recall-based schemes (e.g., DAS [17]), cued-recall schemes (e.g., PassPoints [30]), and recognition-based schemes (e.g., PassFaces/Face [9]).

It is known from the cognitive psychology literature that recognition memory—being able to recognize something previously encountered—is easier and longer-lasting than recall-based memory [20]. Numerous recognition-based graphical password schemes leveraging this human ability have been developed and tested. Users are given a set of pictures, and must recognize and select a subset of them as a password. Most recognition-based gp schemes explored to date have been implemented and tested with relatively small password spaces, e.g., comparable to 4-digit PINs. In general these schemes can be parameterized to yield larger spaces (e.g., using more faces per screen in PassFaces, and/or more than 4 rounds of screens), but usability has not been tested under those circumstances.

GPI and GPIS [3] are recognition-based gp schemes comparable in many ways to PassPoints, including in theoretical password space size, for reasonable parameterizations of each. In GPI and GPIS a password is an ordered sequence of icons (mini-pictures) which represent objects belonging to certain categories.

The categories and objects are based on a category norm study by van Over-schelde et al. [23]. Icons in a common category are grouped and presented in a common row to ease memorizing the password by forming associations between the password, icons and the categories. The idea is that category structures, an organization familiar to the human brain, will enhance memory performance. In GPI, users self-select a portfolio of password icons; in GPIS their portfolio is initially system-assigned and can be changed later. A lab study [3] found GPI less vulnerable to hot-spot issues [29] than Passpoints.

There are two common password manager approaches [14]. The *password wallet approach* uses a master password to encrypt a file of site-specific pass-words, stored in encrypted form and decrypted as required. Numerous manager programs implement this approach, including Apple's Keychain [21], Password Safe [24], and the Firefox browser's built-in password manager; some are im-plemented as browser extensions, and may support advanced features like auto-matic form filling, e.g., LastPass [19], 1Password [1]. In the *hashing approach*, which iPMAN takes, the master password is combined with site-specific infor-mation to generate site-specific passwords. These include early systems [12,2] and browser extension implementations such as PasswordMaker [18], Password Composer [25], PwdHash [26], Password Multiplier [15] and PassPet [31].

Single sign-on solutions (e.g., the OpenID initiative [22,27]) also aim to miti-gate the password fatigue due to the effort required to remember large numbers of passwords. Our anecdotal observation is that only built-in password managers in web browsers are widely used and other password managers appear to be of considerable interest to a minority of users (for personal use), whereas single sign-on solutions seem to be used (and marketed) more by those with enterprise goals. As such, password managers are more a "grassroots" movement, and single sign-on systems more a corporate movement.

A lab study by Chiasson et al. [8] of implementations made publicly avail-able by the original designers of PwdHash [26] and Password Multiplier [15] found major usability problems, and noted the danger of password manager interfaces inducing mental models resulting in security exposures—e.g., users unable to properly activate software may reveal their master password to a visited site.

In a lab study involving a browser-based password manager GPEX, Bicakci et al. [5] found that graphical passwords had better usability characteristics than text passwords. The PassPoints-based user interface involved clicking cells demarked by a visual grid. Lab study results indicated that user performance for common tasks (e.g., login, migrate password) was better than for PwdHash. In contrast to PwdHash, improper usage does not cause security exposures in GPEX as the cued-recall aspect of a GPEX master password precludes it from being submitted to the wrong site. Another study using a graphical password as a password manager is by Govindarajulu and Madhvanath [13].

3 iPMAN Password Manager Implementation

In iPMAN, the hashing approach is used with GPI (see §2) as the password entry interface, thus precluding password reuse across sites.[2] No server-side changes are needed to use iPMAN. A user first double clicks on the password field to activate a dialog box to display a panel of icons (see Fig. 1(a)) and then clicks individual icons to select an ordered set of icons to create their master password. The placement of icons is static, i.e., identical for all users. After the "Enter Password" button is clicked, the panel disappears, and the browser extension converts the master password to a site-specific character-based password, which is automatically inserted in the password field. The iPMAN master password is not stored.

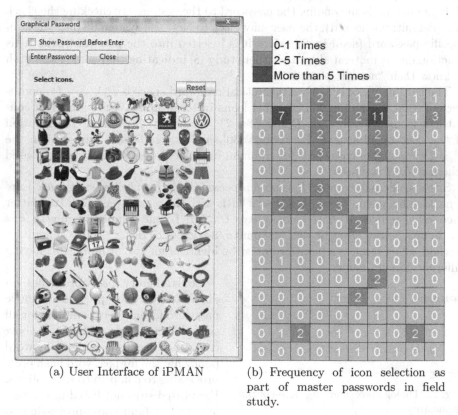

(a) User Interface of iPMAN

(b) Frequency of icon selection as part of master passwords in field study.

Fig. 1. iPMAN Interface and Frequency of Icon Selection in Field Study

The above procedure is the same for both password creation and subsequent password entry; iPMAN has no special session with a different interface to create the master password. This feature is more a technical requirement than a

---

[2] By contrast, in the password wallet approach, if site-specific passwords are user-chosen, password reuse may occur even if users are encouraged to choose unique passwords for different sites.

design choice: a password manager implemented as browser extension cannot distinguish first-time users from existing users, and is thus unable to automatically present a different interface for master password creation. This is also why GPI is used instead of schemes which suggest stronger passwords, such as GPIS [3] above, or the cued-recall PCCP [7] which aims to address user choice issues common in other schemes by persuading users to select more random passwords.

We implemented iPMAN as a Firefox extension, testing on Firefox 3.5 and 3.6.[3] Each interface panel row has 10 icons (each 32 x 32 pixels) belonging to a single category from 15 system-configured categories, for a total of 150 icons and panel size 320 x 480 pixels. The user interface (Fig. 1(a)) includes two other buttons and a check box. The user may press the "Reset" button to start over again, if they wish to change the icons selected. The "Close" button closes the dialogue box without sending the password to the system. By checking the check box (default: unchecked), the user may elect to have the system display the site-specific password (see Fig. 2) before it is inserted into the password field. This functionality is motivated by an earlier study [8] indicating that some users wish to know their "actual" passwords.

The cardinality of iPMAN's theoretical password space is $P(Y, X)$. P denotes permutation, Y the number of panel icons in total, and X the number of constituent icons in passwords. $P(150, 6) \approx 2^{43}$ matches the common configuration of the cued-recall scheme PassPoints [30], and is significantly larger than the $9^4 = 2^{12.7}$ possible passwords for common implementations of recognition-based schemes like PassFaces [9].

Site-specific passwords $SP = post\_process(H(URL\_info\|master\_pswd))$ are generated by hashing part of the site's URL with the master password (the latter encoded as indices of clicked icons); e.g., URL_info may simply be google.com for https://www.google.com/accounts/ServiceLogin?... This generation method suffices unless a password must be identical for two or more sites having different domain names.

Fig. 2. Dialog box showing site-specific password

Contradictory password rules on different sites may preclude a single password format being suitable for all sites. This (and special URLs as above) can be addressed by using a password policy file [26] for password hash post-processing to conform to site policies. For visited sites not listed in the policy file, default post-processing is performed. We introduce a central repository[4] shared between all users to relieve users from the burden of manually updating policy files; iPMAN clients automatically check for an update and retrieve the latest version of a policy file. To avoid security problems, care must be taken to ensure the policy file cannot be controlled by attackers [26].

---

[3] Version 2.1 of iPMAN is available at http://bicakci.etu.edu.tr/iPMANV2.1.xpi

[4] See http://myuceel.etu.edu.tr/rules.xml

Caching the most recent such file allows continued operation should the online connection be temporarily lost.

4   User Study of Password Manager

We conducted a hybrid user study which includes lab and field study components to evaluate iPMAN usability (efficiency, effectiveness, acceptability) and security. While the iPMAN password manager differs from others with respect to its user interface, it also has common features and characteristics, and involves similar user behavior issues to other password managers that use hashing to generate site-specific passwords—e.g., the functionality provided by using a master password, using this one password on different accounts, and attitudes towards password security. Tasks common to such managers include converting existing passwords, remote login, etc. Our study thus provides insight about the usability of both password managers in general, and of graphical passwords as the interface for password managers.

We investigated effects of password rules on the usability of iPMAN. The strength of iPMAN passwords decreases if users choose fewer icons within passwords. A long-standing strategy to reduce weak passwords is password rules. We imposed a password length rule of exactly 6 icons on half the participants; the others chose unrestricted passwords. We compared usability metrics of the two groups to investigate the effects of password rules on login time and login success rate. (In an earlier field study, Tao and Adams [28] compared success rates for creating a new graphical password under various password policies for Pass-Go.)

4.1   Methodology

Our small study, approved by ethics committee of Middle East Technical University, involved 20 students (11 male, 9 female) of average age 21.9 years. None had participated in a password usability study before. Participation was voluntary. Participants could leave the study at any time. At the end of the study, a camera was given to one randomly selected participant. To investigate the effect of a password length rule on usability and security, participants were randomly split into two groups: 10 could choose their own password lengths (Free Choice Group), the other 10 (Six Icons Groups) were required to choose exactly six icons.

Procedure. To begin, we invited participants individually to a lab session for a questionnaire on Internet and password usage. Onto each participant's computer we installed a version of iPMAN that included a logging function to collect data necessary for usability analyses. We informed participants that the software would record information on passwords to their computer; that there were no online data transmissions to remote machines; and that user data including their passwords would be collected at the end of the study by the experimenter. We provided participants detailed written instructions about usage of the system similar to the explanation in the previous section, and answered any questions regarding using iPMAN.[5] We set up a server site allowing users to generate site-specific passwords from computers missing the iPMAN extension (similar to the PwdHash remote-login page [26] but implementing the iPMAN interface as a web application). We showed participants how remote-login works and told them they could use that site/page when desired to login from secondary machines. We provided the site URL in the instruction sheet. The experimenter gave his/her phone number to participants, who were free to ask for help at any time during the study.

Each participant chose their own master password and set it in the lab. There was no practice session. We asked them to use iPMAN on all sites they use. We requested they not use their browser's password auto-complete function during the field study. (Note: any such auto-complete use would not impact our statistics, such as login success rate, as our data collection occurred only for logins in which participants actively click on the icons.) They used iPMAN for 43.6 days on average. After this time, we invited them individually to our lab to collect the passwords and usability data logs on their computer. Users were notified again that their iPMAN passwords were collected but they were not asked to take a particular action. They were free for transition back to normal passwords or to continue using iPMAN with or without changing the master password. They were given a second questionnaire, and a short oral interview on the usability of iPMAN. Finally, 20-25 days later, each was invited to a surprise memory test for their master password.

4.2   Results

Questionnaire on Internet and Password Usage. All participants reported that they use the Internet every day except on vacation. Seventeen reported using Firefox as a browser. In self-rated computer skills, 13 (65%) rated themselves as average users, 4 (20%) as above average, and 3 (15%) as expert. 85% reported using the same regular text password on more than one site. 80% also indicated they were concerned about the security of their password. The two most common criteria cited in password choice were ease for remembering, and difficulty of being guessed by others. The majority of participants' usual text passwords were 8-9 characters and included only mixed case alphanumerics. These results were similar to a previous study [8].

User Support. During the study, 4 of 20 participants called for help. One was unable to change an existing password, because the website rejected passwords with special characters. We updated the password policy file to fix the problem. The other three reported that icons occasionally failed to appear on the panel. We found the problem was Java-related and suggested that participants address

---

[5] Providing information beyond the written instruction was part of our ecological design, and might be expected in an enterprise setting. Our objective was not to assess learning performance itself.

this problem by restarting Firefox. We later modified iPMAN to no longer depend on the Java run time environment. No participants called for a help about how to generate, change or update site-specific passwords with iPMAN.

Effectiveness and Efficiency. The average length of master password was 3.50 icons (min=2, max=6, std.dev=1.08) for the free choice group, and fixed at 6 for the other group. One participant changed their master password during the study. For the following statistical analyses, the level of significance used is 0.05.

During the study participants made a total of 1197 login attempts with iP-MAN. The per-participant average was overall 59.6 (std.dev=29.3, min=31, max=128), for the free choice group 56.9 (std.dev=29.2), and for the six icons group 62.4 (std.dev=30.8). The difference between groups was not significant [t(18)=-0.41, n.s.], suggesting that both groups used iPMAN equally often. On average, participants logged in to 2.35 different sites (stdev=0.48, min=2, max=3) with iPMAN, less than our expectation. Despite the instruction to use iPMAN for all sites, participants preferred to use it for popular sites like Gmail and Facebook but not pages visited less frequently. We view this as a finding of interest (see later discussion), rather than a failure to understand instructions.

Efficiency was measured based on the time taken by users to enter their master password. For each participant average time for correct password entry was calculated. Participants entered their iPMAN password in 6.31s on average (std.dev=1.6): 5.80s for the free choice group (std.dev=1.57), and 6.81s for the six icons group (std.dev=1.51). See Fig.3(a). The difference between the groups was not significant [t(18)=-1.46, n.s.]. As is well-known, failing to find a statistically significant difference between groups does not reflect identity. Our result may also reflect a small difference or low statistical power.

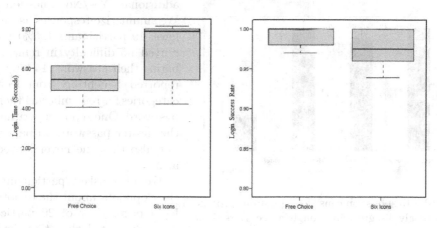

(a) Time to log in with iPMAN   (b) Login success rate with iPMAN

Fig. 3. Login time and success rate across different password rule groups

Effectiveness was measured by number of correct master password entries. Of 1197 total password entries, 1178 succeeded on first attempt (98.4%). For the 19 incorrect password entries, in 11 participants clicked either immediately to the right or left of the correct icon; 5 accidentally clicked the same icon twice; in one the user confused the order of icons. Two of the 19 incorrect entries were consecutive. The login success rate was 98.3% on average (std.dev=1.9%, min=94%, max=100%). There was a significant difference in login success rate between free choice (mean=99.2%, std.dev=1.3%) and six icons group (mean=97.4%, std.dev=2.1%) [t(18)= 2.42, p<.05]. See Fig.3(b). We note that the login success rate was very high in both groups, yielding very low standard deviations, which may affect the significance test. All 19 incorrect logins were made by 10 participants; the other 10 entered their entire master password correctly each time. On average, participants who did not make a mistake logged in 56.6 times (std.dev=28.94, min=31, max=127); those who made a mistake logged in on average 62.7 times (std.dev=30.98, min=34, max=128). There was no correlation between login success rate and number of logins (r(20)=0.084, n.s.).

Questionnaire and Interview. At the end of the study, all participants completed a questionnaire (see [4]). Seven questions were borrowed from an earlier lab-based study on password managers [8], some of which were modified to suit our present study. Fig.4 summarizes responses on a Likert scale (1=strongly disagree; 5=strongly agree). Aggregate scores were: Perceived Security (mean 4.78, std.dev 0.44); Ease of Use (mean 4.45, std.dev 0.52); Perceived Necessity (mean 2.82, std.dev 0.61). Not Giving Control score was: mean 4.50, std.dev 0.76; strongly agree here means participants were fully comfortable with their ability to record, if desired, the resulting site-specific passwords. The free choice and six icons groups did not differ in any of these measures [t(18)<1.18, n.s.].

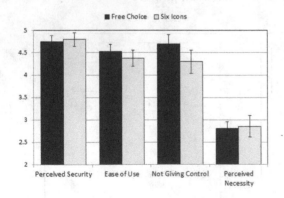

The questionnaire contained additional Yes/No questions. We summarize responses as follows: 19 participants (95%) reported no difficulty in remembering their password; 14 (70%) reported benefiting from icon categories for remembering their password. One reported writing the master password on paper, but also that she never looked at it.

We also asked participants their opinions about the remote login page. Four of 20 participants reported that they had used the remote login feature.

Fig. 4. Response means for question groups. 1=strongly disagree, 5=strongly agree. Bars show std errors.

None found it user-friendly. Participants reported difficulties remembering the web site URL. There were Java-related problems with the page. One participant reported being unable to generate their password with the remote login page. We asked participants if they'd like to continue to use iPMAN after the study. None reported that they would definitely use it; 15 (75%) reported they had not decided yet; 5 (25%) reported that they would definitely not use it. We asked these latter 5 the reason for not using iPMAN furthermore; 4 reported that their original passwords were secure enough.

Memory Persistence. To explore the persistence of memory for master passwords, 20-25 days after the field study ended we invited participants to the lab for a surprise test. All 20 accepted and participated in a test shortly after. We asked each to click their master password. All remembered their password correctly in their first trial although 19 of 20 reported no longer using their iPMAN master password after the field study. The remaining one had continued to use iPMAN.

5   Discussion of Results and Summary Observations

Having collected and reported the user study results, here we analyze and discuss them and their implications for the design of password managers, for conducting user studies on such password manager programs, and also for the specific icon-based graphical password interface of iPMAN. Introducing users to both a new graphical password interface and a password manager makes it hard to separate the effects of each individually. Nonetheless, the results give us the following intuitions packaged as a set of summary observations.

A security analysis is an essential component for a paper exploring usability and security. Fig.1(b) shows the frequency of each icon being selected as a part of master passwords—e.g., the number 7 means that 7 out of 20 or 35% of participants chose "BMW" icon as part of their password. It is a known issue that password schemes allowing free user choice suffer from skewed password distributions. We analyze the passwords collected in our field study with respect to user choice issues. For space reasons, our security analysis is deferred to an extended version [4]. Therein we also present, motivated by our security findings but also of independent interest, a new salt generation method using blind signatures, to protect against offline attacks, decreasing user inconvenience by generating salt significantly faster than earlier work [15].

Users Resist Migrating Their Existing Passwords. A large-scale study conducted in 2007 [10] indicates Internet users have about 25 accounts requiring passwords. The average number of sites our participants logged into with iPMAN was low; they did not follow instructions to migrate all of their passwords to it, and preferred to change their passwords only for frequently visited sites. The convenience of being able to login to multiple sites by entering only a single password is more apparent when so used on larger numbers of accounts. But in iPMAN and similar password managers including those having a text password interface this requires that users have migrated all or most of their old passwords to new ones generated from the master password. Our field study suggests that the short-term hurdle cost of perhaps a few minutes on each site to migrate passwords dominates the perceived longer-term benefit in the minds of users. Another plausible explanation of user resistance is that the "path-of-least-resistance" [11] works against migrating all or most web account passwords. As a result, the impact of the password manager on the web experience of participants was minimal during the field study. This is one reason we believe the perceived necessity score was low and why users were reluctant to continue using iPMAN after the study although they reported that they found iPMAN easy-to-use and secure (in their perception). In the literature, we are not aware of any discussion of the prohibitive nature of this initial one-time cost of migrating passwords. We conjecture that if researchers fail to find an innovative way to reduce the user pain associated with migrating passwords, then the wallet approach to password managers (which avoids migrating passwords) will maintain a major usability advantage over the hashing approach.[6]

There is a Trade-Off between Transportability and Usability. In many existing designs, the available tuning knobs offer a trade-off between security and usability. In password management, there is a third dimension—transportability—which we define as the ability and ease to login from secondary devices other than a user's primary computer. Transportability may be regarded just as one aspect of usability. To explain what we mean by *trade-off*, we first revisit the password wallet approach, which as noted above, has the usability advantage that users can start using it without needing to migrate passwords. On the other hand, it suffers an important deficiency: the master password is useless for login from a secondary machine unless the password wallet is moved to that machine.

In theory, transportability requirements related to password managers can be satisfied by the hashing approach—but not every browser comes with pre-installed password hashing functionality. Thus to support transportability in our field study, we adopted the remote login page method [26]. Our study confirmed previous work [26,8] illustrating usability challenges of the remote login site idea (installing the manager program on the remote machine also raises issues [8]). We thus lean towards the belief that the password hashing approach can address transportability only if the manager is integrated in (all major) browsers rather than implemented as an extension. Otherwise, manually entering site passwords continues to be a more transportable choice (though less usable in other aspects) than using either class of password managers.

Usability Comparison: Master vs. Regular Password. An important advantage of a master password comes from users repeatedly entering the same password time and again for different sites—repetition and habit reinforce memory and usability. This advantage is illustrated by comparing the usability results of our field study on iPMAN with those from the lab study by Bicakci et al. [3] on the stand-alone version of GPI.

---

[6] Our observations differ substantially from those of Yee et al. [31, §7].

Recall that the user interface in iPMAN for master passwords is identical to GPI. The lab study of GPI involved two sessions. First, participants generated passwords with six icons on a GPI interface, then one week later they were invited to a session to login with their GPI passwords; 4 out of 23 forgot their GPI passwords. In contrast in the field study, in a surprise memory test performed 20-25 days after it ended, all participants still remembered their passwords.[7] The difference between the memory performances was significant $[\chi^2(1) = 3.835, p = 0.052]$. We conjecture that the difference is due to participants' repeated rehearsals of their master password while using iPMAN, reinforcing a strong memory of it. In the lab study, the time to enter the correctly remembered password for GPI was 17.5 seconds on average (stdev = 22.30), substantially longer than the average time to login with iPMAN presented in Fig.3(a) $[t(41) = 2.202, p < .05]$. In the final week of the field study, participants entered their iPMAN passwords around 0.5s (on average) faster than the average login time of 6.31s, which also shows that participant login times improved as their experience with the system increased.

It is reasonable to also expect improvements for passwords in regular use as users become familiar with them. For instance, in a field study [28] of the Pass-Go graphical password scheme, login success rates were low in the first three weeks but became stable at around 90% after week 7. Not contradicting the results of previous work, the results of our field study suggest that by habitual use of a single master password across different sites user performance may reach higher levels than when several distinct passwords are used.

Impact of Password Rules on Usability. As another usability result, we observe that forcing users to select six icons did impact the usability of iPMAN as follows. There was no difference between the free choice and six icons groups with respect to login time. But there was a statistically significant difference with respect to login success rate. On the other hand, login success rate was high in both groups (99.2% and 97.4% for free choice and six icons group respectively), and the difference is small (1.8%). We view this as an acceptable usability impact related to the six-icon password rule, albeit lacking a scientific metric.

Comparison of Survey Results. Earlier, we noted the limited number of usability studies on password managers. Using the usability criteria from one exception, Chiasson et al. [8], we put the same survey questions (with minimal necessary changes) to our participants. Our field study results reveal that iPMAN scores well on ease-of-use and perceived security scores which are higher than the scores reported [8] for PwdHash [26] and Password Multiplier [15]. Our survey results also confirm that users are more comfortable if they can learn their site-specific passwords. The only low score for iPMAN is on perceived necessity, which is similarly low for other managers [8].

---

[7] While it is not always appropriate to compare lab and field study results, here the finding that success rates in the lab study were weaker despite its shorter intervening period, appear to only strengthen the observation. Regarding demographics: most participants in both studies were university students with similar web use profiles.

Regarding possible reasons for the low score on perceived necessity in our study, aside from security not being the primary goal of most end users, we conjecture that users are trapped in a vicious downward spiral, in which the small number of web sites the password manager was used for is both cause and effect of low perceived necessity. Our hypothesis, which may be of interest to test in a separate study, is that if we could break the downward spiral and persuade users so that the percentage of a user's passwords migrated to the manager program is increased, the perceived necessity score would also increase.

We conjecture there is a threshold for this migration percentage that, once passed, removes the path-of-least-resistance [11] barrier in favor of continuing with the manager vs. turning back to old passwords.

Limitations. A notable limitation of our study is the small number of users: 20 participants is insufficient, especially for a comprehensive security analysis of user-chosen passwords.

While we highlighted that migration may pose a big challenge to adopting password managers using the hashing approach, this effect may have been amplified by the study design as the users not only had to migrate passwords, but also might feel it necessary to change passwords again after the study as the experimenters gained access to their passwords. It is also possible that part of the reluctance to adopt iPMAN, especially for sensitive accounts, may have been due to a concern about such access to passwords.

The study design involved users adopting both a password manager and a novel graphical password scheme. A design introducing only one of these conditions would allow more convincing conclusions. A future study could compare different user interfaces (e.g., graphical versus text) of password managers.

80% of participants indicated concern about the security of their passwords. Such a concern does not automatically imply security benefits of password managers (e.g., avoidance of password reuse) are understood and appreciated (indeed, 85% also reported reusing passwords). On the other hand, password managers also have usability advantages which may be appreciated more, especially among users who regularly forget passwords. Our study did not ask our participants how often they forgot their passwords. A future study could compare the perceived necessity score and other usability statistics between users who think that they have a password problem and users who already have coping strategies they think work just fine.

6   Conclusion

Our work is the first, to our knowledge, to report in the literature on a field study of a password manager. We believe the knowledge gained will be useful to a broad audience interested in password management. The study found high login success rates and persistent password memory using a manager with an icon-based master password. To counter the observed weakness [4] of user-chosen master passwords—user choice issues now being generally expected in graphical (and text) password schemes which allow user choice—a new method for salt generation is available [4] which supports secondary devices and significantly reduces the waiting time of earlier proposals.

We recognize, as a major obstacle to voluntary widespread use of tools like iPMAN, the secondary importance users give to password security. Another obstacle is the short-term adoption cost, e.g., users must allocate time and attention to migrate existing passwords. We note that "password wallet" approaches have major usability advantages since they do not require that users migrate their passwords. While it is tempting to conclude that the security benefits of a password manager are large, but not fully appreciated by users, we are aware of no clear scientific evidence or convincing metric to support such a claim. It can also be argued, with equal lack of convincing scientific evidence, that users who reject all advice towards increasing password security (typically, to avoid usability penalties) are making a rational choice [16].

Password managers offer to ameliorate a ubiquitous and significant usability issue which also impacts security: requiring users to choose and remember multitudes of passwords. We encourage more research exploring password manager software which stands up to not only security analysis on paper, but critical issues in practice, including password choice and usability as observed in ecologically valid user studies.

Acknowledgements. We thank Hakan Gurbaslar for help in executing the field study, and Robert Biddle, Sonia Chiasson, and anonymous referees for comments that improved the presentation. This research is supported by TUBITAK (The Scientific and Technological Research Council of Turkey) under project number 107E227. The fourth author is Canada Research Chair in Authentication and Computer Security, and acknowledges partial funding from NSERC for the chair, a Discovery Grant, a Discovery Accelerator Supplement, and NSERC ISSNet.

References

1. 1Password, http://agilewebsolutions.com/products/1Password
2. Abadi, M., Bharat, L., Marais, A.: System and method for generating unique passwords. US Patent 6141760 (1997)
3. Bicakci, K., Atalay, N.B., Yuceel, M., Gurbaslar, H., Erdeniz, B.: Towards Usable Solutions to Graphical Password Hotspot Problem. In: 33rd Annual IEEE Int. Computer Software and Applications Conference (2009)
4. Bicakci, K., Atalay, N.B., Yuceel, M., van Oorschot, P.C.: Exploration and Field Study of a Password Manager using Icon-based Passwords. Technical Report, School of Computer Science, Carleton University (April 2011)
5. Bicakci, K., Yuceel, M., Erdeniz, B., Gurbaslar, H., Atalay, N.B.: Graphical passwords as browser extension: Implementation and usability study. In: 3rd IFIP WG 11.11 Int. Conf. on Trust Management (2009)
6. Bonneau, J., Preibusch, S.: The Password Thicket: Technical and Market Failures in Human Authentication on the Web. In: 9th Workshop on the Economics of Information Security, WEIS (2010)1

7. Chiasson, S., Forget, A., Biddle, R., van Oorschot, P.C.: Influencing Users Towards Better Passwords: Persuasive Cued Click-Points. In: BCS-HCI, Liverpool, U.K (2008)

8. Chiasson, S., van Oorschot, P.C., Biddle, R.: A Usability Study and Critique of Two Password Managers. In: USENIX Security (2006)

9. Davis, D., Monrose, F., Reiter, M.: On user choice in graphical password schemes. In: USENIX Security (2004)

10. Florencio, D., Herley, C.: A large-scale study of web password habits. In: 16th Int. Conf. World Wide Web, WWW 2007 (2007)

11. Fogg, B.J.: Persuasive Technologies: Using Computers to Change What We Think and Do. Morgan Kaufmann Publishers, San Francisco (2003)

12. Gaber, E., Gobbons, P., Mattias, Y., Mayer, A.: How to Make Personalized Web Browsing Simple, Secure, and Anonymous. In: Luby, M., Rolim, J.D.P., Serna, M. (eds.) FC 1997. LNCS, vol. 1318, pp. 17–32. Springer, Heidelberg (1997)

13. Govindarajulu, N., Madhvanath, S.: Password management using doodles. In: 9th International Conference on Multimodal Interfaces, ICMI (November 2007)

14. Guttmann, P.: Manuscript chapters, Usable Security,
http://www.cs.auckland.ac.nz/~pgut001/pubs/usability.pdf

15. Halderman, J.A., Waters, B., Felten, E.W.: A convenient method for securely managing passwords. In: 14th International Conf. on World Wide Web, WWW 2005 (2005)

16. Herley, C.: So long, and no thanks for the externalities: The rational rejection of security advice by users. In: NSPW 2009 (2009)

17. Jermyn, I., Mayer, A., Monrose, F., Reiter, M., Rubin, A.: The design and analysis of graphical passwords. In: 8th USENIX Security (1999)

18. Jung, E.: Passwordmaker, http://passwordmaker.mozdev.org

19. Lastpass, http://lastpass.com/

20. Kintsch, W.: Models for free recall and recognition. In: Norman, D.A. (ed.) Models of Human Memory. Academic Press, New York (1970)

21. Mac OS X Reference Library. KeyChain Services Programming Guide,
http://developer.apple.com/library/mac/navigation

22. OpenID Foundation, http://openid.net/

23. van Overschelde, P., Rawson, K.A., Dunlosky, J.: Category norms: An updated and expanded version of the Battig and Montague. norms. Journal of Memory and Language 50, 289–335 (2004)

24. Password Safe, http://passwordsafe.sourceforge.net/

25. la Poutre, J.: Password composer,
http://www.xs4all.nl/~jlpoutre/BoT/Javascript/PasswordComposer/

26. Ross, B., Jackson, C., Miyake, N., Boneh, D., Mitchell, J.: Stronger password authentication using browser extensions. In: USENIX Security (2005)

27. Sun, S.-T., Boshmaf, Y., Hawkey, K., Beznosov, K.: A Billion Keys, but Few Locks: The Crisis of Web Single Sing-On. In: NSPW 2010 (2010)

28. Tao, H., Adams, C.: Pass-Go: A proposal to improve the usability of graphical passwords. International Journal of Network Security 7(2) (2008)

29. Thorpe, J., van Oorschot, P.C.: Human-Seeded Attacks and Exploiting Hot-Spots in Graphical Passwords. In: USENIX Security (2008)

30. Wiedenbeck, S., Waters, J., Birget, J., Brodskiy, A., Memon, N.: PassPoints: Design and longitudinal evaluation of a graphical password system. International Journal of Human-Computer Studies 63(1-2) (2005)

31. Yee, K., Sitaker, K.: Passpet: convenient password management and phishing protection. In: SOUPS (2006)

Ethical Issues in E-Voting Security Analysis

David G. Robinson[1] and J. Alex Halderman[2]

[1] Information Society Project, Yale Law School
david.robinson@yale.edu
[2] The University of Michigan
jhalderm@eecs.umich.edu

Abstract. Research about weaknesses in deployed electronic voting systems raises a variety of pressing ethical concerns. In addition to ethical issues common to vulnerability research, such as the potential harms and beneifts of vulnerability disclosure, electronic voting researchers face questions that flow from the unique and important role voting plays in modern democratic societies. Should researchers worry that their own work (not unlike the flaws they study) could sway an election outcome? When elected officials authorize a security review, how should researchers address the conflicted interests of these incumbent politicians, who may have powerful incentives to downplay problems, and might in principle be in a position to exploit knowledge about vulnerabilities when they stand for re-election? How should researchers address the risk that identifying specific flaws will lead to a false sense of security, after those particular problems have been resolved? This paper makes an early effort to address these and other questions with reference to experience from previous e-voting security reviews. We hope our provisional analysis will help practicing researchers anticipate and address ethical issues in future studies.

1 Introduction

Over the past seven years, computer security researchers have conducted more than a dozen significant studies of vulnerabilities in fielded electronic voting systems (e.g., [2–5, 7, 11, 12, 15, 18, 21–23]). Like many computer security studies, these projects have focused on identifying concrete technological problems and solutions. Yet voting occupies a special place in democratic public life—its integrity is of common concern to all citizens—and security analyses of voting systems can shape a democratic state's actual—and perceived—legitimacy. In this paper, we seek to identify, and describe, some of the ethical choices that are inevitably relevant to security analysis of e-voting systems.

We begin in Section 2 by considering high-level questions: whether researchers should perform such studies at all, and whether, in so doing, they should be concerned with the political consequences of their findings. In Section 3, we consider some of the quandaries that arise when obtaining access to voting systems through means such as leaks, anonymous sources, and direct government authorization of studies. In Section 4, we consider the potential for collateral damage

G. Danezis, S. Dietrich, and K. Sako (Eds.): FC 2011 Workshops, LNCS 7126, pp. 119–130, 2012.
© IFCA/Springer-Verlag Berlin Heidelberg 2012

during the process of studying real systems. In Section 5, we consider issues that arise after the research is complete, such as whether, when, and how to publicly disclose the findings. We conclude, in Section 6, that there is ample room for further inquiry into the ethical issues surrounding voting machine security research. We also suggest that the computer security community might achieve more, in the future, by becoming more involved in public policy debates at an earlier stage—before, rather than after, potentially vulnerable technologies have been adopted.

2   High-Level Questions

2.1   Whether to Perform Such Studies?

Researchers who aim to improve e-voting security must consider whether experimental evaluation of the security of deployed systems actually advances this goal. Many researchers believe that paperless electronic voting machines are inherently insecure, because they lack the transparency or verifiability necessary to prevent attacks by dishonest insiders. Those who accept this view might argue that empirically determining that a particular paperless system is insecure teaches us nothing.

Some in the field, such as Rebecca Mercuri [16], have argued that evaluations that point out specific security problems can actually make the general problem worse. These studies allow officials or vendors to correct some of the immediate problems, then claim that the systems have been tested and fully secured. Moreover, where an evaluation fails to find problems, such a negative result might be hailed by officials or vendors as confirmation of the system's security. Of course, while negative results are a favorable indicator of voting system security, this kind of analysis *cannot* definitively establish that a system is secure: adversaries could always be smarter, luckier, or better funded than testers, and find problems they did not.

Can researchers overcome these objections? One rationale for participating in the e-voting security evaluations is that demonstrating specific security problems may be more persuasive than arguing about abstract architectural weaknesses. Another is that if policymakers, having already heard the arguments about architectural weaknesses, still insist on using the machines, discovering vulnerabilities can provide new information with which to assess the machines' suitability. It may also allow the specific problems to be corrected before they can be maliciously exploited, although in some cases machines have been used in elections with documented vulnerabilities unpatched.

Empirical security evaluations help close the gap between theory and practice, by providing case studies in *how* security fails in practice, in addition to confirmation that it does. Security vulnerabilities remain dangerous even if a voting system provides a paper record of each vote and audits this record to detect fraud—even when they are detected, security or integrity breaches in real elections can still compromise privacy or disrupt elections. By better understanding the kinds of vulnerabilities that arise in deployed systems and seeking their underlying causes, we can hope to strengthen future voting systems, both paperless and not.

2.2   Whether to Consider Near-Term Political Consequences?

The principal goal of electronic voting security research is to ensure high-integrity elections. But in the near term, disclosing findings also has the potential to distort the fortunes of political actors, and the course of political debate, in the places that use these systems. By the same token, the decision to remain silent about known problems may have important political results. Electronic voting vulnerabilities, once detected, may place their discoverers in an inherently political position. Disclosing problems may not only increase the chance they will be remedied (or, the risk that they may empower attackers), but also have immediate and profound effects on voter confidence and turnout.

Even when they are careful to avoid making any claims about the actual integrity of past elections, researchers who identify security concerns in an incumbent voting technology do give voters reason to doubt the legitimacy of that technology, and of the results it has produced. Recent studies of voting system integrity—because they have tended to find major flaws, rather than to offer support for the security or integrity of field-deployed systems—have tended to offer at least implicit or indirect reinfrocement for the electroal integrity concerns of losing candidates and their supporters.[1]

Given these factors, choices made by electronic voting researchers might at the margin change who wins and who loses an election. They could, for example, influence whether a U.S.-aligned political faction in another country does or does not prevail over its domestic rivals. Whatever one's normative views about war and peace, welfare policy, and all the other important choices made by elected officials, these secondary effects of the voting research could easily be the work's most important near-term impact.

It might be tempting for electronic voting researchers to attempt to anticipate, and tailor their actions around, these potential collateral impacts of their work. But we believe this would be a mistake. Political prediction is notoriously difficult even for its foremost practitioners, and effects that help or hurt political incumbents will recede in importance, over time, as different parties trade off in power. Unintended consequences could cut in any number of directions, so researchers could only speculate about what the second-order effects of their work will be.

More broadly, accurate democratic representation based on an honest count of votes is a worthwhile goal in its own right. Voting itself represents a kind of epistemic modesty that denies in principle that any one political actor can

---

[1] See, *e.g.*, [19] (In a Democratic Senate primary, the losing candidate describes the "well-documented unreliability and unverifiability of the voting machines used in South Carolina."); [6]("At last week's hearing, [losing candidate] Rawl trotted out a parade of forensic, academic and computer experts who pointed to security, software and statistical irregularities.").

know what is best for the system as a whole. To speculate about the second-order impact of increased democratic integrity—let alone basing one's actions on such impact—would itself be an anti-democratic choice. Where the release of reserach findings would create a significant risk of physical violence or other clear and concrete harm, researchers might reasonably decide to keep their results temporarily private. But such a choice should be the exception, rather than the rule, and we believe researchers should not pay condition their disclosures on the routine ebb and flow of electoral politics.

3   Obtaining Access

Researchers typically aim to provide a security evaluation that is independent of vendor and official influence. When access is limited, and cooperation with these parties enables otherwise impossible research, researchers must be vigilant to retain as much independence as is feasible—and transparent about the extent to which their end product is informed or shaped by other actors. If vulnerabilities are found, there is a further ethical question about disclosure: Is it ethical for researchers to bind themselves not to disclose such vulnerabilities to the public? On the other hand, how should researchers approach the ethical problems that can arise when their access comes through channels that are not officially approved?

In a typical e-voting security evaluation, researchers analyze a system, design specific attacks against it, and then attempt them in a demonstration or testing environment that mirrors the conditions under which system is actually used. This requires detailed technical information about how the system functions. In practice, researchers obtain this information by analyzing the system's source code or, where source code is not available, by reverse engineering voting machines. Obtaining the necessary access to voting machines or source code is one of the major prerequisite challenges of e-voting research, since vendors and system developers have historically been reluctant to support independent security reviews [17].

There are three main ways researchers have obtained such access: through leaks and anonymous sources (e.g., [11, 15, 22]), through government-sponsored studies (e.g., [4, 21]), and by purchasing government-surplus machines (e.g., [2, 7]).

3.1   Leaks and Anonymous Sources

Leaks and anonymous sources provided access for some of the earliest studies. In 2003, Kohno et al. [15] analyzed source code for components of the Diebold voting system software; this code had been posted to the company's public FTP site, where it was discovered and retrieved by e-voting activist Bev Harris [14]. In 2007, Feldman et al. [11] studied a Diebold AccuVote-TS paperless DRE machine after they were given unrestricted hands-on access to the machine by a nongovernmental source, who provided the machine on condition of anonymity. In 2010, Wolchok et al. [22] analyzed the electronic voting machines used in India by studying a machine given to coauthor Hari Prasad by a government source under condition of anonymity.

Working with leaks and anonymous sources raises several concerns. One is legality: Is the source lawfully permitted to provide the machine? Do intellectual property protections preclude reverse engineering or working with obtained source code? Honoring promises of anonymity may create further risks; for instance, Indian researcher Hari Prasad spent over a week in a Mumbai jail and faces an ongoing legal battle to protect the identity of his source [20]. Researchers should consider whether legal risks may limit their ability to thoroughly evaluate system or disclose their findings.

Another concern is the source's motives. Researchers should questions whether sources that offer to provide or leak material have political motivations. We have argued that researchers have at most a limited duty to predict the secondary political effects of e-voting analyses, but they should be wary about the integrity and authenticity of the machines under study. Sources could hypothetically tamper with them to make them appear more vulnerable or plant evidence of past tampering, jeopardizing the integrity of the study's results. This is particular a concern when working with unknown sources or sources that request anonymity, since readers of the subsequent study will not be able to judge for themselves whether the source is trustworthy. In any case, it creates an extra duty of care for researchers, and it may necessitate clear disclaimers about the provenance of the study material.

3.2 State-Sponsored Studies

Studies sponsored by government entities raise another set of concerns. State-sponsored studies, such as the California secretary of state's Top-to-Bottom Review [21] and the Ohio secretary of state's Project EVEREST [4], provided researchers access to hardware and software for multiple e-voting systems. States' can often compel voting system vendors to provide source code access (for example, California threatened vendors with decertification if they did not), which simplifies the technical aspects of these studies and removes some kinds of legal risk for the researchers; however, cooperating with elected officials leads to other quandaries.

Working with government sources requires clear ground rules about how the study will be performed and how the results will be disclosed. These ground rules often take the form of a legal agreement between the researchers and public officials. Researchers need to ensure that these rules allow them to maintain their independence. If researchers are asked to sign a nondisclosure agreement, they should ensure that the terms allow them to disclose problems they might find, and do not overly restrict their ability to perform future work.

Researchers may also be asked to allow the government to review the findings prior to making them public, or to grant the government the ability to designate certain findings as confidential and prevent public disclosure. Disclosing vulnerabilities to officeholders who were elected (and may face reelection) using the same insecure technologies is deeply troubling, particularly if the vulnerabilities are not fully disclosed to the public and if these officeholders have the authority to decide whether the election technology will continue to be used. Apart from the opportunity to exploit security flaws, public officials may have a strong incentive to downplay information that could cast doubt on the legitimacy of their own past or future elections. Researchers should ensure from the outset that there are clear rules that set appropriate conditions for disclosure, and that set a definitive deadline for all results to become public.

Official studies may require researchers to operate within constraints not applicable to real-world attackers. For example, researchers may be asked to operate within tighter time constraints, while real attackers have potentially unconstrained time to complete their attacks. Such constraints magnify the risk that the study may fail to uncover the full extent of problems. Where conditions are imposed, researchers must decide whether or not it is on balance worthwhile to proceed. In any event, researchers who agree to conduct limited analyses of voting systems should disclose these limitations in their reports, and should emphasize that their findings *cannot* establish that the systems under study are secure, since real-life attackers need not play by similar rules.

3.3   Government-Surplus Equipment

Government-surplus equipment has been obtained by researchers in a number of cases. When Buncombe County, North Carolina replaced its Sequoia AVC Advantage DREs in 2007, Princeton professor Andrew Appel purchased a lot of five machines for $82 [1]; these machines were the subjects of studies by Appel et al. [2] and Checkoway et al. [7]. In 2009, researcher Jeremy Epstein and colleagues purchased two Sequoia AVC Edge DREs for $100 after they were sold by Williamburg, Virginia after the state banned paperless DREs. Halderman and Feldman [13] performed a brief analysis of one of these devices and showed that they could easily alter its software (reprogramming it to play Pac-Man).

In many ways, government-surplus equipment raises fewer concerns that materials from other sources. Such machines often carry less legal encumbrance, and, depending on the chain of custody between government use and the researchers, they may raise fewer doubts about whether the machines under study are the same as the machines actually in use. However, other concerns can arise in later research phases when working with machines that have been used in real elections and may still contain real vote data.

4   Accidents During Analysis

Once researchers have obtained access to machines or source code, the process of security analysis consists of understanding the behavior of the system, identifying vulnerabilities, conceiving attacks, constructing attack demonstrations, and performing experiments to confirm that the attacks work. A number of ethical issues can arise during these efforts as a result of accidental access to data and to other systems.

4.1   Accessing Confidential Voter Information

One concern that may arise when analyzing voting equipment that has been used in real elections is that confidential voter information may remain present on the machines. Whether machines are provided by government or nongovernmental sources or purchased government-surplus, the sources may fail to completely sanitize the storage before turning the equipment over to researchers.

Machines obtained in the India voting study [22] and the AVC Advantage investigations [2, 11] (among several instances), contained vote data from the last elections in which they were used. In several cases the researchers discovered attacks that could deanonymize votes based on this data. Protecting the confidentiality of voters' ballots in instances like these requires researchers to take special precautions to prevent the data they recover from the machines from being publicly disclosed. Researchers may be ethically obligated to erase the data as soon as they discover it (especially if they cannot ensure its security), though this may be complicated by legal requirements for election data retention.

4.2   Risks of Collateral Damage

Other issues arise when testing *Internet* voting systems, such as in the recent public trial of a web-based voting system orchestrated by the Washington, D.C. Board of Elections and Ethics [9]. Researchers from the University of Michigan who participated in the trial [23] (including the second coauthor of this paper) encountered several unexpected ethical quandaries.

The D.C. election officials organized a mock election prior to the start of real voting. They claimed this system was disconnected from unrelated election facilities and promised not to take legal action against well-intentioned efforts to demonstrate security problems in the system. The researchers were able to penetrate the system and take control of the election server, changing votes and compromising ballot secrecy. They were also able to penetrate several other pieces of network infrastructure (routers, switches, and a terminal server) located on the subnet that election officials had initially designated for testing. The researchers noticed that officials were still in the process of configuring this equipment, but they continued their attack on the belief that the insecure components were being prepared for use in D.C.'s real voting system. After the public trial concluded, the researchers learned that these devices were in fact unrelated to the voting trial, and were being prepared for use elsewhere in the D.C. government network—they had discovered a critical security breach, but arguably one outside the intended scope of the testing. Researchers have ethical duty to limit potential for unintentional damage to unrelated equipment like this.

4.3   Risks of Unintentionally Disrupting Real Elections

The Michigan researchers made another unexpected discovery during the D.C. voting trial: they found that election officials, in preparing and testing the system, had uploaded to the test system the credentials that were to be used by real voters following the trial. The researchers only discovered that these credentials were real after they had downloaded them over an insecure connection and transferred them to their own systems.

The researchers in this case had no intention of interfering with a real election, but, had D.C. officials not decided as a result of the trial to refrain from using the system in the real election, the researchers' access to these credentials would likely have constituted an unrecoverable security breach: Any party with access to the credentials would have been able to cast votes on behalf of the real voters, and the researchers had inadvertently exposed these voters to risks of being by malicious third parties. Issuing new credentials was impractical, since they had to be delivered to voters by postal mail, and it was too late to send a new batch. Researchers should weigh the risk of unintentionally disrupting real elections against the potential benefits of participation, and take steps to minimize such risk.

5   Disclosure

After the technical work of evaluation has been completed, researchers need to document their findings and decide what to disclose, to whom to disclose it, and when and how to disclose it. Some of the ethical considerations involved are common to other kinds of security vulnerability disclosures, and others are particular to e-voting security research.

5.1   What to Disclose?

In deciding what to disclose, security researchers must balance the need to convincingly convey the dangers they have found against the potential for making those problems worse by providing details that could aid real attackers. In e-voting research, this problem is complicated by the nature of the decision-making process involved. Researchers could choose to describe certain problems or details only to election officials and vendors, in an effort to limit the potential for misuse. However, election officials and voters have different incentives—officials suffer adverse results from the *appearance* of problems with the voting systems, whereas voters suffer from the existence of such problems, whether visibile or not. Achieving greater security sometimes requires convincing voters that the system is vulnerable, which argues for wider disclosure.

Convining the public that security problems exist does not necessarily require full disclosure of the details of those problems. In practice, researchers often choose to illustrate the problems by creating demonstration attacks that they can perform for officials and journalists and convey to the broader public on video (e.g., [7, 11, 22]).

Researchers have rarely chosen to release full source code for these demonstration attacks. Instead, demonstration videos typically provide evidence that the problems exist without conveying all the technical details required to exploit them. While this practices makes its somewhat more difficult for malicious parties to carry out the attacks, it cuts against the academic norm that research results should be shared in a form allowing reproduction, and it requires voters to take the researchers' word about the findings.

Advocates of full disclosure (and of "responsible disclosure", which gives vendors some time to rectify the problem before making all details public [8]) argue that these practices put added pressure on vendors to produce timely fixes, since they ensure that real attackers will have the information needed to exploit the problem. This argument seems less compelling in the e-voting context, where effectively securing systems like paperless DREs may require replacing them entirely. The governments that own these machines often lack the funds or political will to do so—and, as a result, systems with known vulnerabilities remain in widespread use. For example, Maryland continues to use the Diebold AccuVote-TS DRE that was discredited by researchers in 2005 [11]. This would probably still be the case even if the authors of that study had made attacks even easier by publishing their voting machine virus source code.

5.2   Disclosing Negative Results

If researchers examine a voting system in secret and are unable to discover a way to attack it, should they publicize this fact? On one hand it seems intellectually dishonest to suppress results like this, and it may lead other researchers to waste effort attempting the same thing. On the other hand, as we discussed earlier, this kind of negative says very little about the security of the system, and it may be misrepresented by others to argue that the system has been tested and found to be *fully* secure. We know of no instance where credible researchers have announced a negative e-voting test result.

5.3   When to Disclose?

Unlike most systems studied in security research, election systems are generally used only a few times a year, during elections that are scheduled long in advance. This schedule significantly impacts decisions about when to disclose vulnerabilities. Revealing problems so soon before an election that there is not time to implement any effective remedies would create risks without significant countervailing benefits. On the other hand, if researchers know about problems and there is sufficient time to mitigate them, they may have an obligation to publicly disclose them. Balancing these factors requires, in part, reasoning about what remedies can be practiacally achieved in time.

Researchers might consider giving election officials or voting system vendors advance notice about their findings prior to public disclosure, to allow them to begin implementing mitigations. Though sometimes beneficial, this approach is problemmatic. Researchers who studied systems without authorization may run the risk of political retribution or lawsuits attempting to suppress publication of their results. The mitigations that are implemented may be weaker in the absense of public pressure from voters. The risk of insider attacks, one of the most important categories of threats against voting systems, is certainly not reduced by disclosing new attacks only to insiders. For these reasons, researchers often choose not to disclose problems to officials and vendors in advance of publication.

5.4   Attacking Real Elections

One course of action that is clearly unethical is for researchers to exploit vulnerabilities they have discovered to attack real elections. People outside the research community sometimes suggest that researchers should change an election outcome to an obviously incorrect result in order to demonstrate conclusively that the system is vulnerable in practice. Not would not only criminal, but also a subversion of the democratic process that this body of research serves.

6   Conclusions

We have tried to articulate the scope of ethical concern for electronic voting security researchers, and to describe some of the issues that arise within that scope. Our map of this ethical terrain is far from perfect, but we hope it can be useful—both to researchers facing ethical quandaries, and to the lay public as it considers the value and impact of security research into electronic voting.

This paper explores ethical choices that actually confront today's researchers. Arguably, however, the most important ethical lesson of the electronic voting experience is about what might have been. The troubled modern history of electronic voting owes a great deal to the 2002 passage of the Help America Vote Act,[10] which gave states time-limited funds to purchase computerized voting equipment without setting meaningful standards for its security. Policymakers assumed, or allowed themselves to be persuaded, that widely sold paperless electronic voting machines were as secure as their manufacturers claimed. The vulnerabilities that have since been found may surprise Congress and the public, but they are much less surprising to experts in the field. HAVA's deep flaws reflect our research community's failure to intervene effectively in the public policy debate. In the future, as legislatures consider computerized approaches to emerging challenges in healthcare, defense, and other areas, computer security researchers should do all they can to get out ahead of possible security problems, and to dissuade policymakers from indulging in the kind of wishful thinking that generated the electronic voting morass of the last eight years.

References

1. Appel, A.W.: How I Bought Used Voting Machines on the Internet (February 7, 2007), http://www.cs.princeton.edu/~appel/avc/
2. Appel, A., Ginsburg, M., Hursti, H., Kernighan, B.W., Richards, C.D., Tan, G., Venetis, P.: The New Jersey Voting-Machine Lawsuit and the AVC Advantage DRE Voting Machine. In: Proc. Electronic Voting Technology Workshop/Workshop on Trustworthy Elections (EVT/WOTE) (2009)
3. Aviv, A., Cerný, P., Clark, S., Cronin, E., Shah, G., Sherr, M., Blaze, M.: Security Evaluation of ES&S Voting Machines and Election Management System. In: Proc. USENIX/ACCURATE Electronic Voting Technology Workshop (EVT) (2008)
4. Brunner, J., et al.: Ohio Secretary of State's Evaluation & Validation of Election-Related Equipment, Standards & Testing (EVEREST) (December 2007)

5. Butler, K., Enck, W., Hursti, H., McLaughlin, S., Traynor, P., McDaniel, P.: Systemic Issues in the Hart InterCivic and Premier Voting Systems: Reflections on Project EVEREST. In: Proc. USENIX/ACCURATE Electronic Voting Technology Workshop (EVT) (2008)

6. Carney, E.N.: Voting Without a Net in South Carolina. National Journal (June 21, 2010), http://www.nationaljournal.com/njonline/rg_20100621_7815.php

7. Checkoway, S., Feldman, A.J., Kantor, B., Alex Halderman, J., Felten, E.W., Shacham, H.: Can DREs Provide Long-Lasting Security? The Case of Return-Oriented Programming and the AVC Advantage. In: Jefferson, D., Hall, J.L., Moran, T. (eds.) Proc. USENIX/ ACCURATE Electronic Voting Technology Workshop (EVT) (August 2009)

8. Claburn, T.: Google Seeks Redefinition of Responsible Disclosure. InformationWeek (July 2010),
http://www.informationweek.com/news/smb/security/showArticle.jhtml?article1cleID=226100117

9. Epstein, J., et al.: D.C's Web Voting Test, the Hackers Were the Good Guys. Washington Post (October 2010),
http://voices.washingtonpost.com/local-opinions/2010/10/in_dcs_web_voting_test_the_hac.html

10. Fail, B.: HAVA's Unintended Consequences: A Lesson for Next Time. Yale Law Journal 116 (2006), http://www.yalelawjournal.org/pdf/116-2/Fail.pdf

11. Feldman, A.J., Alex Halderman, J., Felten, E.W.: Security Analysis of the Diebold AccuVote-TS Voting Machine. In: Proc. USENIX/ACCURATE Electronic Voting Technology Workshop (EVT), Boston, MA (August 2007)

12. Gonggrijp, R., Hengeveld, W.-J.: Studying the Nedap/Groenendaal ES3B Voting Computer: A Computer Security Perspective. In: Proc. USENIX/ACCURATE Electronic Voting Technology Workshop (EVT) (2007)

13. Alex Halderman, J., Feldman, A.J.: Pac-Man on the Sequoia AVC-Edge DRE Voting Machine (August 2010), http://www.cse.umich.edu/~jhalderm/pacman/

14. Harris, B.: System Integrity Flaw Discovered At Diebold Elections System. Scoop (Februaary 10, 2003), http://www.scoop.co.nz/stories/HL0302/S00052.htm

15. Kohno, T., Stubblefield, A., Rubin, A.D., Wallach, D.S.: Analysis of an Electronic Voting System. In: Proc. IEEE Symposium on Security and Privacy, Oakland, CA, pp. 27–40 (May 2004)

16. Mercuri, R.: Trust the Vote? Not in DC! OpEdNews (November 8, 2010),
http://www.opednews.com/articles/Trust-the-vote-Not-in-DC-by-Rebecca-Mercuri-101108-990.html

17. Paul, R.: E-vothing Bendor Blocks Security Audit with Legal Threats. ars technica (2008),
http://arstechnica.com/tech-policy/news/2008/03/e-voting-blocks-e-voting-security-audit-with-legal-threat.ars

18. Proebstel, E., Riddle, S., Hsu, F., Cummins, J., Oakley, F., Stanionis, T., Bishop, M.: An Analysis of the Hart Intercivic DAU eSlate. In: Proc. USENIX/ACCURATE Electronic Voting Technology Workshop (EVT) (2007)

19. Vic Rawl for U.S. Senate. Statement of Judge Vic Rawl (June 14, 2010),
http://www.vicrawl.com/vicrawl/post/1023-statement-of-judge-vic-rawl

20. Tyre, J.: 2010 Pioneer Award Winner Hari Prasad Defends India's Democracy. EFF Deeplinks Blog (November 1, 2010),
https://www.eff.org/deeplinks/2010/11/2010-pioneer-award-winner-hari-prasad-defends

21. Wagner, D.A., et al.: California Secretary of State's Top-to-Bottom Review (TTBR) of Electronic Voting Systems (July 2007)
22. Wolchok, S., Wustrow, E., Alex Halderman, J., Prasad, H.K., Kankipati, A., Sakhamuri, S.K., Yagati, V., Gonggrijp, R.: Security Analysis of India's Electronic Voting Machines. In: Proc. 17th ACM Conference on Computer and Communications Security (CCS), Chicago, IL (Oct ober 2010)
23. Wustrow, E., Wolchok, S., Isabel, D., Alex Halderman, J.: Security Analysis of the Washington, D.C. Internet Voting System (2010) (in preparation)

Computer Security Research with Human Subjects: Risks, Benefits and Informed Consent

Maritza L. Johnson, Steven M. Bellovin, and Angelos D. Keromytis

Columbia University, Computer Science Department
{maritzaj,smb,angelos}@cs.columbia.edu

Abstract. Computer security research frequently entails studying real computer systems and their users; studying deployed systems is critical to understanding real world problems, so is having would-be users test a proposed solution. In this paper we focus on three key concepts in regard to ethics: risks, benefits, and informed consent. Many researchers are required by law to obtain the approval of an ethics committee for research with human subjects, a process which includes addressing the three concepts focused on in this paper. Computer security researchers who conduct human subjects research should be concerned with these aspects of their methodology regardless of whether they are required to by law, it is our ethical responsibility as professionals in this field. We augment previous discourse on the ethics of computer security research by sparking the discussion of how the nature of security research may complicate determining how to treat human subjects ethically. We conclude by suggesting ways the community can move forward.

Keywords: Security research, human subjects, responsible conduct, ethics review committee, institutional review board.

1 Introduction

Computer security research frequently entails studying real computer systems and their users. Studying deployed systems is critical to understanding real world problems, so is having would-be users test a potential solution. Oftentimes obtaining these data means interacting with a user, or measuring some aspect of their device. For example, data collection could require installing monitoring software on a user's personal device, instrumenting a website, or conducting a laboratory study. In many cases computer security researchers are doing human subjects research, which is obvious if there is direct interaction with a user, but may also be the case if the collected data was generated by a human. Regardless, it is important for researchers to consider the relationship between the users and the research to ensure the ethical treatment of users.

In this paper we focus on three key concepts in regard to the ethical treatment of users: risks, benefits, and informed consent. These concepts have been used to evaluate the ethics of research in other disciplines and were introduced by the Declaration of Helsinki. They are also widely used by ethics review committees

G. Danezis, S. Dietrich, and K. Sako (Eds.): FC 2011 Workshops, LNCS 7126, pp. 131–137, 2012.

and institutional review boards (IRB). Risk refers to the possibility that something negative will happen to the user as a result of the research. Benefits can be viewed as a something that could positively affect the user, or positively affect a larger population that the user is a member of. Informed consent typically means that the purpose and process of the research are explained to the user, along with the risks and benefits, to allow them to make the decision whether to participate. Researchers may be legally obligated to consider these concepts depending on their location and the nature of the research. In the United States, for example, human subjects research must be evaluated by an IRB, a committee tasked with ensuring people are treated ethically.

As computer security researchers, regardless of whether a committee review is required, we should explore what these concepts mean in regard to our research. Our goal with this paper is to identify some areas for future discussion, argue why our community should take the lead on these concepts, and suggest initial first steps. In the context of computer security research ethics, this paper is concerned with the ethical treatment of human subjects; though the discussion of informed consent, risks, and benefits may be applicable to computer security research that does not involve human subjects in a traditional sense.

Prior work has mentioned this topic as an important piece of the larger discussion of computer security ethics [5]. It's been suggested that perhaps IRBs and ethics committees are in a better position than program committees to provide external ethical review of research [2]. While it may be true that program committees are ill-equipped to conduct an ethical review, based on timing and expertise, turning the issue to the IRB is not an ideal approach. We suggest the community establish best practices for doing human subjects research, similar what has been suggested for vulnerability research [13],

The Ethical Impact Assessment (EIA) framework was introduced to guide the process of determining the potential risks and benefits for stakeholders [10]. The framework is motivated by the same guiding principles that have been used in medical and psychological research [14]. The EIA is a useful starting point for bringing concepts like informed consent and beneficence to the attention of researchers. This paper contributes to the discussion by encouraging researchers to consider how computer security research is the same as medical and psychological research, and how it is different. Exploring these questions will help researchers attain a better understanding of how to apply the concepts of informed consent, risks, and benefits. Usable security researchers have relevant experience, most have interacted with an IRB and have at least a basic understanding of the application of these concepts. They are also able to use their own research as case studies to understand how the research compares to other fields [4]. Since an ethics course is rarely a required part of computer science curriculum, descriptions of how to design a study and how to work with an IRB are instructive [7], as are descriptions of what qualifies as human subjects research [8].

2   Computer Security Research with Human Subjects

As researchers it is in our best interests to determine how risks, benefits, and informed consent apply to our research. We have the deepest knowledge of the area, however, may not have sufficient experience in applied ethics to immediately determine suitable guidelines. We ought to leverage other fields when possible, since this is an issue for other disciplines as well. A step toward achieving this goal is to understand how our research compares to other fields.

To continue the discussion of computer security research with human subjects we ought to compare and contrast our field with medical and behavioral research, the two primary fields of human subjects research. To give a few examples of how our research may differ, in our research there may be the need to collect large amounts of potentially sensitive data, observe login credentials, actively attack the subject, or obfuscate the true purpose of the study [4]. It is reasonable to ask whether our research is different in practice, since many of these examples appear to be quite similar to medical or psychology research. A question that ought to be addressed directly.

Ethics committees and IRBs are tasked with protecting the welfare of human subjects, this includes evaluating whether subjects are sufficiently informed of the risks and benefits of the research, whether the potential risks have been minimized as much as possible, and if expected benefits outweigh the potential risks. Additional factors are considered, but these represent most of the largest concerns. Given that this is an area of expertise for IRB members, but not necessarily for researchers, why would we suggest our community take an active role in discussing how these terms apply to our research? IRBs clearly have expertise in areas that security researchers do not, but it would be a mistake to rely on the existing structure to be the primary source of ethical guidance.

We should look beyond the IRB because, we conjecture, few IRBs have a member with sufficient technical expertise to thoroughly review computer security research. IRBs have deep roots in medical research, other fields that conduct human subjects research have a history of attempting to distinguish themselves from medical research [9,16]. Many institutions have responded by creating a non-medical IRB. However, given the nascency of security research with human subjects, and the wide array of expertise IRBs are expected to have, it's unclear how many IRBs have adapted their membership to include the necessary expertise.

2.1   Risks

Determining the continuum of risks that may be present in computer security human subjects research is critical, and may benefit ethical decision making for other areas as well. Comprehension of the risks involved is an essential part of IRB review, and is also essential to the primary schools of ethics, consequentialism and deontological. Due to the medical origins of regulations guiding human subjects research, behavioral science researchers have aimed to distinguish themselves from biomedical researchers. Behavioral researchers have asserted that the risks involved in their studies tend to be qualitative, compared to the physical nature of biomedical research [12]. The types of risks include physical, psychological, social, economic, legal, and dignity [15]. Computer security research is more like behavioral research in the sense that the risks typically aren't physical, and can be difficult to quantify and to describe.

In order to set forth a continuum of risks, we need to understand the extremes: what are the characteristics of research that involves minimal risk, and what are the characteristics of research the poses the greatest risks?

2.2   Benefits

Expected benefits of the research ought to be considered in terms of the human who directly participated, as well as the potential benefits to the general users. In medical research, the participants may benefit from participating in a clinical trial for a condition they have, especially when effective treatment is not otherwise available. The direct benefit of psychology research sometimes includes a better understanding of oneself. Computer security studies seem to be more aligned with psychology research, where self-education can be a major benefit of participation. However, the benefit of knowing more about computer security may prove to be quite useful, like when knowledge such as how to avoid a phishing attack can be imparted [11].

2.3   Informed Consent

Informed consent has two primary facets, the first is that the participant is presented with the potential risks and benefits of participation, the second is that the participant is given an opportunity to decide whether to participate. Important differences may exist for our field with the first aspect. Empirical studies have shown that the typical user has an incorrect mental model of basic security primitives [17], and the execution of common attacks like phishing. If they are asked to install monitoring software on their personal device, can they be expected to properly evaluate the risks of participating unless the potential risk is very clearly explained in layman terms? IRB review evaluates whether the consent form is understandable to potential subjects, how do we ensure that both parties comprehend the necessary details? Is a text-based consent form effective? Researchers from other fields have attempted to evaluate the effectiveness of various mediums [1]. In some cases it may be useful to engage in a conversation where the researcher explains key ideas and the participant can ask questions, or to include a brief quiz to gauge comprehension [6].

In some cases disclosing the research purpose in the consent form may threaten the validity of the results. For example, if a researcher plans to study how users respond to an attack, or measure a user's security mindedness, revealing the purpose of the study will influence the participant's behavior. To avoid this researchers can request a waiver of informed consent, or obfuscate the true purpose of the study. Obtaining a waiver typically requires demonstrating that the potential risks are minimal and that other study designs will not suffice. If IRB review is required, the IRB will sometimes request that participants are debriefed once the study is completed, this can serve as a tool to reduce the perceived risks and to ensure the participants questions are answered.

Debriefing takes place after the person has completed the study, it is an opportunity for the researcher and subject to discuss the study and perhaps the true nature of the study. A waiver for debriefing can be granted if revealing the true research protocol may cause the participant distress, and there is minimal risk involved [7]. In our field, debriefing can be an opportune time to increase the benefits of participation by providing the participant with security education. Particularly when participants are being attacked or are answering questions related to their security knowledge and practices. However, it can be difficult to design an effective debriefing message, especially when users participate remotely and are not present in person. Depending on the research topic, the researcher may be in the position to give advice that is known to be effective [11], or they may feel debriefing will raise more concerns than it is able to effectively address thus causing unnecessary distress to participants [7]. It would be useful to have guidelines to help a researcher decide when each technique is appropriate or desirable, perhaps it depends on the amount of risk involved.

3   Moving Forward

This paper raises more issues than it addresses; in this section we will suggest ways that the community can make progress in this area. The first of which is to continue identifying the similarities and differences between our field and fields that have a history of conducting human subjects research. This includes working toward an understanding of the continuums of risks and benefits.

We recommend empirically evaluating our suspicion that most IRBs are unprepared to review research protocols in our field. This conjecture was formed based on our knowledge of IRB membership, the nascency of security research involving human subjects, and the technical nature of some protocols. A better understanding of the expertise and backgrounds of IRB members, and a survey of their level of comfort reviewing various types of protocols would be useful. The study design could be modeled after Buchanan and Hvizdak's evaluation of IRB concerns with research conducted via the Internet [3]. Additional data that could be collected include measuring IRB experience with reviewing computer security research, the number of protocols computer science departments submit each year, and when the first was submitted. It would also be useful to collect data on the sort of questions that arise when reviewing computer security protocols.

Our community could form a community of researchers who have experience with ethics or the IRB process. Researchers could consult with this board during the early stages of the research, and IRBs could also consult with the committee when they need external assistance for the review of a protocol.[1]

---

[1] IRB membership 45 CFR 46.107 (2009).

Perhaps we need a repository of IRB protocols or study methodologies to encourage the discussion of ethical decision making. This could increase expertise by allowing researchers to gain an understanding of the tradeoffs that were made during the initial stages of the research. Researchers could also describe any IRB concerns that arose, and how they were addressed.

4   Conclusion

We suggest that it is our community's responsibility to explore concepts such as informed consent, risk, and benefits as they pertain to our research. We selected these concepts as the focus of this early discussion because of the important role they play in the IRB review process and because they are the concepts where our research may diverge from other fields. We assign the task to our community because the alternative is to wait for an outside body to impose regulations. The expertise of IRBs and their members will serve as a useful guide, but we must use our intimate knowledge of the domain to ensure the necessary concepts are satisfactorily explored. Much of this paper is dedicated to research with human subjects, however, an understanding of the risks and benefits associated with this research may benefit the larger discussion of computer security ethics.

The recommended directions for moving forward will advance the discussion and lead to a better understanding of the issues at hand. In this paper we introduce a preliminary set of concerns, and suggest possible next steps. We should continue to explore best practices for our field to ensure the ethical design of research methodologies, borrowing from fields where similarities can be found and identifying pertinent differences.

Acknowledgments. The authors would like to thank the anonymous reviewers for their feedback. This work was supported by the NSF through Grant CNS-09-14845. Any opinions, findings, conclusions or recommendations expressed herein are those of the authors, and do not necessarily reflect those of the US Government or the NSF.

References

1. Agre, P., Campbell, F.A., Goldman, B.D., et al.: Improving informed consent: The medium is not the message. IRB: Ethics and Human Research 25(5), S11–S19 (2003)
2. Allman, M.: What ought a program committee to do? In: WOWCS 2008: Proceedings of the Conference on Organizing Workshops, Conferences, and Symposia for Computer Systems, pp. 1–5. USENIX Association, Berkeley (2008)
3. Buchanan, E.A., Hvizdak, E.E.: Online survey tools: Ethical and methodological concerns of human research ethics committees. Journal of Empirical Research on Human Research Ethics: An International Journal 4(2), 37–48 (2009)
4. Cranor, L.: Ethical Concerns in Computer Security and Privacy Research Involving Human Subjects. In: Sion, R., Curtmola, R., Dietrich, S., Kiayias, A., Miret, J.M., Sako, K., Sebé, F. (eds.) RLCPS, WECSR, and WLC 2010. LNCS, vol. 6054, pp. 247–249. Springer, Heidelberg (2010)

5. Dittrich, D., Bailey, M., Dietrich, S.: Towards community standards for ethical behavior in computer security research. Tech. Rep. 2009-1, Stevens Institute of Technology (April 2009)
6. Ess, C.: AoIR: Ethical decision-making and Internet research: Recommendations from the ethics working committee (2002), http://aoir.org/reports/ethics.pdf
7. Finn, P., Jakobsson, M.: Designing and conducting phishing experiments. In: IEEE Technology and Society Magazine, Special Issue on Usability and Security (2007)
8. Garfinkel, S.L.: IRBs and security research: myths, facts and mission creep. In: UPSEC 2008: Proceedings of the 1st Conference on Usability, Psychology, and Security, pp. 1–5. USENIX Association, Berkeley (2008)
9. Gunsalus, C.K., Bruner, E., Burbules, N., Dash Jr., L.D., Finkin, M.W., Goldberg, J., Greenough, W., Miller, G., Pratt, M.G.: The Illinois White Paper - Improving the System for Protecting Human Subjects: Counteracting IRB Mission Creep. Qualitative Inquiry 13(5), 617–649 (2005)
10. Kenneally, E., Bailey, M., Maughan, D.: A Framework for Understanding and Applying Ethical Principles in Network and Security Research. In: Sion, R., Curtmola, R., Dietrich, S., Kiayias, A., Miret, J.M., Sako, K., Sebé, F. (eds.) RLCPS, WECSR, and WLC 2010. LNCS, vol. 6054, pp. 240–246. Springer, Heidelberg (2010)
11. Kumaraguru, P., Cranshaw, J., Acquisti, A., Cranor, L., Hong, J., Blair, M.A., Pham, T.: School of phish: a real-world evaluation of anti-phishing training. In: SOUPS 2009: Proceedings of the 5th Symposium on Usable Privacy and Security, pp. 1–12. ACM, NY (2009)
12. Labott, S.M., Johnson, T.P.: Psychological and social risks of behavioral research. IRB: Ethics and Human Research 26(3), 11–15 (2004)
13. Matwyshyn, A.M., Cui, A., Keromytis, A.D., Stolfo, S.J.: Ethics in security vulnerability research. In: IEEE Security and Privacy, pp. 67–72 (2010)
14. National Commission for the Protection of Human Subjects of Biomedical and Behavioral Research: The Belmont report - ethical principles and guidelines for the protection of human subjects of research
15. National Research Council: Protecting Participants and Facilitating Social and Behavioral Sciences Research. National Academies Press, Washington D.C. (2003)
16. White, R.F.: Institutional review board mission creep: The common rule, social science, and the nanny state. The Independent Review XI(4), 547–564 (2007)
17. Whitten, A., Tygar, J.D.: Why Johnny can't encrypt: A usability evaluation of PGP 5.0. In: 8th USENIX Security Symposium, pp. 169–184 (1999)

Human Subjects, Agents, or Bots: Current Issues in Ethics and Computer Security Research

John Aycock[1], Elizabeth Buchanan[2], Scott Dexter[3], and David Dittrich[4],*

[1] University of Calgary
[2] University of Wisconsin-Stout
[3] Brooklyn College
[4] University of Washington

Abstract. In this panel, we explore some of the issues surrounding the ethical review of computer security research by institutional review boards (IRBs) and other ethical review bodies. These issues include interpretation of legal language defining how ethical review is to be performed, the impact of information and communication technologies (ICT) on research methods and ethical analysis, how terms like "risk" and "harm" must be interpreted in the light of ICT. We examine two case studies in which these issues surface, and conclude by providing some ideas on the path forward.

1 Introduction

This statement addresses issues of human research ethics boards/institutional review boards and the concept of computer security research from the perspectives of four researchers, including computer scientists, ethicists, and computer security experts. We frame this discussion from the extant regulations, particularly those from the United States Code of Federal Regulations at 45/46 [1], and the Canadian Tri-Council Policy Statement: Ethical Conduct for Research Involving Humans [3]. As computer security research has grown in such forms of bot research, malicious software, and denial of service attacks [4], attention from and interest by review boards to these forms of research has correspondingly grown [7].

However, on such review boards, there is a lack of expertise and representation on boards, with anecdotal evidence from 2009 showing that of computer security researchers, only 4 out of 200 at the Network and Distributed System Security Symposium reported serving on review boards, while a lack of knowledge on US institutional review boards around computer science and computer security research has been reported. Buchanan and Ess [2] found that in their respondents, 75% of 700 boards did not have a technical expert to review internet-computer related research protocols, and, 75% of boards did not provide training for their boards in this area. While some years earlier, Hall and Flynn [5] conducted a

---

* Copyright © 2011, IFCA. Primary source of publication is `http://www.spinger.de/comp/lncs/index.html`

survey of Computer Science departments in the UK regarding human subjects research ethics in software engineering (SE) research with a response rate of 47% (44 department heads). At that time, they found several trends that point to a lack of culture of support surrounding human subjects research ethics. Few other empirical studies have been conducted to disprove what Hall and Flynn, and Buchanan and Ess, have found. Unfortunately, it appears that both the current state of CS departments and IRBs are not in sync around human subjects and ethics awareness just yet.

2   Specific Computer Security Issues: Risk

The traditional principles of research ethics include respect for persons, beneficence, and justice. IRBs have the mission to protect *human subjects* of *research* and serve as the advocate for research subjects in evaluation and review of research. A particular area of concern for computer security revolves around risk. According to the Office of Human Research Protections [9], "risks to research subjects posed by participation in research should be justified by the anticipated benefits to the subjects or society. This requirement is clearly stated in all codes of research ethics, and is central to the federal regulations. One of the major responsibilities of the IRB, therefore, is to assess the risks and benefits of proposed research." At 45 CFR 46.102(i) [1], the regulations require researchers only to *minimize*, not *eliminate*, risks to research subjects. In IRB discourse, many computer security protocols would fall into the realm of minimal risk – CS research presents many different possibilities for reconceptualizing this regulatory concept of minimal risk. The concepts of universal precautions, individual precautions and responsibility are key. Researchers and boards must balance presenting risks related to the specific research with risks related to the technologies in use.

With computer security research, major issues around risk arise, for society at large especially. The risk may not seem evident to an individual but in the scope of security research, larger populations may be vulnerable. There is a significant difficulty in quantifying risks and benefits, in the traditional sense of research ethics, and an ultimate question that is emerging is, can the computer security researcher articulate those in terms that an IRB understands and can quantify appropriately? The goal of the IRB in general is to protect human subjects, while ensuring appropriate methods and ethics in research. Meaningful assessment of computer security research may involve understanding technical details well outside the area in which IRB members are trained; effectively, the methods are concealed. However, if computer security research is opaque as to methods, it is opaque as to ethics, as methods and ethics are inherently intertwined. This is a challenge for both security researchers and for IRBs.

Moreover, in computer security research, the distance between researcher and "subject" or participant influences how an IRB will review the risk-benefit. For instance, as the "distance" between the researcher and subject/author/ participant decreases, we are more likely to define the research scenario as one that involves "humans" [8]. As the distance increases, we are more likely to define the research scenario as one that does not involve "humans." For instance, an aggregation of surfing behaviors collected by a bot presents greater distance between researcher and respondent than an interview done in a virtual world between avatars. This distance leads us to suggest that computer security research focus less concern around human subjects research in the traditional sense and more concern with human harming research. As an IRB reviews a computer security research protocol, it is imperative that they consider the larger picture beyond the individual. This is in keeping with novel review forms, such as those corresponding to community-based participatory research [10].

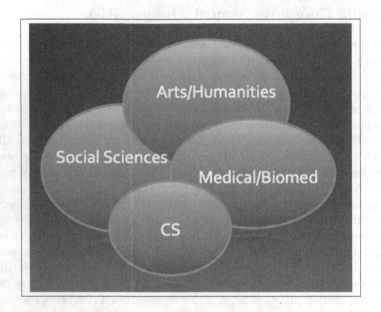

Fig. 1. Where does CS fit in?

2.1   CS Specificity

Computer security is a sub discipline, not analogous with biomedical or social sciences, and thus, fails to fit smoothly within regulatory and practical IRB language. IRBs have little expertise available to them to know all of these potential risks to protected data, let alone how to identify when a researcher is not adequately explaining the full range of protective measures that are necessary to prevent data breach, or other risks involved with computer security research that go beyond just data.

In the realm of IRB discourse, specific language has been used to review all disciplinary research, though, as noted, novel interpretations are emerging [10]. It is common to see in an IRB application for a research study involving collection of personally identifiable information phrases such as:

– "No others will have access to the data."
– "Anonymous identifiers will be used during all data collection and analysis and the link to the subject identifiers will be stored in a secure manner."

These phrases are boilerplate, in that they inherit the standard means of protecting data stored on pieces of paper physically located in a locked cabinet in a locked researcher's office in a building with a guard at the front desk. They give very little detail as to the methods used to secure data, but an IRB committee that includes no experts in computer security may be satisfied with these assurances. Only after a breach would questions arise.

More and more, researchers are learning about the policies and practices of data security being enforced as part of the compliance regime at university medical centers. These policies follow years of records breaches that seem to be growing in scale and scope.[1] IRB applications now contain language such as:

– "Data files that contain summaries of chart reviews and surveys will only have study numbers but no data to identify the subjects. The key [linking] subject names and study identifiers will be kept in a locked file."
– "Electronic data will be stored on a password protected and secure computer that will be kept in a locked office. The software 'File Vault' will be used to protect all study data loaded to portable laptops, flash drives or other storage media. This will encode all data using Advanced Encryption Standard with 128-bit keys (AES-128)."

These statements are more explicit about protection of *data*, because the risk of disclosure (or exposure) of subject identities is a well-known risk. But what does it mean to store data in a "locked file?" Is the lock the username/password required to disable the screen saver or log in to the user account? Or does it mean a password protected ZIP archive file or Excel spreadsheet? What is the quality of the password (e.g., is it the word "password" or is it the the same string as the user name?) or the encryption algorithm that is used? Is the password written on a note stuck to the monitor? Who else has access to the directory in which the file is kept, have they undergone the same ethics training and signed the same confidentiality agreements other research staff have signed? Is that directory configured so as to be openly readable from any computer on the local network or anywhere on the internet? Is the data copied to a USB thumb drive that requires no password at all to mount and read from another computer? Even when specifying the details of using whole-disk encryption with File Vault, if the password is trivially guessable, even military-grade encryption does little good in terms of protecting stored electronic data.

Securing data is about more than just a password, or using a particular encryption algorithm. Data must be protected not only at rest, but in transit over the network, and while it is being processed (when it must exist in decrypted form in order to be of use to a researcher.) It must also be securely destroyed when no longer needed. Simply deleting a file does not, by itself, over-write the

---

[1] http://www.privacyrights.org/data-breach

sensitive data contained in the file: it simply makes the space on disk that the data occupied available for potential re-use when new files are created and can often be trivially recovered by anyone with rudimentary knowledge of computer forensics and the proper software tools to recover deleted files.

But the risks go even farther than just data breach. Some computer security research puts at risk the integrity and/or the availability of information and information systems. Altering or destroying data, or causing a computer system to crash, can have just as serious harms as disclosure of patient records could have (perhaps even more). There is a long way to go before current IRB review mechanisms will adequately handle the breadth and depth of risks and benefits associated with computer security research.

To assist researchers and IRBs as they struggle with the complexity of data security, Harvard University has recently devised a tiered system of data management [6]. Specifically, Harvard outlines responsibilities for researchers, IRBs, and the IT departments within the university. In addition, they have designated different types of data along a continuum and apply appropriate standards of protection to those various forms of research data. For example, in Harvard's Information Security Categories range from Level Five: "Extremely sensitive information about individually identifiable people;" to Level Four: "Very sensitive information about individually identifiable people;" to Level Three: "Sensitive information about individually identifiable people;" to Level Two: "Benign information about individually identifiable people;" to finally, Level One: "De-identified research information about people and other non-confidential research information." Harvard's approach is a meaningful and practical approach that stands to assist researchers and IRBs in their understanding and appropriate evaluation of data security. Yet, there remain obstacles to the computer security field moving more readily to a research ethics awareness, or, towards an suitable model that best fits the specificity of the discipline, while ensuring the basic principles of research protections.

3   Best Practices and Suggestions

As this current WECSR Workshop has shown, the community of computer security researchers themselves need to identify and promulgate best practices, develop curriculum standards, self-regulate, perhaps through the model of an extra-institutional review board, and develop and apply "ethical clean bill of health" standards for publications. For instance, the Journal of the American Medical Association has an explicit statement for ethical considerations[2], asserting: "For all manuscripts reporting data from studies involving human participants or animals, formal review and approval, or formal review and waiver, by an appropriate institutional review board or ethics committee is required and should be described in the Methods section. For those investigators who do not

---

[2] http://jama.ama-assn.org/site/misc/ifora.xhtml#EthicalApprovalofStudies
    StudiesandInformedConsent

have formal ethics review committees, the principles outlined in the Declaration of Helsinki should be followed. For investigations of humans, state in the Methods section the manner in which informed consent was obtained from the study participants (ie, oral or written). Editors may request that authors provide documentation of the formal review and recommendation from the institutional review board or ethics committee responsible for oversight of the study."

Similarly, and in a positive directive, the Symposium on Usable Privacy and Security (SOUPS)[3] has recently moved in a similar fashion and adopted an ethics statement for papers and publications: "Papers should mention how the authors addressed any ethical considerations applicable to the research and user studies, such as passing an IRB review." Specific examples from SOUPS include[4]:

"Example descriptions of ethical considerations:
- This study was approved as a minimal risk study by our university's IRB.
- Study participants were debriefed after the study to make them aware of the deception used in the study and to inform them of how they could protect themselves had this been an actual phishing attack. This study, including our use of deception and subsequent debriefing procedure, was approved by our university's IRB.
- Our organization does not require human subjects review.
- According to the rules of our institution, this study did not require IRB approval because all human subjects data was gathered from previously-published publicly available data sets."

In order to expose the next generation of researchers to broader, more appropriate research ethics models, we advocate for a number of pathways. These include pedagogical, professional, and regulatory. In the realm of the pedagogical, we recommend CS classes with a "research methods" component allow instructors to serve as *ex officio* members of an IRB in order to strengthen faculty-IRB connections and expose students to IRB motivations and methods. Academic environments, in conjunction with professional societies should develop short modules on research ethics which could be used in a variety of courses (security, computer ethics, software engineering, HCI, etc), that expand in scope and detail the current Collaborative Institutional Training Initiative (CITI) models, which are used internationally as an online research ethics training program. In addition, the field of CS needs to explore the importance and centrality of ethics in such initiatives as NSA and the Department of Homeland Security (DHS) jointly sponsored National Centers of Academic Excellence in IA Education (CAE/IAE) and CAE-Research (CAE-R) programs (CAE/IAE or CAE-R criteria), and clearly comprehend and articulate the standards for federally-funded research.

In terms of industry connections, as Shou [11] has shown, the opportunity for industry-academy partnership around ethics is possible. His work on the ethics of

---

[3] http://cups.cs.cmu.edu/pipermail/soups-announce/2011/000055.html
[4] http://cups.cs.cmu.edu/soups/2011/ethics-examples.html

data sharing shows that industry and academia can share in their ethics frameworks for the betterment of research in general. In terms of regulation, we need to engage as a discipline in significant risk assessment evaluation: Does security research carry the possibility of harm at the levels of, say, pharmaceutical research or research involving infectious diseases/nuclear materials? As such, regulations will be formed accordingly. Current laws around computer security are mixed, and ambiguous, and for researchers, this complexity in law contributes to confounding ethics.

4   Conclusion

We have seen some of the issues surrounding the ways computer security researchers communicate with IRBs, how well IRBs do or do not understand the risks inherent in computer security research, and some ways in which the computer security research community can move forward towards improved ethical evaluation capacity.

References

1. 45 CFR 46, http://www.hhs.gov/ohrp/humansubjects/guidance/45cfr46.htm
2. Buchanan, E., Ess, C.: Internet Research Ethics and the Institutional Review Board: Current Practices and Issues. In: ACM SIGCAS Computers and Society, vol. 39 (2009)
3. Canadian Institutes of Health Research, Natural Sciences and Engineering Research Council of Canada, Social Sciences and Humanities Research Council of Canada. Tri-Council Policy Statement: Ethical Conduct for Research Involving Humans (December 2010),
   http://www.pre.ethics.gc.ca/pdf/eng/tcps2/TCPS_2_FINAL_Web.pdf
4. Dittrich, D., Bailey, M., Dietrich, S.: Towards Community Standards for Ethical Behavior in Computer Security Research. Technical Report CS 2009-01, Stevens Institute of Technology (April 2009)
5. Hall, T., Flynn, V.: Ethical issues in software engineering research: A survey of current practice. Empirical Software Engineering, 305–317 (2001)
6. Harvard University Information Security. Harvard Research Data Security Policy Protection Memo (October 2010),
   http://security.harvard.edu/harvard-research-data-security-policy-protection-memo
7. Kenneally, E., Bailey, M., Maughan, D.: A Framework for Understanding and Applying Ethical Principles in Network and Security Research. In: Sion, R., Curtmola, R., Dietrich, S., Kiayias, A., Miret, J.M., Sako, K., Sebé, F. (eds.) RLCPS, WECSR, and WLC 2010. LNCS, vol. 6054, pp. 240–246. Springer, Heidelberg (2010)
8. Markham, A., Buchanan, E.: The Distance Principle in Internet Research Ethics. International Journal of Internet Research Ethics (forthcoming, 2011)

9. Office for Human Research Protections (OHRP). Institutional review board guidebook (1993), http://www.hhs.gov/ohrp/archive/irb/irb_chapter3.htm
10. Ross, L., Loup, A., Nelson, R.M., Botkin, J., Kost, R., Smith, G., Gehlert, S.: Human subjects protections in collaborative community-engaged research: A research ethics framework. Journal of Empirical Research on Human Research Ethics 5(1), 5–17 (2010)
11. Shou, D.: Ethical Considerations of Sharing Data for Cybersecurity Research. In: Danezis, G., Dietrich, S., Sako, K. (eds.) FC 2011 Workshops. LNCS, vol. 7126, pp. 169–177. Springer, Heidelberg (2012)

Enforced Community Standards for Research on Users of the Tor Anonymity Network

Christopher Soghoian

Center for Applied Cybersecurity Research, Indiana University
chris@soghoian.net

Abstract. Security and privacy researchers are increasingly taking an interest in the Tor network, and have even performed studies that involved intercepting the network communications of Tor users. There are currently no generally agreed upon community norms for research on Tor users, and so unfortunately, several projects have engaged in problematic behavior – not because the researchers had malicious intent, but because they simply did not see the ethical or legal issues associated with their data gathering. This paper proposes a set of four bright-line rules for researchers conducting privacy invading research on the Tor network. The author hopes that it will spark a debate, and hopefully lead to responsible program committees taking some action to embrace these, or similar rules.

1   Introduction

Over the past few years, the Tor network has grown from an academic research project [4] to one of the most widely used privacy enhancing technologies, with several hundreds thousand of active users [9]. While little is known about the average Tor user, it is safe to assume that it is used by individuals seeking to protect their privacy, either denying their own ISP or government the ability to learn what they are doing online, or to stop websites from learning anything about their visitors. In order to achieve this degree of privacy protection, Tor's users pay a significant penalty, both in latency, as well as in general usability (as many popular plugins such as Flash must be disabled in order to prevent data leakage).

Just as privacy-seeking users have flocked to Tor, so too have researchers interested in learning more about its users and their use of the network. In some cases, these researchers specifically wish to observe Tor users in order to learn how it is being used. However, in others cases, the researchers simply seek to study general Internet behavior, and Tor is just a quick way to easily observe the traffic of thousands of Internet users – perhaps because major ISPs will not permit some kinds of traffic interception and network attacks on their customers, even in the name of research.

There are currently no widely accepted or publicized research community norms for studies on Tor and its users. As such, each team of researchers interested in studying the use of the network is left to determine what is right and

G. Danezis, S. Dietrich, and K. Sako (Eds.): FC 2011 Workshops, LNCS 7126, pp. 146–153, 2012.

wrong for themselves. While many researchers have gone out of their way to protect the privacy of Tor users as they collect data from the network [9], some are not getting it right, at least in the opinion of this author.

This paper will present two case studies in which researchers setup their own Tor servers, specifically in order to monitor the traffic that flows over the network. The paper will examine several ethical issues, and attempt to establish bright line rules for determining if the Tor network should be used to answer particular research questions. Finally, the paper will conclude by proposing that conference and workshop program committees play a strong role in establishing norms for this type of research, and enforcing these norms by rejecting papers that do not adhere to a few basic guidelines.

2   Prior Academic Studies on Tor Users

This section will summarize two academic research studies performed on the Tor anonymity network, one published in 2008, and one in 2010. These are not the only studies to involve the collection of data on the Tor network ([9] includes references to several others), but these papers are noteworthy in that they received strong post-publication criticism from the privacy community regarding the degree to which the researchers needlessly violated, or put at risk the privacy of Tor users. The purpose of this section is not to demonize the researchers, but to highlight the fact that the privacy community has failed to establish and enforce ethical norms for research studies that involve monitoring the Tor network.

2.1   Shining Light in Dark Places: Understanding the Tor Network

In 2008, McCoy et al. published the results of a study [11], which sought to determine the kind of traffic flowing over the Tor anonymity network [4]. In order to gather this data, the researchers setup a Tor exit node server on the University of Colorado's high-speed network, and added it to the publicly distributed list of Tor servers. During a four day period in December 2007, the researchers logged and stored the first 150 bytes of each network packet that went through their server their network. This revealed the kind of traffic that was crossing the Tor network, and the specific websites that users were accessing. In a second part of the study, the researchers ran an entry node to the network for fifteen days, which allowed them to determine the source IP address of a large number of Tor users. They used this to learn which countries use Tor more heavily than others.

Before starting their study, the researchers did not seek or obtain a thorough evaluation of the legality of their activities. When later questioned by this author, one of the researchers stated that they "spoke informally with one lawyer, who told us that that area of the law is ill defined." Based on this, he said, the researchers felt that it was "unnecessary to follow up with other lawyers [14]." Similarly, the researchers did not seek the guidance and approval of their university's Institutional Review Board (IRB). "We were advised that it wasn't necessary," one of the researchers said, adding that the IRB review process is used "used more in medical and psychology research at our university," and was not generally consulted in computer science projects [14].

The researchers did not receive a warm welcome after presenting their work at the Privacy Enhancing Technologies Symposium. Several outspoken members of the academic privacy community were in the audience, as well as core developers of the Tor project, many of whom reacted harshly to the news that the researchers had monitored traffic on the network. As one example, when questioned by an audience member after the presentation, the researchers admitted that they had retained a copy of the logged Tor traffic, and further, that it was not held on an encrypted storage device. This disclosure was met with boos from the audience, even after the researchers stressed that the data was kept in a "secure" location [14].

Within days of the researchers' presentation, the University of Colorado announced that a post-review of the project had determined that the researchers did not violate university policies, specifically finding that:

"Based on our assessment and understanding of the issues involved in your work, our opinion was that by any reasonable standard, the work in question was not classifiable as human subject research, nor did it involve the collection of personally identifying information. While the underlying issues are certainly interesting and complex, our opinion is that in this case, no rules were violated by your not having subjected your proposed work to prior [IRB] scrutiny. Our analysis was confined to this [IRB] issue [10]."

2.2   Private Information Disclosure from Web Searches

In 2010, Castelluccia *et al.* revealed a privacy flaw in several major search engines, in which an attacker can use a sniffed authentication cookie to reconstruct a users' search query history [3]. In addition to demonstrating the flaw, the researchers also sought to determine the degree to which users are vulnerable, that is, how many users conduct web searches when "logged in" to a search engine, and how many of them have enabled Google's Web History feature. In order to determine this information, the researchers collected data via three different methods: First, network traces for the 500-600 daily users at their own research center were collected and analyzed. Second, the researchers established a Tor exit node server, and examined the network traffic exiting from it. Third, the researchers received opt-in consent from 10 users, whose Google session cookies the researchers sniffed, and then used to actively reconstruct the individuals' search history information.

During the one week period in which the researchers collected data from the Tor network, 1803 distinct Google users were observed, 46% of which were logged into their accounts. For each of these logged-in users, the researchers used the sniffed Google session cookies and attempted to access the users' first and last name; locations searched using Google Maps (along with the "default location", when available); blogs followed using Google Reader; full Web History (when accessible without re-entering credentials); finance portfolio; and bookmarks. In their paper, the researchers stress that their research application did not store any individual users' data – only aggregate statistical information was retained.

The researchers treated the three groups of users (the volunteers, co-workers at their research center and Tor users) quite differently. For example, the researchers did not actively attack the accounts of their colleagues, they merely passively analyzed the network traces, whereas users of the Tor network had their accounts actively attacked, and some of their data downloaded from Google's servers (although not retained). In their paper, the researchers do not reveal the reason for the restraint they showed in choosing to not actively attack their colleagues" accounts.

Similarly, the researchers did not actively probe the search history of either their colleagues' accounts or the Tor users, and restricted the use of this attack to just the 10 volunteers who had consented to assist with the study. The researchers describe the motivation for this difference, writing in their paper that "it would have been otherwise impossible to conduct our study on uninformed users without incurring legal and ethical issues." It is unclear from the content of the paper why the researchers found it ethically acceptable to actively attack Tor users' Google accounts, but not to download their search history.

When the researchers presented their paper at the Privacy Enhancing Technologies Symposium in 2010, they received a similar reaction from the audience as McCoy *et al.* had in 2008. The reaction of the audience is not terribly surprising, given that most of the people attending the conference spend their time working to protect users' privacy. What is surprising, and extremely relevant to the focus of this paper, is that the researchers presenting their paper in 2010 had not learned about the strong reaction from the community to the paper by McCoy *et al.* presented at the very same conference two years earlier.

2.3 Analyzing and Comparing the Two Studies

The academic privacy and security community can learn a few things by contrasting these two research papers. First, the published proceedings from the 2008 and 2010 Privacy Enhancing Technologies Symposia include the McCoy *et al.* and Castelluccia *et al.* papers, but nothing documenting the strong reactions from the audience. As such, any future researchers looking through previously published papers in this community may reasonably believe that such studies are appropriate, and blessed by the community.

Second, it is quite easy to differentiate between the McCoy and Castelluccia studies. The former specifically sought to learn more about users of the Tor network, whereas the latter simply used Tor users' network activity to assist in drawing broader conclusions about general Internet behavior. The fact that Castelluccia *et al.* performed only passive network monitoring on their own colleagues but actively attacked the accounts of Tor users likely indicates that the researchers knew they were engaging in morally and ethically dubious behavior. If there were no problems with what they were doing, why would they not do it to their friends and colleagues, but were willing to do it to users who had specifically signaled a desire to protect their own privacy?

Third, neither group of researchers submitted their studies for Institutional Review Board approval – McCoy *et al* did not believe they had to, while Castelluccia *et al.* did not have an IRB at their research institution.

Finally, Castelluccia *et al.* specifically designed their research tool to analyze individual user' data in-memory, and only retained aggregate statistical data. On the other hand, McCoy *et al.* retained individual users' browsing data, and performed statistical analysis of it after the fact. The former approach is clearly more privacy preserving, but the latter is more resistant to researcher-error. That is, had Castelluccia *et al.* made a mistake in their code, they would have had to collect new user data in order to analyze and aggregate it. By retaining individual users' data McCoy *et al.* were free to tweak their code as much as they wanted, as they could always re-run it against their previously collected data.

3   Towards a Community Standard

Program committees can and should play a major role in both establishing and enforcing community standards for research. Even if just one or two conferences establish and publicize such rules, it will send a clear signal to researchers and help them to take appropriate steps to protect user privacy as they design their studies. Furthermore, since most of the Tor related research seems to be published at the Privacy Enhancing Technologies Symposium, it is likely that a strong set of community norms can be established via the decision of a single program committee. In this section, I propose four bright-line rules for Tor related research – these are not exhaustive, and it is still quite possible for researchers to meet these guidelines and still engage in irresponsible, privacy invading research. However, should researchers follow these rules, they should at least be able to avoid several privacy pitfalls present in earlier research studies.

Research should be focused on users of the Tor network. Researchers seeking to gather Tor network usage data should be specifically focused on studying users of the Tor network, and should not be using Tor as as a convenient method of studying general Internet users' activity online. Researchers may be tempted to establish their own Tor exit node, as it is a very quick way of getting access to the Internet traffic of thousands of users. This may be a particularly attractive option for those researchers without close ties to a large Internet service provider, as well as for those researchers whose academic institutions will not permit them to conduct the study on their colleagues and students. In spite of this temptation, it is simply not appropriate to violate the privacy of Tor users just because it is easier to do so than to get approval to monitor the network at one's own university. If the privacy of Tor users is to be intruded upon, it should at least be to answer questions specific to the Tor community, and not something that could be learned another way.

Minimize user data collection and retention. Researchers should ensure that user data is examined in-memory only, and that the only data retained is aggregate in nature. The researchers should not put themselves in a position where they could be later compelled (by law enforcement agencies, for example) to disclose any identifiable data either about specific users (such as originating IP addresses), or the specific web sites and web pages that Tor users visit.

Ensure that the research study is legal in the country where it is performed. There are significant questions surrounding the legality of much network monitoring research, particularly when it is conducted in the United States, where communications privacy and interception law is exceedingly complex [12]. Computer scientists are simply not equipped to evaluate the legality of the research they perform, and as such, it is important that researchers seek the assistance of qualified legal experts as they design their studies. Program committees should require that the researchers identify the legal expert with whom they consulted, and should independently contact the named legal expert in order to verify that they do indeed believe that the researchers' study did not violate the law.

Research studies should be vetted by an IRB, if one exists. While Institutional Review Boards exist at most research universities in the United States, they are far less common in many other countries. It is certainly true that there are legitimate concerns about the lack of technical expertise on many IRBs, however, these will lessen over time, as more and more computer scientists interact with IRBs. Furthermore, even if the IRB does not provide much in the way of useful technical oversight, the self-evaluation that the researchers have to perform as part of the review process (listing the kinds of possible harms that test subjects may face, and the steps they have taken to mitigate them) may be be useful.

4   Related Work

Loesing *at al.* presented two case studies in which data was gathered from the Tor network in a responsible, and privacy-preserving manner [9]. Drawing from these case studies, the researchers proposed three general guidelines for future Tor data collection: data minimalism, source aggregation and transparency. The researchers goal for the paper was to start a discussion, but they do do not call for enforcement of these rules.

Dittrich *et al.* proposed an ethical framework to guide and evaluate applied security research, motivated by a frustration among researchers, program committees, and professional organizations over the current state of affairs [6,5]. Their goal too was to encourage a dialog, which would hopefully lead to some form of community consensus.

Allman examined the role that conference program committees may play in guiding researchers towards ethical research methodologies [1]. Allman does not however propose a clear set of rules that program committees should adopt. Likewise, Landwehr has called on professional societies to develop ethical guidelines for their members who are facing these issues [8].

Allman, Garfinkel and Landwehr [1,8,7] all suggested that Institutional Review Boards may play a positive role, but have voiced concerns about the degree to which IRB members lack enough computer security skills and an awareness of the existing values of the computer science community to to effectively judge the risks involved in such research.

Sicker *et al.* [12] outlined several areas of potential legal liability for researchers engaging in network monitoring research. The authors strongly encourage the broader network monitoring community to establish community norms, but do not suggest what these norms should be. On a similar note, Burstein and Soghoian each offered specific recommendations to security researchers engaging in cybersecurity and phishing research in order to avoid specific legal pitfalls [2,13].

5 Conclusion

In this paper, I have proposed four easy, bright-line rules that can be used to evaluate and guide researchers seeking to engage in studies involving the Tor anonymity network. The community has largely failed, thus far, to establish and enforce any standards for this type of research. Both of the problematic research projects summarized in this paper were published at a highly ranked peer reviewed conference. This creates two incentive problems: the researchers who conducted the earlier studies pay no real long-term price for recklessly violating the privacy of Tor users, and future researchers who read through the published conference proceedings may be reasonably lead to believe that the methods employed in these studies are legitimate and blessed by the community.

The community must promptly agree upon, establish and enforce a set of easy to understand guidelines for acceptable Tor research (those presented in this paper, those created by Loesing *at al.*, or a different set). Future Tor related research projects that violate these guidelines should be rejected from the Privacy Enhancing Technologies Symposium, as well as other top-tier privacy and security conferences.

References

1. Allman, M.: What ought a program committee to do? In: Proceedings of the Conference on Organizing Workshops, Conferences, and Symposia for Computer Systems, pp. 9:1–9:5. USENIX Association, Berkeley (2008)
2. Burstein, A.J.: Conducting cybersecurity research legally and ethically. In: Proceedings of the 1st Usenix Workshop on Large-Scale Exploits and Emergent Threats, pp. 8:1–8:8. USENIX Association, Berkeley (2008)
3. Castelluccia, C., De Cristofaro, E., Perito, D.: Private Information Disclosure from Web Searches. In: Atallah, M.J., Hopper, N.J. (eds.) PETS 2010. LNCS, vol. 6205, pp. 38–55. Springer, Heidelberg (2010)
4. Dingledine, R., Mathewson, N., Syverson, P.: Tor: the second-generation onion router. In: Proceedings of the 13th conference on USENIX Security Symposium, SSYM 2004, vol. 13, p. 21. USENIX Association, Berkeley (2004)

5. Dittrich, D., Bailey, M., Dietrich, S.: Have we Crossed the Line? The Growing Ethical Debate in Modern Computer Security Research. In: (Poster at) Proceedings of the 16th ACM Conference on Computer and Communication Security (CCS 2009), Chicago, Illinois, USA (November 2009)
6. Dittrich, D., Bailey, M., Dietrich, S.: Towards community standards for ethical behavior in computer security research. Technical Report 2009-01, Stevens Institute of Technology, Hoboken, NJ, USA (April 2009)
7. Garfinkel, S.L.: Irbs and security research: myths, facts and mission creep. In: Proceedings of the 1st Conference on Usability, Psychology, and Security, pp. 13:1–13:5. USENIX Association, Berkeley (2008)
8. Landwehr, C.E.: Drawing the line. IEEE Security and Privacy 8, 3–4 (2010)
9. Loesing, K., Murdoch, S.J., Dingledine, R.: A Case Study on Measuring Statistical Data in the Tor Anonymity Network. In: Sion, R., Curtmola, R., Dietrich, S., Kiayias, A., Miret, J.M., Sako, K., Sebé, F. (eds.) RLCPS, WECSR, and WLC 2010. LNCS, vol. 6054, pp. 203–215. Springer, Heidelberg (2010)
10. McCoy, D., Bauer, K., Grunwald, D., Kohno, T., Sicker, D.: Response to tor study (July 25, 2008), http://www.verisign.com/static/039933.pdf
11. McCoy, D., Bauer, K., Grunwald, D., Kohno, T., Sicker, D.C.: Shining Light in Dark Places: Understanding the Tor Network. In: Borisov, N., Goldberg, I. (eds.) PETS 2008. LNCS, vol. 5134, pp. 63–76. Springer, Heidelberg (2008)
12. Sicker, D.C., Ohm, P., Grunwald, D.: Legal issues surrounding monitoring during network research. In: Proceedings of the 7th ACM SIGCOMM Conference on Internet Measurement, IMC 2007, pp. 141–148. ACM, New York (2007)
13. Soghoian, C.: Legal Risks For Phishing Researchers. In: Proceedings of eCrime Researchers Summit (2008)
14. Soghoian, C.: Researchers could face legal risks for network snooping. Surveilance State (July 24, 2008), news.cnet.com/8301-13739_3-9997273-46.html

Ethical Dilemmas in Take-Down Research

Tyler Moore[1] and Richard Clayton[2]

[1] Center for Research on Computation and Society, Harvard University, USA
tmoore@seas.harvard.edu
[2] Computer Laboratory, University of Cambridge, UK
richard.clayton@cl.cam.ac.uk

Abstract. We discuss nine ethical dilemmas which have arisen during the investigation of 'notice and take-down' regimes for Internet content. Issues arise when balancing the desire for accurate measurement to advance the security community's understanding with the need to immediately reduce harm that is uncovered in the course of measurement. Research methods demand explanation to be accepted in peer-reviewed publications, yet the dissemination of knowledge may help miscreants improve their operations and avoid detection in the future. Finally, when researchers put forward solutions to problems they have identified, it is important that they ensure that their interventions demonstrably improve the situation and do not cause undue collateral damage.

1 Introduction

This paper is a case study of the ethical dilemmas we have faced in our computer security research. We do not set out any over-arching ethical theories of behavior. Instead, we discuss our personal experiences and those of other researchers, reporting with the benefit of hindsight when we did the right thing and perhaps also when we did not.

Over the past few years we have researched and published a number of papers about 'phishing', where criminals entice people into visiting websites that impersonate the real thing and dupe them into revealing passwords and other credentials, which will later be used for fraud. The main countermeasure to phishing is the removal, or 'take-down', of the fake websites. In some papers, notably [15], we consider take-down of other types of Internet content.

Our research approach might very loosely be described as econometrics. We obtain large numbers of measurements of real-world activity, particularly of website take-down times. From this data, and particularly from variations in this data, we tease out an understanding of the underlying criminality. This approach has been extremely valuable, in that it has allowed us to explain the relative success of some criminal gangs, and to reveal the harm caused by a lack of information sharing between companies offering take-down services.

Our research also lies in the general field of 'security economics', the relatively recent understanding that computer and networking security problems are better explained by economic considerations than by considering the more technical

G. Danezis, S. Dietrich, and K. Sako (Eds.): FC 2011 Workshops, LNCS 7126, pp. 154–168, 2012.

'computer science' aspects of the situation [2]. Our research can also be seen to be criminological, in that we are looking at crime scenes, gauging the rates of victimization and assessing the effectiveness of crime prevention measures.

Because what we're looking at is criminal activity in the real world, with real victims suffering real monetary losses, we have found ourselves facing a number of ethical dilemmas, and it is those dilemmas upon which we focus in this paper. In Subsection 1.1 we describe our take-down research in more detail to better explain what we have been doing over the past few years that has triggered ethical headaches. In Section 2 we set out four ethical dilemmas that arise in the context of measuring criminal activity. In Section 3 we discuss two further ethical dilemmas that arise when explaining how take-down works, and then in Section 4 we explain three ethical dilemmas to be confronted when writing about 'fixes' for the original problem. Thereafter Section 5 discusses related work and finally in Section 6 we draw some conclusions.

1.1   An Overview of Our Phishing Research Papers

In order to avoid continually having to break off from our later discussion of ethical dilemmas to explain details of our research, we will now present a quick overview of relevant aspects of our phishing research papers. Our account here is superficial and incomplete, and – for those concerned more about phishing than ethics – no substitute for consulting the original work.

For our first paper in 2007 [14] we measured phishing website lifetimes. We found that some websites, operated by the 'rock-phish' gang, were using a technically innovative scheme whereby the website host name resolved to a different set of intermediary machines every few minutes. These intermediaries relayed the website traffic to a hidden 'mothership'.

In order to calculate the harm done by phishing, we fetched 'world-readable' log-summary files (created by The Webalizer[1]) from a subset of compromised machines. This gave us data from which to estimate the number of visitors that a phishing website received, a figure that was previously unknown. We were surprised to find that some visitors turned up weeks after it was first reported.

We also found that a small number of websites were storing the credentials they had stolen in files on the websites themselves. We inferred the locations of these credentials and found that about half appeared genuine and the rest took the form of messages, mainly abusive, directed at the criminals. Determining the proportion of visitors who were actually fooled into divulging real credentials allowed us estimate the total harm that phishing was causing.

In 2008 we wrote [15], in which we considered a range of different types of content for which a 'take-down' regime exists: defamation, copyright violations, child sexual abuse images, phishing, and various types of fraudulent website. Our conclusion was that lifetimes were determined more by the incentives of those trying to remove the content, than by the nature of the content or the technical arrangements used to host it.

---

[1] http://mrunix.net/webalizer/

Also in 2008, we revisited our website lifetime statistics using 'feeds' of phishing website URLs from competing take-down companies. We were able to show in [16] that, because these feeds were not being shared with competitors, websites which were not universally known about were not removed.

In 2009 we took a further look at Webalizer data in [17,18]. In particular we considered what was revealed about the search terms that had been used to locate the phishing website. We were able to demonstrate that search was an important way for criminals to locate websites that they were able to compromise, and that being findable in this way was a contributory factor to recompromise rates.

2   Measuring Take-Down

A natural tension exists between conducting accurate, reproducible research and reducing the harm caused by the content that is being removed. We explore some of the issues which arise in the following four dilemmas.

Dilemma 1: Should researchers notify affected parties in order to expedite take-down? In our research investigating phishing website take-down [14], we observed that many fake websites remained online for several weeks. Furthermore, our measurements suggested that consumers continued to visit such long-lived websites, indicating that their continued presences caused direct harm. Consequently, we discussed whether we should bring these websites to the attention of the banks being impersonated.

On one hand, it seems like a no-brainer: passing the information along might reduce the harm caused by phishing. However, there are several compelling reasons why we might prefer not to share this information. First, doing so could taint our measurements. One aim of our research was to independently measure the lifetime of phishing websites. Security companies had reported short takedown times, yet we found high variation that fitted a lognormal distribution. If we had notified banks and firms immediately, we could never have accurately measured the slow take-down speed.

Second, had we chosen to notify others, who should we tell? In some cases the relevant bank contact details could be easily inferred, but in other cases not. Significant additional effort would have been required to identify the appropriate points of contact for several hundred banks. Many banks hire specialist take-down companies to take down phishing websites on their behalf. Without knowing the arrangements a bank had put in place, we could not readily determine who we should be sharing our findings with.

Third, even if we had wanted to share, our arrangements with data sources precluded this. We negotiated real-time 'feeds' of phishing reports from two large take-down providers, but signed non-disclosure agreements to secure access. Notifying banks about long-lived phishing websites would have violated these agreements and could have caused financial harm to the feed providers.

In the end, we decided to mainly keep the reports to ourselves. After conducting the initial research and publishing our first paper, we began sharing reports with individual banks and take-down companies on a one-off basis as requested, but we chose not to attempt to notify all banks. We later discovered that the primary explanation for long-lived phishing websites is that take-down companies do not exchange their lists with each other. We published a paper highlighting the adverse effect of firms' refusal to cooperate and called for greater data sharing [16], but we decided that it was entirely inappropriate for us to even consider being the long-term conduit for exchanging relevant information.

For a long time, researchers conducting clinical trials have balanced individual ethics – the needs of the next eligible patient – and collective ethics – the obligation to develop correct policies for the future [25]. Clinical trials can and should be stopped prematurely once the results become statistically significant and the divergence in treatment outcome is substantial. While security researchers are rarely afforded the luxury of controlling a randomized trial (for more on that see Dilemma 3), we could still learn from the procedures adopted by clinical researchers. In particular, we recommend that researchers avoid direct interference during data collection, but once the conclusions have been drawn, assistance to relevant stakeholders should be encouraged.

Dilemma 2: Should researchers intervene to assist victims? Security researchers often stumble upon information that identifies victims. For example, we gathered 414 user responses with personal information published on phishing websites [14]. We used the information to answer a research question (what proportion of user responses to phishing emails are legitimate?). Having gathered the information, were we obligated to notify the victims of their risk? We notified banks where we had existing contacts and where fast intervention was possible, but we did not notify all banks.

Unfortunately, ours is a common dilemma. Researchers investigating the Torpig botnet observed 180 000 infections and gathered over 70 GB of data collected by the bots, including over 1 million Windows password logins, 100 000 SMTP account logins and 12 000 FTP credentials [30]. In a subsequent presentation one co-author lamented the headaches introduced by collecting such data [11]. The co-author's conclusion is that researchers should go out of their way to avoid collecting such data because of the resulting obligation to notify victims.

If victims should be notified, what form should the notification take? One option might be to attempt to notify victims via pop-up messages on victim computers. In March 2009 the BBC's Click program purchased access to a botnet and demonstrated the evil that could be done with it. They then changed the 'wallpaper' on the individual members of the botnet to warn the owners that their machines were compromised. They have vigorously defended their actions as being in the public interest [23] – but they were heavily criticized for paying money to criminals and for the likelihood that in accessing machines without permission and altering content they had committed offenses under the UK's Computer Misuse Act 1990 [24].

We must beware the unintended consequences of intervention. Rod Rasmussen, CTO of InternetIdentity, a take-down company, relates [27] that they had problems getting a phishing site disabled on a machine in a small West Virginia county:

> The normal admin for the machine had been deployed to Iraq as part of his National Guard unit, and his backup was busy and hundreds of miles away that weekend because of his father's funeral. There were plenty of people looking at the machine (as in had their physical eyeballs on it) including the local sheriff, but no one was touching it since it ran the 911 Dispatch system and no one had the knowledge (as in passwords and expertise) to fix it.

> We've also had take-downs on machines that were in hospitals, railroad stations, airports, and government facilities. While those could be just public access terminals, there's no way we can tell from the outside if that is the case or they are running life-saving equipment, switching operations, air-traffic control systems, or have sensitive data on them respectively. That's why we have a very bright line barring any sort of 'write access', resetting or otherwise monkeying with content on compromised servers. Not only is it usually illegal in the US, someone's life can literally be on the line!

Dilemma 3: Should researchers fabricate plausible content in order to conduct 'pure' experiments of take-down? With few exceptions, empirical research in information security does not employ a similar design to that of randomized experiments. Instead, researchers must rely on observational data, as is commonly done in the social sciences. Incidents regularly occur, which prompts defenders to respond. Researchers observe this process and collect data describing it. Observational studies present many difficulties, notably the potential for sample bias, correlation/causation issues, and the presence of multiple confounding dependent variables.

Some researchers looking at the response to copyright violations have attempted to create 'pure' experiments by introducing content and observing the take-down response. The US and EU have different regimes for dealing with claims of copyright violation online, and some have argued that the EU approach encourages greater ISP compliance with dubious take-down requests. At least two groups have performed experiments to test the claim.

In 2003 an Oxford research group posted material onto UK and US websites [1]. The material was an extract of John Stuart Mill's 1869 'On Liberty', discussing freedom of speech. The experimenters then wrote anonymously to the two hosting ISPs, falsely claiming that the material was still in copyright. The UK ISP removed the material, whereas the US ISP insisted upon the provision of the legally necessary "on pain of perjury" declaration on the DMCA notice. In 2004 a similar experiment was performed by the Netherlands-based 'Multatuli

Project' [21]. They placed some out-of-copyright material from a famous 1871 tract onto webspace provided by ten different Dutch ISPs. Their results were mixed, with some ISPs losing their first complaint and only acting on a follow-up message. By the end of the experiment, seven of the ten ISPs had removed the material, taking between 3 hours and 3 days to do so.

While both copyright experiments had substantial design issues that undermined the results obtained, the underlying ethical question is whether such experimentation is appropriate for researchers to pursue. The main argument in favor is that such methods may be used to improve scientific knowledge. Yet this raises the question whether a randomized experimental design is really necessary to advance knowledge. Might we instead make do with using observational studies instead? Observational studies have the advantage of studying the response to real incidents. Fabricating plausible incidents may be hard, and there is a history of difficulty in other areas of information security that have tried to rely on 'synthetic' data, notably in intrusion detection [12].

Furthermore, individual ethics must also be considered. Wasting the time and energy of frontline responders on fabricated requests suggests real harm is caused by the experiments. In particular, the responders typically have substantial resource constraints and already find it difficult to keep up with the number of legitimate take-down requests. In sum, we believe the fabrication of reports to study take-down is usually unethical.

Dilemma 4: Should researchers collect world-readable data from 'private' locations? Our final 'measurement' ethical dilemma concerns the type of data that is suitable for collection. Researchers must often be creative to identify suitable data sources.

Many websites make use of The Webalizer, a program for summarizing web server log files. It creates reports of how many visitors looked at the website, what times of day they came, the most popular pages on the website, and so forth. It is not uncommon to leave these reports 'world-readable' in a standard location on the server, which means that anyone can inspect their contents. We have repeatedly collected Webalizer reports from websites that have been compromised and loaded with phishing pages.

But is it ethical to collect such 'world-readable' data in order to conduct research? In practice, most website operators who make their Webalizer logs public did not take an explicit decision to do so, and we expect that many would choose to make them private once they became aware they were in fact publicly available. We decided to collect the data for two main reasons. First, it enabled us to answer research questions that otherwise would not have been possible. Second, the data available through logs does not include personally-identifiable information, which lessens the scope for harm by collecting the data.

On balance, we feel the opportunities for scientific advancement outweigh the risks to an individual website operator in collecting the data. However, it is a judgment call, and one that should be weighed on a case-by-case basis.

3   Explaining Take-Down

This section considers the two main dilemmas that we have encountered when analyzing criminal activity.

The first dilemma is that our analysis may be superior to that of the criminals, and our insights will assist them in becoming more efficient. This concern about having a superior analysis is subtly different from the ethical question of whether criminality should be studied at all, which is usually seen as being a case of catching up with the bad guys. The usual answer put forward in defense of a 'full disclosure' policy is that the criminals already know how to be bad, and it is beneficial for the good guys to have a fuller understanding. As Hobbs put it back in 1853 in the context of studying the insecurity of locks [9]:

> Rogues are very keen in their profession, and know already much more than we can teach them respecting their several kinds of roguery.

Or as Bishop John Wilkins put it two hundred years earlier [35]:

> If all those useful Inventions that are liable to abuse, should therefore be concealed, there is not any Art or Science which might be lawfully profest.

The second dilemma is that we may be explaining weaknesses in the criminals' systems that can be used by investigators to get an 'edge'. Once those weaknesses are explained, the criminals may be able to fix them. As researchers, we may be completely unaware of what use the weaknesses are being put to, and so any public discussion will carry the risk that we are making the situation worse, rather than better.

Dilemma 5: What if our analysis will assist criminals? In our first paper about phishing [14] we analyzed the relative take-down performance of traditional phishing websites and botnet-hosted fast-flux systems. We observed that although the lifetime of individual servers was less on the fast-flux systems it was still substantial. The criminals clearly expected to have much lower lifetimes because they used five or more servers in parallel to compensate for failures. We didn't spell out that our figures showed this was unnecessarily cautious, and the criminals have continued to use multiple servers in parallel, which has considerably simplified detecting the use of fast-flux systems.

In that first paper we also observed that since the server lifetimes were so high, setting appropriate time-to-live values would be likely to keep the criminal sites available in the DNS caches of large ISPs, even when domain names were taken down. Once again we didn't especially stress this point, and we are not aware of criminals taking this approach, but once again our measurements and analysis had shown the use of sub-optimal trade-offs in criminal system design, and our dilemma had been the extent to which we should improve the intellectual value of our paper versus the help we might give the criminals. In the event, we chose to sacrifice some clarity in our exposition, and the criminals missed our point, and have yet to do anything imaginative with time-to-live values.

Dilemma 6: Should investigatory techniques be revealed? It is not appropriate to write computer security papers which keep some parts of the methodology secret. Experiments should be reproducible by others to confirm the accuracy of results (never mind that in computer security it is almost impossible to find a venue that will publish papers that merely confirm what others have found, triggering doubt as to how often such reproduction is attempted).

The main effect has been that we have failed to conduct some research or publish some results because we would need to reveal how we knew what we did. For example, the existence of 'back doors' in phishing kits was widely known about before Netcraft decided to write about it on their blog [20]. The freely available phishing kits sent details of compromised victims not only to the criminal who deployed them, but also, in various obfuscated ways, to webmail accounts operated by the 'Mr Brain' gang. We speculate that tipping off criminals to the existence of such back-doors will have impeded law-enforcement investigations by eliminating central repositories of victim details.

As a further example, the location of the rock-phish gang's 'motherships' could only be determined by inspecting traffic that traversed one of the relay machines. Consequently, as part of our research we spent some effort in providing live feeds of their location to police forces so they could visit active machines and monitor the traffic. We then discovered a technique for remotely identifying the mothership location.[2] Even now this technique may be of use to future investigators, so we still have chosen not to reveal it here.

Many researchers do not see these types of issues as a dilemma, falling back on 'full disclosure' arguments. Recently Billy Rios, a "security engineer for a major software firm" took a look at a kit for Zeus, a major component of criminal attacks on banking customers that are netting many millions of dollars [31] (and pounds [8] and rubles [33]) a month. His blog post [28] explained how a file injection vulnerability in the code could be leveraged to inspect the internals of this crimeware. There are said to be several hundred Zeus-related botnets and many are under active investigation by law enforcement (only a few days later a major series of arrests were made). Disclosing this vulnerability could well have jeopardized some of these investigations. Rios, however, did not seem to mind:

> There are some fascinating things to consider when finding bugs in software that is used primarily by criminals, but I won't bore you with that now. Instead I'd like to share with you some of the more interesting parts of my research.

Rios argues that the information he has disclosed will assist in defending against the Zeus threat, although in what he has published thus far he has not explained what this assistance might be.

---

[2] For some time, one of the motherships was located at a hosting provider in suburban Seattle, a most convenient place for investigators to visit.

4   Fixing Take-Down

During the course of our research, we have gained a better understanding of how to make take-down a more effective tool for improving information security. This has led to several dilemmas over the choices we face in 'fixing' take-down. We discuss three of them here. First, those who identify content that should be removed must decide whether to publish lists of this content, since this will help researchers and defenders but can also aid criminals. Second, when recommending a change in policy, we must balance between what we believe to be right and what we know to be achievable. Third, while take-down may improve security, it can sometimes conflict with the principles of a free and open society. Consequently, the benefits of any mechanism that expedites take-down in the short term must be weighed against the potential for its abuse by others.

Dilemma 7: When should datasets be made public or kept secret? Given the many types of online material targeted for take-down, a natural question arises: should a public record be kept, or would society's interests be better served by keeping the information secret? In a few contexts, public lists are kept. For example, PhishTank (`phishtank.com`) reports known phishing websites, Chilling Effects (`chillingeffects.org`) documents DMCA take-down requests, and Artists Against 419 (`aa419.org`) publishes records of websites that support advanced-fee fraud.

Publishing reports offers several advantages. It increases transparency, important given that so much take-down is coordinated by the private action of volunteers. It enables research to be reproducible, while creating the potential for richer investigation by people who otherwise would not have access to the information. Finally, it can help defenders expedite the take-down process. For instance, we found that phishing websites reported to PhishTank were less likely to be recompromised than websites which only appeared in secret lists [18].

Of course, there are downsides to publishing take-down lists. The list could help the attacker by revealing what the defender knows, as well as providing a source of future targets. It could even help criminals copy caches of credentials from each other, much as we ourselves did and discussed in Dilemma 2. Sometimes knowledge of the content being taken down is problematic: publishing locations of child sexual abuse images would certainly be harmful.

Finally, publishing a record of offending content will 'name and shame' responsible parties and victims, which they may not appreciate. In [17], we explained how `chat2me247.com` had been repeatedly compromised through targeted web searches and loaded with phishing pages. In October 2010, the webmaster of `chat2me247.com` wrote us to complain that we had publicly discussed the website's security problems. We chose not to ask for the website's permission before writing about it because the information we gathered was public: some of the phishing pages on `chat2me247.com` had appeared on PhishTank, and the Webalizer logs we collected were also made publicly available.

Given these downsides, some have devised alternative arrangements to public disclosure. One popular compromise is to publish a cryptographic hash of the records, so that anyone can still verify whether a record is present in the list without making the entire list public. For example, the Google Safe Browsing API[3] only allows users to verify whether suspected URLs are malicious. This strikes a balance that protects users without letting the world know which websites have been infected. There are significant downsides to this approach, however, which should be considered. Secondary research is severely limited. Outside researchers cannot answer even basic questions, such as whether the number of take-down requests grows or shrinks over time. Defenders can also be hampered by the hashing arrangement. For example, a hosting provider who manages many websites cannot easily determine whether they are present in the blacklist, and so cannot proactively respond.

Some researchers have opted for a completely private exchange of information. For instance, groups such as Team Cymru (`team-cymru.org`) and Shadowserver (`shadowserver.org`) directly pass along lists of machines suspected of participation in botnets to the relevant ISPs. These informal arrangements have low overhead and ensure a timely response and shield the ISP from any fear of public humiliation. The downsides to this arrangement are similar to those of hash-based arrangements, with the added cost of requiring explicit cooperation between all partners for positive gains to be realized.

Why is selecting a method of publishing an ethical issue? We argue that those involved in take-down should consider how to protect individuals from harm while creating an opportunity for research to advance the understanding of how to better perform take-down. Opting to keep information private can be even more dangerous than the reckless publication of information that aids attackers. The harm may be more difficult to directly observe (slowed take-down speed, lack of pressure to improve practices, etc.) but equally destructive.

Dilemma 8: Is the fix realistic, and does it consider the incentives of all the participants? As we explained earlier, we believe that security stems in a large part from getting the economics of the situation correct, and that often means aligning incentives and making an entity that is able to fix the security issue responsible for doing so – even if the original problem was not of their making.

This analysis has led us to make controversial recommendations for information sharing in the anti-phishing community. Our paper conclusively demonstrated that damage was being done by the compartmentalizing of data about where the websites were located – our 'sound-bite' is that "bank phishing websites are taken down in four hours when the banks know about them, and four days if they don't". We suggested that the take-down companies should be forced to share information by their customers (the banks) renegotiating their contracts. This suggestion did not impress the take-down companies, and Eric Olsen wrote a comprehensive rebuttal [22], suggesting that we would destroy the incentives to improve the quality of feeds and permit 'free riding'. We responded to this [13] with a suggestion as to how feeds could be shared for payment in such a way as to keep the incentives in place, and the following year one of us co-authored

---

[3] http://code.google.com/apis/safebrowsing/

a paper on a data sharing protocol, with strong information-hiding guarantees, that would support the sharing-for-payment concept [19].

In this case: at best our initial paper exemplified classic academic naïveté in proposing a system that would not work in the real world, at worst we were wrong to put the idea forward without further explanation, and through the unnecessary controversy we reduced the impact of some important measurements whose implications needed to be understood by the whole take-down industry.

Measurements we made (in [15]) of data from the Internet Watch Foundation mean that we can add to our sound-bite, "and child sexual abuse image websites are removed in four weeks". This quite scandalous statistic arises, we believe, because the 'hot-lines' who share information about this type of content fail to tell the hosting companies that they are providing services to criminals. The hot-lines do tell the police, but their lines of communication can be slow, and policing incentives are more to do with catching the criminals than in getting the website taken down.

Once again our recommendations for improvement have been seen as unrealistic – in particular we understand that INHOPE,[4] the international association of hot-lines, forbids members from contacting hosting providers located in a country where another INHOPE member operates. This is clearly obstructive and so we continue to believe that our recommendations about sharing are the ethical ones, even though they do not currently appear to be practical without the disbandment or restructuring of INHOPE.

Dilemma 9: What if the fix is worse than the problem? We believe that when we put forward solutions to problems we have an ethical responsibility to ensure that we will not be making things worse.

We could, for example, make a clear case for the benefits of restricting the registering of misleading domain names, and of being able to precisely identify who was making the registrations, but we believe that such measures would be incompatible with a free and open society. For every fake `barklays.com` that was blocked[5] there would also be the restriction to free speech of blocking, say, `barclayssucks.com`.[6] The Peoples' Republic of China has chosen to make it compulsory to provide photographic identification of `.cn` domain registrants [3] with the stated intention of tackling pornography, but many commentators have suggested that the real intent is to suppress dissident use of the Internet.

In this context we note with some alarm the recent RPZ proposal by Paul Vixie which codifies a method for suppressing DNS results [32]. Vixie envisages that the new system will be used to disrupt malware rendezvous and command-and-control mechanisms. However we believe that politicians worldwide could immediately understand the message to be "there is now a standard

---

[4] `http://www.inhope.org`

[5] In fact `barklays.com` is owned by a small business in Oshawa, Canada and currently redirects to the website for a Canadian fishing (`f` not `ph`) TV show. It has nothing to do with the global banking group Barclays plc.

[6] `barclayssucks.com` currently appears to be registered by Barclays themselves, but at present it is 'parked' with no Barclays-related content.

and
easy-to-deploy method of insisting that particular domains must be censored".
They might bring forward a whole raft of censorship initiatives, to block access to child sexual abuse sites, offshore gambling, adult pornography, political dissidents, and even, in Turkey, `richarddawkins.com`.

This type of blocking, 'DNS poisoning', has been implemented in ad hoc mechanisms for years despite clear evidence of unintended collateral damage [6] and relatively simple evasion [4]. The difference Vixie has made is to make the mechanism standard, to provide the functionality in the normal code base, and to provide authorities with the ability to identify conformance by the inspection of configuration files. The RPZ will probably have an impact on botnet design, and will be outflanked as other rendezvous systems come to the fore. Time will tell if the short-term disruption to the criminals is outweighed by the harm that we predict will stem from this well-meaning, but ethically dubious, proposal.

5   Related Work

Information security researchers have encountered numerous ethical dilemmas. In one early work, Spafford argued that, under most circumstances, unauthorized access to a computer is unethical [29]. Indeed, in most countries such unauthorized access is also illegal. More recently, following the rise of botnets, researchers and practitioners have argued over whether defenders could or should intervene to remediate botnet-infected computers. Dittrich et al. [5] discuss this and several related open ethical questions regarding how best to fight botnets.

Perhaps most closely related to the dilemmas we discuss in this paper is the quandary facing researchers who infiltrated a portion of the Storm botnet in order to measure its activity [10]. To obtain a more accurate measurement of Storm activity, the authors took control of a portion of the botnet and allowed it to continue operation rather than shut down the machines under its control. The authors followed a self-declared ethical principle of "strictly reducing harm": no additional spam was sent out than otherwise would have been, and they blocked purchase of goods advertised by the spam. Nevertheless, consumer machines under their control sent slightly modified spam as directed by the botnet's controller. This led to unprecedented measurements of botnet activity, but at the cost of permitting some harm that they were in a position to reduce.

6   Conclusion

This case study has set out the nature of nine ethical dilemmas we have faced over the past few years as we conducted research into the take-down of criminal websites. Our aim has not been to set out ethical principles that could guide others, or to promote our ethical choices as if we were paragons to be emulated, but rather to provide a rich set of 'war stories' which illuminate the issues we have faced and document the choices we have made. Undoubtedly, others might have done things differently, and with the benefit of hindsight we might have been more cautious in our handling of credentials and more circumspect in our recommendations. We hope that, at the least, our experiences will make others pause before rushing into research activity, and at best we have offered deeper thinkers than ourselves access to practical material for testing their ethical principles.

References

1. Ahlert, C., Marsden, C., Yung, C.: How 'Liberty' disappeared from cyberspace: the mystery shopper tests Internet content self-regulation (2004),
   http://pcmlp.socleg.ox.ac.uk/text/liberty.pdf
2. Anderson, R., Moore, T.: The economics of information security. Science 314(5799), 610–613 (2006)
3. Chao, L.: China Porn Measures Raise Fear Of Censors. Wall Street Journal, page A10 (December 17, 2009),
   http://online.wsj.com/article/SB126098577403994051.html
4. Clayton, R.: Anonymity and Traceability in Cyberspace. Technical Report UCAM-CL-TR-653, University of Cambridge Computer Laboratory (2005)
5. Dittrich, D., Leder, F., Werner, T.: A Case Study in Ethical Decision Making Regarding Remote Mitigation of Botnets. In: Sion, R., Curtmola, R., Dietrich, S., Kiayias, A., Miret, J.M., Sako, K., Sebé, F. (eds.) RLCPS, WECSR, and WLC 2010. LNCS, vol. 6054, pp. 216–230. Springer, Heidelberg (2010)
6. Dornseif, M.: Government mandated blocking of foreign web content. In: von Knop, J., Haverkamp, W., Jessen, E. (eds.): Security, E-Learning, E-Services: Proceedings of the 17. DFN-Arbeitstagung über Kommunikationsnetze, Düsseldorf, Lecture Notes in Informatics, pp. 617–648 (2003)
7. Franklin, J., Paxson, V., Perrig, A., Savage, S.: An inquiry into the nature and causes of the wealth of Internet miscreants. In: Proceedings of the 14th ACM Conference on Computer and Communications Security (CCS), pp. 375–388. ACM Press, New York (2007)
8. Gill, C.: Hi-tech crime police quiz 19 people over Internet bank scam that netted hackers up to £20m from British accounts. Daily Mail (September 29, 2010),
   http://www.dailymail.co.uk/news/article-1316022/Nineteen-arrested-online-bank-raid-netted-20m.html
9. Hobbs, A.C. (Tomlinson, C. (ed.)): Locks and Safes: The Construction of Locks. Virtue and Co., London (1853)
10. Kanich, C., Kreibich, C., Levchenko, K., Enright, B., Voelker, G.M., Paxson, V., Savage, S.: Spamalytics: an empirical analysis of spam marketing conversion. In: Proceedings of the 15th ACM CCS, pp. 3–14. ACM Press, New York (2008)
11. Kemmerer, R.: How to steal a botnet and what can happen when you do. Google Tech Talk (2009), http://www.youtube.com/watch?v=2GdqoQJa6r4
12. McHugh, J.: Testing intrusion detection systems: a critique of the 1998 and 1999 DARPA intrusion detection system evaluations as performed by Lincoln Laboratory. ACM Transactions on Information and System Security 3(4), 262–294 (2000)
13. Moore, T.: How can we co-operate to tackle phishing? Light Blue Touchpaper (October 27, 2008),
    http://www.lightbluetouchpaper.org/2008/10/27/how-can-we-co-operate-to-tackle-phishing/
14. Moore, T., Clayton, R.: Examining the impact of website take-down on phishing. In: 2nd Anti-Phishing Working Group eCrime Researchers Summit (APWG eCrime), pp. 1–13. ACM Press, New York (2007)

15. Moore, T., Clayton, R.: The Impact of Incentives on Notice and Take-down. In: Eric Johnson, M. (ed.) Managing Information Risk and the Economics of Security, pp. 199–223. Springer, New York (2008)
16. Moore, T., Clayton, R.: The consequence of non-cooperation in the fight against phishing. In: Anti-Phishing Working Group eCrime Researchers Summit (APWG eCrime), pp. 1–14. IEEE (2008)
17. Moore, T., Clayton, R.: Evil Searching: Compromise and Recompromise of Internet Hosts for Phishing. In: Dingledine, R., Golle, P. (eds.) FC 2009. LNCS, vol. 5628, pp. 256–272. Springer, Heidelberg (2009)
18. Moore, T., Clayton, R.: The impact of public information on phishing attack and defense. Communications and Strategies 81(1), 45–68 (2011)
19. Moran, T., Moore, T.: The Phish-Market Protocol: Securely Sharing Attack Data Between Competitors. In: Sion, R. (ed.) FC 2010. LNCS, vol. 6052, pp. 222–237. Springer, Heidelberg (2010)
20. Mutton, P.: Mr-Brain: Stealing Phish from Fraudsters. Netcraft Blog (January 22, 2008),
   http://news.netcraft.com/archives/2008/01/22/mrbrain_stealing_phish_from_fraudsters.html
21. Nas, S.: The Multatuli project: ISP notice & take down. In: SANE (2004),
   http://www.bof.nl/docs/researchpaperSANE.pdf
22. Olsen, E.: A Contrary Perspective – Forced Data Sharing Will Decrease Performance and Reduce Protection. Cyveillance Blog (October 28, 2008),
   http://www.cyveillanceblog.com/phishing/a-contrary-perspective-%E2%80%93-forced-data-sharing-will-decrease-performance-and-reduce-protection
23. Perrow, M.: Click's botnet experiment. BBC Editors blog (March 13, 2009),
   http://www.bbc.co.uk/blogs/theeditors/2009/03/click_botnet_experiment.html
24. Masons, P.: BBC programme broke law with botnets, says lawyer. Out-law news (March 12, 2009), http://www.out-law.com/page-9863
25. Pocock, S.J.: When to stop a clinical trial. British Medical Journal 305(6847), 235–240 (1992)
26. Provos, N., Mavrommatis, P., Rajab, M., Monrose, F.: All your iFrames point to us. In: 17th USENIX Security Symposium, pp. 1–15 (2008)
27. Rasmussen, R.: Personal Communication (August 13, 2010)
28. Rios, B.: Turning the Tables – Part I (September 27, 2010),
   http://xs-sniper.com/blog/2010/09/27/turning-the-tables/
29. Spafford, E.H.: Are computer hacker break-ins ethical? Journal of Systems and Software 17(1), 41–48 (1992)
30. Stone-Gross, B., Cova, M., Cavallaro, L., Gilbert, B., Szydlowski, M., Kemmerer, R., Kruegel, C., Vigna, G.: Your botnet is my botnet: analysis of a botnet takeover. In: Proceedings of the 16th ACM CCS, pp. 635–647. ACM Press, New York (2009)
31. US Department of Justice: Manhattan U.S. Attorney Charges 37 Defendants Involved in Global Bank Fraud Schemes that Used 'Zeus Trojan' and Other Malware to Steal Millions of Dollars from U.S. Bank Accounts (press release September 30, 2010), http://newyork.fbi.gov/dojpressrel/pressrel10/nyfo093010.html

32. Vixie, P.: Taking Back the DNS. CircleID (July 30, 2010),
    http://www.circleid.com/posts/20100728_taking_back_the_dns/
33. Warner, G.: Is Russia joining the Zeus hunt? Cybercrime & Doing Time (October
    4, 2010),
    http://garwarner.blogspot.com/2010/10/is-russia-joining-zeus-hunt.html
34. Weaver, R., Collins, M.P.: Fishing for phishes: applying capture-recapture meth-
    ods to estimate phishing populations. In: Anti-Phishing Working Group eCrime
    Researchers Summit (APWG eCrime), pp. 14–25. ACM Press, New York (2007)
35. Wilkins, J.: Mercury: Or the Secret and Swift Messenger. Maynard and Wilkins,
    London (1641)

Ethical Considerations of Sharing Data
for Cybersecurity Research

Darren Shou

Symantec Research Labs, Culver City CA 92030, USA
darren_shou@symantec.com

Abstract. Governments, companies, and scientists performing cyber security research need reference data sets, based on real systems and users, to test the validity and efficacy of the predictions of a given theory. However, various ethical and practical concerns complicate when and how proprietary operational data should be shared. In this paper, we discuss hypothetical and actual examples to illustrate the reasons for increasing the availability of data for legitimate research purposes. We also discuss the reasons, such as privacy and competition, to limit data sharing. We discuss the capabilities and limitations of several existing models of data sharing. We present an infrastructure specifically designed for making proprietary operational data available for cyber security research and experimentation. We conclude by discussing the ways in which a new infrastructure, WINE, balances the values of openness, sound experimentation, and privacy by enabling data sharing with privacy controls.

Keywords: Data sharing, ethics, security.

1 Introduction

1.1 Data Needs of Cybersecurity Research

Real world data is necessary for research and there is broad consensus in the security research community on what kind of data is needed [5]. Access to the large scale datasets needed for security research is limited primarily to the organizations that curate information for operational use in products. This access limitation is primarily due to intellectual property and privacy risks. These practical concerns are pitted against the ethical principle that access to data should be open and the scientific need for data to confirm experimental predictions. An increased availability of data would increase the research that could be performed and the usefulness of the results. Done properly, the availability of common datasets would enable peer review of cyber-security research. For the above reasons, increased data sharing has the potential to improve cyber-security research. In this paper we examine the practical and ethical aspects of data sharing, discuss the capabilities and limitations of several existing models of data sharing and propose a model of data sharing for data generators. An example infrastructure that accommodates the concerns of this model is titled the Worldwide Intelligence Network Environment (WINE).

G. Danezis, S. Dietrich, and K. Sako (Eds.): FC 2011 Workshops, LNCS 7126, pp. 169–177, 2012.

1.2 Existing Data Sharing Models

Companies and operators currently share data with academic and institutional researchers in several ways. Three approaches for data sharing are: using interns as data envoys, ad hoc sponsored research and data clearinghouses. Companies often hire interns from academic labs to experiment on the company's data. By using interns, companies maintain intellectual property rights and diminish the risk of data leakage. Unfortunately, the scale of using interns is limited by funding and the interns' time. As a result, the duration of such a data sharing project is often too short to accomplish significant results. Companies often contract research with university groups in order to share data. Again this does not scale well and benefits a relatively small group of researchers. Data clearinghouses like the Internet Traffic Archive collect datasets and make them publicly available for researchers. We list several specific examples below and elucidate their capabilities and limitations.

The Internet Systems Consortium provides a private information sharing framework, the Security Information Exchange (ISC SIE). It allows participants to contribute live feeds to be consumed by other members [12]. A limitation of this model is that does not provide a data preservation mechanism.

The Department of Homeland Security maintains a data archive known as PREDICT, the Protected Repository for the Defense of Infrastructure Against Cyber Threats. PREDICT acts as a clearinghouse between data providers and researchers [8]. A limitation of PREDICT is that data providers can retire datasets, making it impossible to reproduce past experiments.

The Internet Measurement Data Catalogue (DatCat) model is a searchable registry of donated data [10]. The DatCat model promotes reproducible research since researchers can cite the dataset handle in their research. Unfortunately, the database is down indefinitely.

The Internet Traffic Archive (ITA) contains mostly filtered network traffic traces [13].

The SIE, PREDICT, DatCat, and ITA models for data sharing have certain valuable capabilities but are limited in that none of them are data generators; they all rely on others for data contribution. Relying on donations from data generators is fundamentally problematic since data generators such as network operators and software companies often view the data they produce as intellectual property and a competitive advantage. Yet, a large amount of the interesting data needed by security researchers is collected, curated and preserved by such companies. Thus, a model for data generators to safely share their operational data without giving up control to a data collector would benefit the research community.

2 Ethical Considerations of Data Sharing

A number of statutes govern the legality of certain activities related to conducting cyber-security research [1][2][3]. However, ethical actions are not the same as legal actions; there exist legal activities that are not ethically permissible.

The ethics addressed in this paper refer to well-founded standards of right and wrong. In the rapidly evolving field of data gathering it is possible to amass information on billions of people around the world in seconds. Not only must researchers ask whether their experiment is scientifically valuable, they must consider certain ethical questions. Researchers should ask, "Is this the right way to go about doing this experiment?" One can frame the applied ethics by relating to norms in research, such as knowledge, truth and the avoidance of error. In this paper we will examine three specific aspects of scientific ethical concerns: openness, privacy, and sound experimentation. To begin, there exists tension between privacy and openness. The issue is, how can those with data allow external research on that data in a manner that is both secure, with respect to privacy in particular, and also open? Only if this can be accomplished can we then enable meaningful confirmation of experimental research results.

2.1 Balancing Privacy Rights

As we consider sharing data to improve research and thus deliver technology value to society, we may observe that the ethical principle of privacy is seemingly in conflict with the ethical principle behind our desire to share: openness. Openness calls for sharing data, tools, ideas and results, whereas privacy calls for freedom from observation.

Specifically, sharing data involves two parties: those that have the data and those that want to conduct research. There is a moral objection based on the principle of privacy that is raised with regards to both parties. First, the data is collected from consenting research participants who have the right to protect their personally identifiable information (PII). Second, companies that generate data from these research participants have good reason to maintain secrecy with regards to data that they have collected and enriched. These datasets may represent intellectual property (IP) and a competitive advantage. In sum, companies have IP concerns and research participants have PII concerns. Any model of data sharing must balance the privacy risks of both groups to the potential benefits that accrue from openly sharing data for research results.

The issue is that much of the data needed for critical cyber-security research relies on data from real networks and users. For example, intrusion detection is dependent on large volumes of traffic so that researchers may generate signatures that minimize false positives and false negatives. There are of course several privacy laws that limit access to network traffic or address the storage of this information. In the US, there is the Wiretap Act that prohibits interception of the contents of communications, the Pen/Trap statute that prohibits real time interception of the non-content, and the Stored Communications Act that prohibits providers from knowingly disclosing their customer's communications [1][2][3]. The Health Insurance Portability and Accountability Act (HIPAA) of 1996 attempts to balance privacy protection while still making information available for research [11]. HIPAA restricts disclosures of health information but provides means for researchers to obtain information with and without individual consent. HIPAA is both an example that provisions to make information available for research should be built into privacy laws and that improper regulation may inadvertently decrease the amount of such information. Unfortunately, unlike HIPAA, the current cyber privacy laws contain no research exceptions.

But these laws lack complete guidance when it comes to data that is volunteered with informed consent for the purpose of research activities. Thus we must establish ourselves how we ought to protect privacy but still enable sharing to capture the value of open research. To do this, we must examine the benefit and harm to the user that volunteers the data. Data curators should strive to be responsible stewards of the user's information they hold, protecting the ability for people to seclude themselves or reveal their information selectively. The use of the data should also be restricted to activities that provide value back to those whose information was volunteered. The main privacy concern in security research exists mainly because sensitive personally identifiable information may be present in the data we are looking to conduct research on and there are those that would expose or use this PII in ways that do not benefit those that volunteered data. Typically, the response to this concern has been technological. Technology can mitigate the risk, namely data handling tools such as anonymization and data leak protection (DLP) tools. Carefully anonymized datasets can be useful since they reveal very little about individuals while still allowing researchers to learn from the data. However, the possibility of re-identification is changing the belief that perfect anonymization is possible [7][16]. Given that we can not rely on anonymization as a panacea, we must seek additional protections.

First, we note that as a subset of researchers, rarely do academics have the motive to re-identify people in data as part of their experiments. And so, data curators may prefer to share data with only trusted researchers such as the academic community. Of note, academics are already making use of data sets made available on an ad hoc basis or via a partnership with a data generator or which they obtained themselves. Given that some researchers already have access to datasets that may be subject to privacy concerns, expanding the availability of data to a larger number of the same community should not make the situation morally worse. Yet increasing the broad sharing of datasets, if only to academics, does make the situation of openness morally better. In addition, the feared consequences of re-identification can occur, in some cases, regardless of any new plan to increase sharing with academic researchers. Fortunately, a carefully planned model of data sharing for cyber security research may improve the situation by implementing technology, data handling techniques, and access policies such as restricting access to only trusted parties [16]. Taken one step further, those wishing to share private data publicly may do so by restricting the data access to be on-site where data handling can be more strictly enforced and motive may be further examined.

We have seen how we can protect the PII of research participants using trusted relationships and data handling policy. Yet we also have to address the secrecy of the organizations that have this data from the participants to share. However, the compromise to use trusted parties to not reveal PII may also be of help with

IP. That is, restricting proprietary data access to the same trusted relationship, academic researchers, keeps the research largely pre-competitive.

In sum, it is possible for companies and operators to strike a balance between privacy and openness to protect both PII and IP. If we can remove some of the more serious moral privacy objections, like PII exposure risk, to data sharing, what additional challenges remain?

2.2   Openness

As we have seen, there exists tension between openness and privacy. There are also additional objections to the ethical principle that data, results and ideas should be shared and made available for peer review. Those that wish to conduct research on the data have concerns about priority and recognition in addition to the PII risk issues. Those that have the data, such as companies and operators, have aforementioned intellectual property issues, as well as motive issues. To implement a broad data sharing program, a data curator would have to consider operational expenses and the benefit of such an investment.

Consider first the issue of priority and recognition. For example, a situation where a computer security researcher has proprietary access to a massive network trace dataset and conducts research that identifies a particular threat and a novel approach to addressing the threat. Should the author share the dataset although doing so may allow others to conduct research she might have interest in: and allow them priority and recognition [18]? The central question is how to weigh the benefit of the additional research that will follow from her sharing of the data against her personal ambitions. Her sharing the dataset with other researchers would serve not only the advancement of knowledge but also the public security interest.

Now consider the second issue of motive to share for a data curator. Practical financial considerations must be addressed when companies practice scientific openness. First, can private data be liberated in a way that it is truly democratically available? Should a public company with petabytes of operational data be compelled to provide this data to its competitors as well as to educators and researchers? The costs of storing, transmitting, maintaining and protecting large amounts of data are not inconsequential; who should bear the costs?

A solution for both researchers and data curators may be found in a model of data sharing that makes several concessions. First, a potential compromise is for public companies to make data broadly available for non-competitive purposes such as academic research. If an academic team has an idea for improving detection rates of say, malware, the team may use company data in their experiments. In this case, the academics would own their IP but not the shared data. Thus there is still an incentive for data curators to share since they can license IP generated. Arrangements can also be made to encourage publication of the research results, but not the data (so as to protect any PII), in a manner that protects priority and recognition for researchers.

A consequence of our model of sharing is that it enables confirmation and sound experimentation. With the data centrally shared, repeatability is straightforward. Given trusted party access to data and open publication of experiments, we can then minimize experimental errors and more securely trust in experimental results.

2.3   Enabling Sound Scientific Experimentation

Earlier we described how the availability of data is necessary for additional and better scientific experimentation. Experimental results must be independently confirmable if they are to be accepted by the scientific community and useful to commercial enterprises. Peer review and reproducibility are fundamental elements of the scientific method; these are the primary methods for identifying flaws in scientific research; everything from falsified data to statistically insignificance or misleading results. Scientific peer review is a self-correcting mechanism that eventually catches those that try to cheat the system, but it is imperfect; misleading, erroneous or fraudulent research can go undetected for years.

Confirmation is the best guard against flawed science and fraud. Two particular causes of flawed scientific research are the use of inadequate data sets and experimentation on data that is not archived for future access. If researchers do not have access to the appropriate data, then they cannot criticize fully or make comparisons between competing claims. Furthermore, if a given technology is only tested on a dataset that is knowingly orders of magnitude smaller than what is possible, then is any resulting error misconduct or accidental? Accidental experimental dataset errors will be reduced if scientists have access to the most comprehensive datasets as reference sets. The availability of such data sets would allow researchers to make fruitful comparisons between competing mechanisms, broadly measure progress, and validate or refute the claims of others. An example of this is the National Science Foundation policy that researchers must archive their data and methods so that others may test the methods and data [15]. In sum, the availability of archival data is essential for experiments to be verified through reproduction and for reliability to be measured with statistical analysis.

ITA and similar aforementioned models address the cost issue from a technical standpoint since they offer to maintain a central repository of data for multiple researchers. However, given the risks associated with intellectual property and proprietary information facing operators and companies, it is more likely that most companies will want to host their own datasets onsite. Furthermore, if an operator restricts to onsite access only, it can provide more than just data. It can provide computing resources, subject experts and experimentation facilities. Having researchers onsite with companies' datasets encourages cross-fertilization of ideas amongst researchers and employees, potentially resulting in increased commercial technology.

3   Conclusion

In this paper we have discussed the need for cyber security research that is based on data from real users and systems. The idea of sharing scientific data for the public good was the impetus for the sharing mandates and guidelines in the America COMPETES Act. Specifically, the America COMPETES Act (or the "America Creating Opportunities to Meaningfully Promote Excellence in Technology, Education, and Science Act") requires civilian federal agencies to facilitate the open exchange of data and research between agencies and the public. This underscores the importance of information sharing for the public good [4].

In addition, data sharing is good for the cyber security research community. The health care research community recognizes the benefits of sharing to accelerate progress of research as well as the application for the public good [14]. But medical researchers are also aware of the hazards of data withholding. For example, within their literature there are studies showing demonstrated negative effects of data withholding including delayed research, inefficient training, and a detrimental quality of relationships with other scientists [21].

However, while research collaborations involving data sharing are happening in the medical community, it is lacking in the cyber security community. In order to implement data sharing in a responsible manner for our discipline, we must make it subject to appropriate safeguards. We have already proposed controls to protect the privacy of individuals as well as an approach that preserves the incentives of curating proprietary information. And this model of data sharing provides scientists a mechanism for confirming experimental results.

Symantec's Worldwide Intelligence Network Environment (WINE) is an existing implementation of such a data sharing model. WINE addresses two related shortcoming of the various existing data sharing models, SIE, PREDICT, Dat-Cat, and ITA; these models rely on volunteered data and the continued availability of the data is subject to the whims of those that volunteered the data.

WINE provides academics with access to precisely those security related data feeds that many data generators choose not to volunteer. WINE makes available telemetry data from over 75 million participating machines, including every attack on both the file system or network. Such attack data includes a rich set of metadata including anonymized attacking addresses, OS version, process name, geographic local, language, URL the file or attack came from, etc. In addition, the dataset includes 5.5 million malware, 100,000 spam emails, and 60 TB of binaries' metadata gathered from millions of sensors, honeynets and decoy accounts: [19]. Where applicable, tools, scripts, and documentation will also be archived with datasets. Furthermore, WINE retains datasets indefinitely, as permitted by cost and legal restrictions. This allows scientists to reproduce past experiments and compare the effectiveness of older algorithms to newer ones.

In the WINE model, researchers browse a catalogue of datasets and construct a proposal along with a data request. The validity of the proposals and the availability of the requested data are evaluated by an advisory board of external and internal researchers. The intellectual property developed by the researchers using WINE is theirs and they are encouraged to publish their results responsibly.

The WINE model thus encourages data curators to share, minimizes the privacy risks to participants, and maximizes benefits to researchers, participants, curators and the public good. We sincerely hope that, for the benefit of cybersecurity research, other companies choose to establish models similar to the guidelines set out in this paper.

References

1. 18 U.S.C. §2510-2522. Wire and Electronic Communications Interception and Interception of Oral Communications
2. 18 U.S.C. §2701-2711. Electronic Communications Privacy Act: Stored Wire and Electronic Communications and Transactions Records Access
3. 18 U.S.C. §3121-3127. Pen Registers and Trap and Trace Devices
4. H.R. 2272–110th Congress: America COMPETES Act (2007) GovTrack.us, http://www.govtrack.us/congress/bill.xpd?bill=h110-2272
5. Camp, J., Cranor, L., Feamster, N., Feigenbaum, J., Forrest, S., Kotz, D., Lee, W., Lincoln, P., Paxson, V., Reiter, M., Rivest, R., Sanders, W., Savage, S., Smith, S., Spafford, E., Stolfo, S.: Data for Cybersecurity Research: Process and Wish List. In: National Science Foundation Workshop on Cyber Security Data for Experimentation (2010)
6. Chesbrough, H.: Open Business Models: How to Thrive in the New Innovation Landscape. Harvard Business School Press, Boston (2006)
7. Coull, S., Wright, C., Keromytis, A., Monrose, F., Reiter, M.: Taming the Devil: Techniques for Evaluating Anonymized Network Data. In: Proceedings of the Network and Distributed System Security Symposium, NDSS 2008, San Diego, California (2008)
8. Department of Homeland Security: Protected Repository for the Defense of Infrastructure Against Cyber Threats, https://www.predict.org
9. Google: Security, http://www.google.com/corporate/security.html
10. Internet Measurement: The Internet Measurement Data Catalogue (DatCat), http://imdc.datcat.org
11. 42 U.S.C. §17935. Health Insurance Portability and Accountability Act
12. Internet Systems Consortium: Security Information Exchange, https://sie.isc.org
13. Internet Traffic Archive: The Internet Traffic Archive (ITA), http://ita.ee.lbl.gov
14. Brest, P., Walport, M.: Sharing Research Data to Improve Public Health, http://www.wellcome.ac.uk/About-us/Policy/Spotlight-issues/Data-/sharing/Public-health-and-epidemiology/WTDV030690.html
15. National Science Foundation: Dissemination and Sharing of Research Results: NSF Data Sharing Policy, http://www.nsf.gov/bfa/dias/policy/dmp.jsp
16. Ohm, P.: Broken Promises of Privacy: Responding to the Surprising Failure of Anonymization. SSRN eLibrary (2009)
17. Powner, D.A. , Wilshusen, G.C: Key Challenges Need to Be Addressed to Improve Research and Development. Technical Report, GAO-10-466 (2010)
18. Resnik, D.B.: What is Ethics in Research and Why is it Important? National Institute of Environmental Health Sciences, http://www.niehs.nih.gov/research/resources/bioethics/whatis.cfm

19. Symantec Corporation: Internet Security Threat Report. Technical report, Syman-
    tec Managed Security Services (2010)
20. Symantec Corporation: Symantec Responsible Disclosure Policy,
    http://www.symantec.com/research/Symantec-Responsible-Disclosure.pdf
21. Vogeli, C., Yucel, R., Bendavid, E., Jones, L.M., Anderson Melissa, S., Louis, K.S.,
    Campbell, E.G.: Data Withholding and the Next Generation of Scientists: Results
    of a National Survey Academic Medicine 81(2), 128–136 (2006)

Moving Forward, Building an Ethics Community (Panel Statements)

Erin Kenneally[1], Angelos Stavrou[2], John McHugh[3], and Nicolas Christin[4,*]

[1] Cooperative Association for Internet Data Analysis, Elchemy
[2] George Mason University
[3] Redjack
[4] INI/CyLab, Carnegie Mellon University

Abstract. The organizing question around which this panel at WECSR 2011 rallied was how to move toward building a nation-state-agnostic ethics community in computer security research.

1 Ethics as a Three-Legged Stool

To jumpstart the discourse, panel moderator Erin Kenneally framed the issue of ethics in computer security research as a metaphorical three-legged stool consisting of principles, the applications of principles, and implementation of those applications. Accepting that model, the problems that define the current state of affairs of ethics in computer security research expose frailties along each of the three appendages, as well as that of a domain-agnostic yet nebulous fourth limb.

Specifically, the security research community and the larger domain of information and communication technology research (e.g., network measurement, computer-human interface, software engineering) lack shared community values - guiding principles around which 'right and wrong' research conduct can be assessed, systematized, influenced, and defended[3]. The growth and persistence of debate among relevant conference program committees over the ethical propriety of certain research offers a glimpse of this disharmony. Arguably, the problem may be less one of disagreement over principles than a failure to galvanize principles into a coherent delivery vehicle.

Moving on to the second leg of the ethics stool, the community is faced with a dearth of domain guidance and technical enablers to translate the abstract and theoretical ethics principles into practicable actions. Specifically, there is a lack of both formal institutional and ad hoc peer guidance in ethical decision management, thereby reinforcing the vacuum within which first order ethics principles are embraced at the community-level. Further, assuming the existence of guidance, there are nary few tools that embed, consistently reproduce, and

---

* Copyright © 2011, IFCA. Primary source of publication is http://www.spinger.de/comp/lncs/index.html

G. Danezis, S. Dietrich, and K. Sako (Eds.): FC 2011 Workshops, LNCS 7126, pp. 178–183, 2012.
© IFCA/Springer-Verlag Berlin Heidelberg 2012

scale such expert ethics advice. Together, these deficiencies all but relegate an ethics-by-design goal for the computer security community fantastical.

Finally, there is a shortage of forcing functions that would carry the weight of the third leg of the stool, implementing the applications of ethics principles. Specifically, while Institutional Review Boards (IRB) have carried the mandate to ensure ethics in research involving human subjects, their relevance and capabilities in computer security research is under debate. Furthermore, it is unclear the extent to which other institutions, such as conference program committees or funding agencies, can or are willing to provide the oversight and quality control to ensure that ethics are identified, applied, and evaluated in research endeavors. Incentives are the implicit fourth element of the structure that directly relate to implementation. Currently, the community of researchers are neither presented with carrots - e.g., accolades, competitive advantage by way of funding or publication, nor faced with sticks - e.g., termination of funding, conference rejection.

Lest the panel end before it got started, Kenneally segued the discussion by highlighting a path forward paved by promising mechanisms to shore up the three-legged stool. Specifically, the Menlo Report is a multi-year work in progress by a collection of community stakeholders to galvanize ethics principles and their applications. The document is modeled after the Belmont Report, a bellwether guide for biomedical and behavioral research, which roots U.S. federal regulations governing ethical protections of human subjects in research. As for tools to help elucidate and systematize the application of ethics principles, an emerging solution is the Ethical Impact Assessment (EIA)[4]. Modeled after security requirements documents (if you are a techie) or privacy impact assessments (if you are a policy wonk), the design goals of the EIA are to lower the barrier of entry for researchers and oversight or advisory entities to operationalize the application of the Menlo principles into their research design, implementation, and assessment activities. These mechanisms are a path forward for the community to embrace a self-regulatory approach to embedding ethics in their respective research so as to evolve a more mature and community-built notion of what is ethically defensible. One alternative is to wait for an unfortunate event to trigger hasty, top-down forcing functions that will likely not bear the input of this community that will shoulder much of the consequences.

2 Computer Security Ethics, Quo Vadis?

Panelist Angelos Stavrou rhetorically imparted the question, "CS Ethics, Quo Vadis?" to jumpstart his commentary.

Research Ethics has been a subject of active debate in health and human-related sciences including medicine, biology, and behavioral sciences. In those fields, researchers have to submit their research plans to an Institutional Review Board (IRB) or Ethical Review Board (ERB). Such committees are formed within the researcher?s institution to approve, monitor, and regulate conducted research that involves human subjects. The mission of these committees is to provide an independent mechanism to protect the rights and well being of the participating subjects from the effects of the conducted research.

Although the mission of the IRB and ERBs encompasses the entire research that is conducted in an institution, its role has been limited to sciences that involve human or living subjects. Their design and requirements for fields such as computer science has been vastly inadequate to capture the ?essence? of what needs to be protected and how. Researchers find themselves in a conundrum when requesting and IRB approval for research that does not involve direct human interaction but involves human activity (for instance human generated network traffic). The IRB committee either provides a ?carte blanche? to the researcher or denies the request based on unspecified concerns for harming the rights of the human subjects. In the first case, the CS researcher is compelled to explain the risks and potential harm to the human subjects only to find out that her research plan has been denied because the IRB committee does not have the mechanisms and expertise to apply medical and behavioral protocols to the new brave world of computers and computer generated information.

Moving forward, it is the duty of the computer science researchers to discuss and take action on the Ethical issues, risks, and mitigating factors for collecting, processing, and storing human generated information. We, as a community, are responsible to form the right mechanisms that will allow unequivocally and without bias experimentation in the CS field. Indeed, it seems that now is the right time to analyze what older and more mature scientific fields have done regarding ethics rules and adapt them to the Computer Science research.

3   Be Careful What You Wish For

John McHugh further enhanced the dialogue by cautioning, "Be Careful What You Wish For."

Over the course of the last few years, there has been a movement to draft a set of ethical standards for the conduct of research in computer security. While there is a clear need for such standards, the effort and its resulting guidelines, commonly known as the "Menlo Report" are primarily directed at the academic community.

To a large extent, the Menlo Report is an attempt to adapt the earlier "Belmont Report" which provides ethical guidance primarily for medical research involving human subjects. The Belmont report was a result of widely publicized abuses of human subjects by researchers in the period leading up to, during, and after the Second World War. The report and regulations stemming from it place restrictions on research involving human subjects funded by the US department of Health and Human Services. Identical regulations have been adopted by some 14 other U.S. government agencies. The regulations effectively cover any research being performed at an institution receiving funds from one of these agencies, whether government funded or not. Most academic researchers have learned to accommodate the requirements, factoring into their research plans the time needed to obtain Institutional Review Board approval and documenting their research approach and process accordingly. Since most of the medical and pharmaceutical research in the U.S. involves academic participation, the regulations also affect substantial industrial research programs, as well. In recent years though the pharmaceutical industry has turned to the third world to conduct clinical trials under conditions that would not pass IRB scrutiny in the U.S.[1]

Academic computer security research (and academic computer science research, as well) is already in a state of crisis, largely due to pressure to publish early and often. When the author obtained his PhD in the early 1980s it was often the case that a new graduate's first conference or journal publication resulted from the work that led to the degree and was excerpted from the dissertation. Today, it is not uncommon for graduate students (and their advisers) to amass several publications per year out of work leading to the degree. For several years, I have been involved in an effort to raise the quality of academic research in the field by insisting that experimental papers contain an explicit description of the research question or hypothesis being investigated and detailed description of the experimental setup and methodology used to conduct the experiment. At a recent IFIP workshop, these suggestions were met with substantial resistance by a number of well known researchers in the fault tolerant and dependable systems area, largely on the grounds that the effort involved would slow the pace of the student's publication, jeopardizing employment prospects upon graduation.

I note that, to a large extent, the process that I advocate for research in general would be required for IRB approval in cases where human subjects are directly involved, and that much of the effort might be required in building a case that IRB approval should be waived for research with only a tenuous connection to real human subjects. One of my concerns is that imposing such conditions might result in driving students away from meaningful research questions requiring IRB interactions on the grounds that other research will produce more publications with less effort. Another concern is that this will exacerbate the current trend towards rapid (though trivial and largely useless) research leading to quick publications.

Unlike the medical area, a substantial amount of computer security research is conducted outside academia. Much of this work receives no government funding whatsoever and is largely beyond the reach of the processes proposed by the Menlo report. In a keynote address at the 6th European Conference on Computer Network Defence, Felix 'FX' Lindner of Recurity Labs gave a talk entitled "On Hackers and Academia" in which he took the academic community to task for concentrating on largely irrelevant approaches in an area that desperately needs useful results to help solve real problems. Recurity Labs is but one of hundreds of organizations that conduct research in computer security. These organizations have been largely left out of the ethics discussion although their actions in areas such as vulnerability disclosure and the development of both attack and defense techniques have the potential to cause serious societal harm on a broader scale the work of many academic researchers and they should be brought into the discussions.

---

[1] See "Deadly Medicine", Donald L. Barlett and James B. Steele, Vanity Fair, January 2011 on line at
http://www.vanityfair.com/politics/features/2011/01/deadly-medicine-201101?printable=true&currentPage=3#ixzz18NY8yGh9

There is a need for an open dialog on ethical issues in the community. Insofar as I can tell, the topic is completely ignored in most academic training programs at both the graduate and undergraduate levels. When it is approached, it is often couched in a legalistic rather than in an ethical framework. The Menlo report is, perhaps, too human subjects centric in its emphasis on IRB involvement. The issue is much broader than that and needs to be placed in a context of societal expectations for ethical behavior that apply inside and outside of the research arena. Although imposing an ethics review process on academic research sounds like a good idea initially, we need to be careful to ensure that it does not alter the research landscape so that valuable lines of research are avoided or pushed underground, out of academia, because the approval process is viewed as too onerous or time consuming.

4   Incorporating Cultural Differences

Finally, Nicolas Christin rounded out the topic with yet another insightful angle.

The 2011 edition of the WECSR workshop has focused a number of discussions on legal liabilities, and how transnational studies and research could result in interesting legal problems. In particular, a fair amount of time was devoted to arguing about United States vs. international law. Yet, this legal focus leads me to believe that we have ignored a more important point related to ethics: the need to be sensitive to cultural differences.

Specifically, the very definition of ethics varies depending on the culture considered. While I am not an ethicist, I have done research both in the United States and in Japan, and have, as is common for information security specialists, interacted with a large number of scientists from different cultures.

The West usually distinguishes between three different types of ethics. Utilitarian ethics, where the criterion to decide on whether or not a given action is ethical is whether society as whole would be better off – even though the action itself may hurt some individuals. Deontological ethics decide on whether an action is ethical or not, based on its consequences. Virtue ethics, on the other hand, use the character of the agent performing the action as a decision criterion.

From the discussions that preceded, it seems that a fair number of computer security experts use such a utilitarian view. In particular, the paper by Moore and Clayton presented earlier in the workshop uses this utilitarian argument to justify certain experiments that were conducted.

Yet, it is interesting to note that, in Asia for instance, the notions of ethics are completely different. Buddhist ethics can be construed to some extent as a combination of deontological and utilitarian ethics ("anatta"), while some (e.g., Gier[2]) have compared them to virtue ethics. In addition, a certain amount of modesty would be considered as an ethical necessity. The author that uses a large dataset, potentially hurting a large number of people in the process may be viewed as unethical if s/he does so to publish a research paper to further his/her reputation,

---

[2] See http://www.class.uidaho.edu/ngier/307/buddve.htm

even though, from a purely utilitarian standpoint, the action would be ethical if the benefits to society are considerable.

In another ethical puzzle, in Japan, it is often the case that, when exposed to a scandal, top management of a company resigns *even if they are (and are believed to be) personally innocent.*[3] In the West, this would amount to an admission of guilt. Again, our ethical frames are colored by our cultural backgrounds.

Where does this leave us for Computer Security research? My thesis is that, when dealing with data coming from geographically diverse origins, we need to adopt ethical frames of reference that match the culture or ethnic groups we are considering rather than ours. For instance, when a large number of Mechanical Turk users participating in online behavioral experiments (e.g., [1]) are from India, we need to apply ethical notions relevant to our Indian users; if we study frauds or online scams prevalent in a single country, like One Click Fraud[2] we need to adopt a definition of ethics consistent with the predominant culture in that country.

References

1. Christin, N., Egelman, S., Vidas, T., Grossklags, J.: It's all about the Benjamins: An Empirical Study on Incentivizing users to Ignore Security Advice. In: Danezis, G. (ed.) FC 2011. LNCS, vol. 7035, pp. 16–30. Springer, Heidelberg (2011)
2. Christin, N., Yanagihara, S., Kamataki, K.: Dissecting one click frauds (October 2010)
3. Dittrich, D., Bailey, M., Dietrich, S.: Towards Community Standards for Ethical Behavior in Computer Security Research. Technical Report CS 2009-01, Stevens Institute of Technology (April 2009)
4. Kenneally, E., Bailey, M., Maughan, D.: A Framework for Understanding and Applying Ethical Principles in Network and Security Research. In: Sion, R., Curtmola, R., Dietrich, S., Kiayias, A., Miret, J.M., Sako, K., Sebé, F. (eds.) RLCPS, WECSR, and WLC 2010. LNCS, vol. 6054, pp. 240–246. Springer, Heidelberg (2010)

---

[3] See http://ccbs.ntu.edu.tw/FULLTEXT/JR-PHIL/wargo.htm for anecdotes.

Author Index